MALCOLM CHRISTIE

The Reality of the Dream

First Edition.
First published 2022

Published by:
Morgan Lawrence Publishing Services Limited
16a Main Ridge West
Boston
Lincolnshire
PE21 6QQ
www.morganlawrence.co.uk
email: info@morganlawrence.co.uk
Company number: 12910264

ISBN: 9781838232948

A CIP catalogue record is available for this book from the British Library.

Photographs are courtesy of: Middlesbrough Football Club, PA Images, Andrew Varley (Varley Picture Agency), Action Images/Tony O'Brien, Action Images/Michael Regan, Action Images/Darren Walsh, Action Images/John Sibley, *Derby Telegraph,* Alamy

Cover Photography: Emma Christie
Cover Design: LC Graphix

Proofreading by Amy Memory

Printed and bound in the United Kingdom by Clays Ltd.

Contents

Sponsored by

frontlinerecruitment.co.uk

Foreword
by Steve Round

When I was just 24 years old, a surgeon told me that my career as a footballer with Derby County was over. Derby offered me a coaching role starting the following summer, but in the meantime, I needed to prove to myself that I could still play. My best pal was playing centre forward for Nuneaton Borough, so I went to play for them for a few months. I really enjoyed it and made some good friends.

A few seasons later I was managing Derby's reserve team when my mate rang me and said, "I've got a young centre forward here by the name of Malcolm Christie and he's not bad."

I watched him four or five times and really liked what I saw, so I showed Jim Smith, our first team manager, some footage of Malcolm in action for Nuneaton.

"I'm telling you, Jim, you need to sign this boy. He can start off in the reserve team and push forward. He's got a chance," I said. To be fair to Jim he backed me and we made the deal.

Mally was ballistically quick and he always looked capable of nicking a goal. He came into my group, worked really hard in training, listened, learned and took on board everything we said. He developed really quickly at that stage and when he got his opportunity, he took it well.

He's probably best known by Derby fans for the great goal he scored against Manchester United that kept us in the Premier League. What a lot of people have forgotten is that he also had an unbelievable chance to make it 2-0 with ten minutes to go, but he missed. We went mad on the touchline, and I think if Jim could have got on the pitch, he'd have killed him! I had to hold him back. But what a goal!

I later joined Middlesbrough as Steve McClaren's assistant. We inherited an aging side and were looking to do some squad balancing, by bringing in some more vibrant young players to push for a first team place. Malcolm had all the attributes we were looking for: he had pace, could adapt well to the Middlesbrough mentality, would be able to settle in the area, and could play on the shoulder. Best of all, we didn't think he'd reached his full potential.

He still had a lot of development ahead of him because he'd come into the game late, but we felt Malcolm had a chance of getting into the England squad. Whether he would have or not, who knows. But he was heading in the right direction. He'd scored goals for the Under 21s and had scored goals in the Premier League.

He was a similar type of player to Jamie Vardy who followed a comparable path into the game. Whether he could have been as good as Jamie, I don't know, but he was on that trajectory. We had a lot of faith in him and thought he had a chance.

Sadly, Malcolm suffered a really bad leg break, a potential career ender. I'd been there myself, so I had a pretty good appreciation of what he was going through. Those dark days are really tough and we gave him lots of support and rehab. He worked so hard, did everything the physios asked of him. Unfortunately, he lost a little bit of edge and didn't quite have that same sharpness, the same zip that his game was all about. But it is testament to Malcolm's character that he did come back to play and score in the Premier League again.

Off the pitch, Mally had the worst moustache I've ever seen! He could barely grow one and he got hammered for it. He also had some pretty bad clothes, his fashion sense left a lot to be desired, let's put it that way. The combination of his tash and dress sense meant he looked like something out of *Only Fools and Horses*!

But he was a good lad, popular in the dressing room and liked by all. I'm sure his book will be a tremendous read.

Foreword
by Steve McClaren

Our paths crossed briefly during my final months at Derby County, but it was in 2001 when I was Manchester United's assistant manager that I really became aware of Malcolm Christie.

We had already won the Premier League, while Derby was fighting for their lives. I remember the goal vividly. Malcolm steered the ball in with his left foot to put the Rams one up. There was still a lot of time left and I thought we'd get back in the game, but we didn't. Derby won 1-0 to stay up. Jim Smith was happy, and Malcolm had scored the winning goal at Old Trafford – not many people can say that.

Malcolm impressed me that day and I kept an eye on him over the next couple of seasons. During the summer of 2002, as manager of Middlesbrough, I was on the lookout for a young striker and Malcolm was one of the players I was interested in.

In the end, I went with Massimo Maccarone instead because he won Player of the Tournament at the Under 21 European Championships, and we thought we could get him cheaper. Maccarone made a blistering start for us and later wrote himself into Boro folklore for his exploits in the UEFA Cup, but I was still looking for someone to come in and play alongside him.

We kept tabs on Malcolm and in January 2003, an opportunity arose to release Alen Boksic which freed up the money to sign Malcolm and his Derby teammate Chris Riggott, two young talents we felt we could develop.

They got off to a great start, with both scoring against Sunderland in what is a huge game for Middlesbrough.

My great memory of Malcolm is when we went to Southampton at the end of September 2003. We'd had a difficult start to the season and were yet to win away. Before the game, I told the staff that we needed to pick up three points or we'd be in trouble. Malcolm scored a great goal, squeezing it in at the near post to give us a vital 1-0 victory. That goal, and the one he scored against Brighton in the League Cup kick started our season and helped us on our way to a very successful period in the club's history.

I'll never forget that horrendous day in training when Malcolm broke his leg. I've never seen anything like it before or since. Such an innocuous challenge resulted in a very serious injury. It takes a special type of character to come back from what could have been a career-ending injury. His bravery and strength is why he was able to fight back from such devastation. People looking in from the outside don't understand what it's like for a footballer to be injured and how tough that is.

He was a goal scorer who had great belief in himself. We signed him because of his attitude, work rate, and the fact he was a team player. What I also liked about Malcolm was that he was fearless and wasn't afraid to go in where others wouldn't. It's one of the reasons he scored so many goals, but also a factor in why he picked up so many knocks and injuries.

Malcolm had an innocence about him because he hadn't been brought up in the football system and he was different from the other players. He came into the game late and was playing catch up with all the banter, but the lads loved him, and he was a good guy to have around.

I know that Malcolm experienced some dark days when his career finished, but I'm delighted to see that he's recaptured his enthusiasm for football again and I wish him the best of luck with his coaching journey.

Stacking shelves to the Premier League – it's a hell of a tale!

Introduction by Gareth Southgate

Malcolm joined Middlesbrough in January 2003, when I was club captain. Steve McClaren was trying to bring in some younger, more athletic players and Malcolm fit the bill, especially as we didn't have anyone with his speed in the squad.

I much preferred playing with Malcolm than against him. In fact, I'd describe him as a pest! Pace wasn't something I was particularly blessed with, so players like Malcolm, looking to run in behind, were always a little more complicated for me to deal with than strikers who are happy to drop back.

His journey into professional football was unique, and he was a player who played with a hunger that comes from having experienced a life outside of football. There was a rawness about the way he played and in his approach to the game.

When I think of Malcolm, I am taken back to the 24th September 2003. We were playing Brighton in the second round of the League Cup and weren't on a particularly good run at the time, but we won that game with Malcolm scoring the winner in the 94th minute.

Whenever you look at teams who have won trophies there are always moments along the way that are really key, although a lot of people don't remember them. But I remember that goal because it was a significant moment that led to us winning the League Cup that season.

Sadly, by the time the final was played, Malcolm had broken his leg and he never got to experience the latter stages of that cup run and the excitement that surrounded it. He was in the role of frustrated, injured player and that is a really lonely place to be.

Malcolm's story really encapsulates how difficult it is to be a professional footballer. People often read about the top players who play in the biggest matches and achieve things, but for the majority of professionals trying to make their way in the game, it is a difficult slog full of set backs and injuries. Football is a tough sport, much harder than people envisage.

The one thing about being a footballer is that you are going to have to have a second career unless you retire at 35 and do nothing for the rest of your life which for most people is neither an option nor a desire. What Malcolm experienced in his career, and his journey into the game, I'm sure will prepare him for anything else that he is going to go through in his life.

The resilience that Malcolm displayed to come back from a series of potentially career ending injuries and play first team football again at the very top level is a credit to Malcolm as a person.

Prologue

Saturday, 5th May, 2001
Old Trafford, Manchester.

The Theatre of Dreams was packed to the rafters, with almost 70,000 Manchester United fans creating a carnival atmosphere while we warmed up on the pitch before the game. After the match, United were being presented with the Premier League trophy and their jubilant supporters were keen to start the celebrations early.

However, before the party could begin, the champions were facing my team Derby County. We were fighting for our lives at the foot of the table, needing a miracle to avoid relegation from the Premier League.

The odds were firmly stacked against us; United had lost just once at home all season, whereas we had only won one match on our travels. Our captain, Darryl Powell, was injured on the morning of the match and our top scorer, yours truly, hadn't scored a league goal for almost five months. There weren't many people inside that stadium who were expecting us to win, that's for sure.

But we had belief, we had nothing to lose, and we were determined to spoil United's party.

With 34 minutes on the clock, our Italian midfielder Stefano Eranio, chipped the ball to me. With my back to goal, I felt a Manchester United defender closing in. I was facing the corner flag and running out of options. I turned towards the edge of the United box, took two touches with the outside of my right foot to create some space and I finally saw the goal open out in front of me.

Time seemed to slow down as I looked up and saw the faces of the Manchester United fans sitting in the Stretford End. A few years ago, my dream was to sit amongst them and cheer on my beloved United, and now here I was standing in the penalty area at Old Trafford, with the ball at my feet.

How amazing is this? I thought to myself.

With no other options available, I smashed the ball with my left foot, aiming for the top corner. As I watched the ball fly towards the goal, I knew straight away that it was going in. Not even Fabien Barthez, United's World Cup winning goalkeeper, could stop this.

Seconds later I saw the net bulge and the realisation hit me – I've scored!

CHAPTER 1
All about United

There's nothing quite like it.

Hearing the cheers from the supporters as the ball ripples the net, receiving the acclaim of my teammates, knowing that I've helped my side. There's no doubt about it, scoring a goal is the best feeling in the world.

I bagged my first goal playing for St George's Primary School in Stamford, a quaint little town in Lincolnshire. I'm not sure why, but I realised from a very early age that I was just that little bit better at football than everyone else. My PE teacher, Mr Thompson, saw a little bit of flair in me and he quickly selected me for the school team where I lined up alongside boys three years older than me. I loved it because my older brother, Gavin, was in the same team so I got to play with him. Even though everyone towered over me, no one could keep up when I had the ball, so I used to knock it past my opponents, sprint by them and then smash the ball into the back of the net. I got kicked a lot, which wasn't nice at the time, but it helped me to develop a steely resolve.

After school, my brother and I would go back to our home on Drift Road, drop our bags off and have a quick snack before heading over the road to Stamford College which had a huge football pitch and lots of green land. It was perfect for 11-a-side matches, but we also played all the popular street games, like headers and volleys, and World Cup. It was good fun, but even then, my focus was on winning and, more importantly, scoring goals. I knew that if I scored, my side were likely to win, so the two always went hand in hand.

We'd play football whenever we could, staying out until Dad came out and gave us a loud whistle, signalling that it was time for us to go in. I don't remember ever returning home before he called us. Having that field so close to my house helped me massively, and I wonder if things would have worked out differently for me had I grown up somewhere else.

We had a pretty good school football team and we usually won by a large margin. I remember one day after a game, Mum came to pick me up and she asked if we'd won.

"Yes," I replied. "15-0."

"15-0?" She asked in disbelief.

"Yes, and I scored 10!"

"What! You scored 10?" She couldn't quite believe it.

My uncle Trevor was quite a talented footballer in the local leagues, and my dad claims that he was a tricky winger, so maybe it was in my genes. All I know is that football was something that came naturally to me.

*****

I, Malcolm Neil Christie, came into the world on 11th April 1979. I'm told that when the midwife passed me to my dad she said, "Here's another one for your five-a-side team." She must have known I was going to be a footballer!

My dad, Bill, was a printer by trade and worked at Potters, a local printing firm. His real name is actually Anthony, but when he was a child he used to dress up as a cowboy like Billy the Kid, a character from a popular television series at the time, so everyone called him Billy or Bill and the name stuck. My mum, Sue, also worked at Potters, so I spent a lot of time there myself as a youngster

I am blessed to have been brought up by two loving parents who worked hard to provide me and Gavin with everything we needed or wanted. We weren't rich, by any means – we didn't have a big house or flash cars – but my parents spent every penny they earned on us and rarely bought things for themselves.

My first passion was Superman. I can still vividly remember when my mum bought me my very own Superman costume, complete with flowing red cape. I wore it around the house all the time, pretending to fly and fight off the bad guys. In those formative years, I wanted to be Superman.

I spent hours watching the movies, *Superman, Superman II,*

Superman III and *Superman IV,* it got to the stage where I could almost recite all four films the whole way through.

For me Superman *is* Christopher Reeve. I've watched the more recent movies starring Brandon Routh and Henry Cavill, but it's just not the same. I was in floods of tears when I heard that Reeve had been paralysed in a horse riding accident.

In addition to Superman, I was obsessed with football, and Manchester United, in particular. United were going through a barren spell in the eighties, and most of my friends supported Liverpool or Everton, the two sides that dominated the decade. Gavin chose Everton – glory hunter! – but it was always Manchester United for me. I can still remember the excitement I felt when Dad brought me my first football top from a jumble sale – a United replica shirt. Seeing the famous Red Devil emblem, knowing that this was the same jersey my heroes wore was incredible. Wearing that shirt made me feel part of something special.

From that moment on, everything was about Manchester United. My bedroom became a shrine to United. Every inch of my wall was covered in posters; Corinthian figures and bobble heads adorned my shelves. I had the duvet and pillow set, curtains, light fittings, mouse mats, anything and everything Man United that you can think of, I had it. It's very difficult to find a photo of me as a child where I am not wearing something football related. The world as I knew it revolved around Manchester United.

At the start of every season, I'd beg my parents to take me down to the local sports shop, Hardingham's, so I could get the latest United shirt. In those days the shop sold the kits in black presentational boxes, it was a magical experience taking the top out of the box and putting it on over my head, pretending that I was a Manchester United player. I treasured those shirts and only wore them for best. Although I was always playing football, I never wore my United top. No, those shirts were sacred, and I'd only ever wear them around the house. When I was playing football, I'd put on a raggy, old top that I didn't mind getting dirty.

Every year, United released a long-padded promotional jacket, as worn by the manager Sir Alex Ferguson. Mum knew that I was desperate for one and one day she came home from work with a huge grin on her face, holding a present for me. I quickly guessed what it was and my heart was bursting out of my chest with excitement as I opened the package only to realise that the jacket wasn't made by Umbro, Manchester United's kit manufacturer, and, more importantly, it wasn't a United one. I was gutted. The proper gear was so special, the snidey stuff just wasn't the same. She had the right idea, though.

With very little football on television during the eighties, VHS cassettes were popular, and my library was full of Manchester United videos. My favourite was Jimmy Greaves' *Six of the Best*, a collection of six classic United games. I watched it so often that the tape began to wear out! My friend James Strickley, a fellow Red Devil, would come over to my house and we'd watch it over and over again, before heading across the road with a football where we'd pretend to be our heroes. Later on, when computer games came along, we'd also play *Sensible Soccer* and *Championship Manager.*

It was Man United first, closely followed by England. Most years I'd take a trip into Stamford with my parents, and I'd get the latest England replica kit which I always wore when I watched the Three Lions play on television. In those days, English clubs were banned from Europe, and the European leagues weren't broadcast in the UK, so the international scene opened my eyes to a whole host of new players.

I was eight when I was given a VHS called *Hero*, the official film of the 1986 World Cup, narrated by Michael Caine. I couldn't believe my eyes when I saw footage of legends like Careca, Michel Platini, and especially Diego Maradona.

I remember thinking that Peter Shilton should have jumped higher for the infamous 'Hand of God' goal in the quarter final, but what really excited me was Maradona's stunning second goal when he took on almost the entire England team. I lost count of the number of times I tried to replicate that goal on the park, while I recited Bryon Butler's commentary in my head: "Maradona turns like a little eel. He comes away from trouble, little squat man. . ."

The football played during the big international tournaments was on another level and I enjoyed standing in my front room, passionately belting out 'God Save The Queen' before each England match. As the camera panned along the line up, Gavin and I would look to see who was singing and how loudly. I felt hurt, almost insulted, if a player didn't sing the National Anthem. It was like they weren't bothered about representing their country.

It became my dream to one day stand in that line up, and I knew that if that ever happened, I'd be singing with pride.

The other highlight of international tournaments were the Panini sticker albums. Completing them became another obsession and I spent many hours with my friends going through our swap piles – got, got, need. I enjoyed collecting the random stickers from teams like South Korea and UAE, whose players only had half a sticker each, whereas the bigger nations like England and Italy were allocated a two-page spread because their players were deemed worthy of a whole sticker to themselves.

I was immersed in football throughout my childhood, but it was all from afar. I was never really exposed to the live professional world, so my love of football was through television, magazines, merchandise, and playing with my friends and my school team.

Peterborough United were the closest professional club to me, but their London Road ground was a 30-minute drive or train ride away from my house which, as a kid, felt like the other side of the country. Professional football was just a dream, I couldn't see it ever becoming a reality for me. Stamford had not produced a single player of note who had gone on to play league football, so there was no one to aspire to.

The closest I got to the big clubs was writing to footballers asking them to sign a poster. I did it every week without fail, and not just United players either. Mum and Dad would sometimes take us to Walker's Bookshop in Stamford, and while Gavin was buying the latest *Transformers* magazine, I'd get the football ones; *Shoot, Match*, you name it, I read it. When I got home, I'd flick through the magazine looking at the posters and when I saw one that I liked, I'd carefully cut it out, write a letter to the player featured requesting their autograph, add a self-addressed envelope, and take it to the post box.

I then had the anticipation and excitement of waiting for the postman each morning. I'd practically stalk him as he delivered mail down the street; standing in the bay window at the front of our house, watching him approach the front door, focussing on what was in his hands. If he was holding a brown envelope, my stomach was full of butterflies as I tried to guess whose autograph was enclosed. It became addictive and gave me a huge buzz. As soon as the post had been pushed through the letter box, I'd tear the envelope open to see what treasures I had received. My autograph collection included players and managers such as, David Beckham, Alex Ferguson, Ryan Giggs, David Seaman, Tony Adams, and Matt Le Tissier.

Most of the players replied to me, but some only sent a photocopy of their signature and that was always so disappointing. I remember wondering how a footballer could possibly think *that* is good enough to send to a fan. It had to be real ink and a proper autograph for me, nothing else would do. I have kept them all to this day.

Bryan Robson was my earliest football hero; he was the captain of England and Manchester United, the main man and a true leader. Even though I was a centre forward, I used to pretend to be Robson when I was playing at the park.

The strikers I admired were Mark Hughes, Gary Lineker, and Ian Rush. I'd study their movement, the runs they made, and I absorbed it all like a sponge. Even though Lineker and Rush played for United's rivals, they were the type of forwards that I aspired to be. They didn't necessarily score spectacular strikes, but I wasn't bothered about that, I just wanted to score goals – and lots of them.

I excelled at any sport I turned my hand to. At Primary School, I entered everything I could and, more often than not, I won. One year, I entered the slow bike race where the person who came last was crowned the winner. We lined up, the teacher blew his whistle, and out of a whole field of kids I won riding my BMX. I'd never done it before and hadn't even practiced. My dad videotaped the awards ceremony from my final year at Primary School and I cringe when I watch it back because I won everything: Athlete of the Year, Footballer of the Year, team captain, and so on. I'm sure the other kids and their parents used to go home and say, "We hate him!"

When I was 11, I experienced my first real taste of disappointment. I sat an exam to see if I would be accepted into the local grammar school, Stamford Boys' School, but I narrowly missed out. I was gutted, and so were my teachers because it was the first time I hadn't achieved what I had set out to do. It turned out to be a blessing in disguise because they didn't play much football at the grammar school, it was all cricket and rugby, so it could have hampered my progress. Instead, I attended Queen Eleanor Secondary School which was perfect for me as break times were spent playing football and swapping stickers on the playground.

I was soon selected for the school team, but I also wanted to know what it was like to feel part of a non-school football club. The problem was that there weren't any youth football teams on my doorstep. It was actually my mum who found an article in the local newspaper about Northborough Football Club who were looking for boys to play in their Under 13 side. The following week, I turned up for training, met the other lads – who were great to me – and that was really the start of my football journey.

I trained every week and soon became the centre forward. *Yes*, I thought, *I'm going to be the one who scores the goals for the team.* Even though I was only 12, I was incredibly driven and set myself an ambitious target of scoring in every game.

Once I'd settled into the side, I managed to convince a few of my school mates to join me at Northborough. One of whom was Graeme Theodore, a childhood friend, and a good goalkeeper. We spent hours practising with each other on the green space near Stamford College. It was perfect for both of us really, as he'd don his gloves, we'd put down some jumpers to use as goalposts, and I'd take shots at him from various angles. He became a better keeper, and I improved my finishing. We did it every single night. Later on, they built a swimming pool on that field, with an enclosed five-a-side pitch behind it, which was great as we finally had proper facilities to use. All the pieces were there to help me develop as a footballer.

As well as playing with my mates, I also spent a lot of time practising on my own and that is probably where I developed the most. There was a row of three black bricks that broke up the brickwork on the swimming pool wall and I spent hours and hours aiming for those bricks, hitting them time after time. Another thing I did was face the wall and smash a ball against it. When the ball rebounded, I'd turn, sprint to the other side of the grass and take a shot, re-enacting a goal or situation that I'd seen on television. In those moments, in my head I was a real footballer running towards goal. I'd pretend to take the ball past the defenders and around the goalkeeper before finishing from various angles into a makeshift goal. I'd do that drill for hours on end and it eventually paid off, as we'll come to later on.

Years later, a sports facility was built on the land which I was asked to open, so there is a plaque there with my name on it. It was a huge honour and is very surreal because that's the place where I honed my craft.

CHAPTER 2
A boy with a dream

No one could ever accuse me of being lucky. I achieved everything through sheer hard work. I trained every weekend and every single night in pursuit of becoming a footballer. Although I dreamt of becoming a professional, it didn't feel like a dream I would ever realise. Especially after my first experience with a pro club left a bitter taste in my mouth.

My PE teacher at secondary school, Stuart Gray, was a scout for Peterborough United and he recommended me to their School of Excellence. I felt that I was taking the first step on my journey as I went along to Peterborough's ground on London Road, one Thursday night, only to find myself disappointed when I discovered that we would be training in the car park. A concrete surface for kids to play football on is just comical.

Malcolm Hird and former Posh striker Dominic Genovese ran the sessions and I hated it. Absolutely hated it. It was so regimented, and the pressure was intense. I hadn't signed anything, it was a just a case of turning up and training, so I felt that I had to perform every single week. The coaches left me wondering if each session would be my last and it got to the stage where I didn't really want to get out of the car when we arrived because I just didn't enjoy it. Some of the lads there played for Northborough's rivals and there were a lot of egos there. It wasn't organised, we weren't a team, and we didn't even play any games.

Despite all that, when Graham Scarff, the youth team manager, called me into his office one day and told me that he was going to offer me schoolboy forms, I was delighted and thought that I was taking my first step on the ladder. But it all fell through a month later when Scarff and his coaches left the club and were replaced by Kit Carson who had been the youth team manager at Norwich City, and he changed everything. After all those weeks training, I was back to square one. He invited me to a trial which I assumed would be for the small group of us who'd been verbally offered schoolboy forms.

I was wrong.

When I arrived for the trial, I saw Thomas Smith, Leigh Mytton, and Lawrence Shaw, friends of mine from school. I asked what they were doing there, and they told me that they were attending the trial too. I was shocked as I'd been led to believe it was an opportunity for Carson and his coaches to have a good look at me, but it turned out to be an open day that anyone could just turn up to, regardless of their ability. There were hundreds and hundreds of kids arriving on buses, some of whom couldn't even kick a football. The whole thing was a joke.

The coaches explained that they would be observing us while we played a game and then they would decide who would be offered schoolboy forms. There were so many people there, and we were asked to put our hands up for each position. They started with centre forward and everyone's hand shot in the air. I knew I had no chance, so I offered to play at right back, a position no one else wanted. We went out onto the pitch, and I hardly kicked the ball.

It was a horrible experience and a few days later I received a letter from the club explaining that I wouldn't be invited back. When I look back now, I think the trial was just a box ticking exercise so they could say that they'd given an opportunity to the local kids before Carson brought in all the best youngsters he'd worked with at Norwich.

It was a huge disappointment as I would have jumped at the chance to play for my local club. Peterborough had every opportunity to sign me; my dad later wrote them a letter asking them to come and watch me play, but they replied with a bog standard response explaining that they already had a full quota of playing staff.

Peterborough United did give me my first experience of watching live, professional football. When I was 14, Gavin, some friends, and I would catch the train from Stamford, and travel to London Road to stand behind the goal and cheer on the Posh. They had a decent team in those days: Mick Halsall was the captain, Tony Philliskirk was the big centre forward and Fred Barber was the goalkeeper. Barber was a right character who used to run out of the tunnel wearing a Freddie Kruger mask and perform hand stands during the warm up. He even wore the mask when walking out at Wembley for the 1992 Play Off Final!

Although I was still obsessed with United, Manchester was too far for me to travel for a match, so the few occasions I visited London Road gave me the opportunity to enjoy the buzz of the crowd and soak up the atmosphere of a live game.

But the thrill of watching Peterborough was nothing compared to the feeling I experienced when my grandad, a fireman, took me to Wembley for the first time to watch England Schoolboys.

The Stamford fire station managed to get tickets from the FA and laid on coaches to take all the families of the fire fighters down to Wembley, with a stop at Biggleswade for fish and chips on the way. Although the journey took less than two hours, it seemed like we were going on a trip to a different country.

I remember one of the first games I saw, a schoolboy international against West Germany when England were captained by a young lad called Ryan Wilson, who later changed his name to Ryan Giggs.

It became an annual tradition, visiting the best stadium in England, seeing the Twin Towers, buying a rosette and a scarf as a souvenir – it was magical. Sitting in the stands, looking onto the pitch, I tried to imagine how amazing it would be to play at the famous ground, and it became one of my dreams.

In 1993, I left Northborough to join Deeping Rangers, a successful amateur team based in nearby Market Deeping. A very well-run club, they operated teams from youth level all the way through to the men's league. Deeping Rangers, and the wonderful coaches I met there, gave me a magnificent footing in football and moulded me into the player I later became. They also instilled in me respect towards my opponents and referees.

I started out in the Under 14 side and immediately set my sights on breaking into the first team. Although I still dreamt of playing at grounds like Old Trafford and Anfield in the Premier League, that was all it was – a dream. After Peterborough had rejected me, I felt that becoming a professional was no longer a realistic goal for me, so I instead focussed on what I could see before me. If I could make it into Deeping's first team squad then, and only then, would I set my sights on the next rung of the ladder.

Alan Hughes was my manager at Under 14 and Under 15 level, and when I think of people who helped me and had an influence on my career, Alan is one of the first people I recall. He brought out the best in me, made me feel special, and I always wanted to play for him and make him proud.

Bromley Clarke became my manager when I joined the youth team, and he did as much for me as anyone. He taught me so much about football because until that stage I had been self-taught. Bromley played me in every position other than goalkeeper which was a genius move because when I returned to my favoured position, centre forward, I had an edge. I had learnt how to think like a defender, I knew where they wanted to stand in certain situations, and I used that knowledge to my advantage. We were an all-conquering youth team, winning both the league title and the County Cup. I was so confident that it wasn't a matter of *if* I would score, more a case of *how many* I would score.

By the time I turned 15, I was promoted to the reserve team – the men's league – which was a real eye opener as I was coming up against players bigger and more experienced than me, who were likely twice my age. It didn't faze me though, I just played my normal game – get the ball, knock it past the defenders, race by them, and score. Pace was my biggest asset and I soon discovered that no one at that level could keep up with me.

It didn't take long before I made my first team debut in the Peterborough and District Premier Division, and that was a huge thing for me. They played on a different pitch to the reserve and youth teams with a little stand where some spectators congregated to watch the games It made me feel that I was playing in a proper match.

It was exciting and challenging in equal measure. I felt nervous and a little on edge as I adapted to the men's environment. Although I never doubted my ability on the pitch, little things like seeing the players walking around the dressing room completely naked was totally alien to me. I never had a shower after games in those days. *Shower naked with grown men? No thanks!* I'd go home and have a wash in the privacy of my own bathroom instead.

The first team manager at the time was Paul Bentley. Paul helped me massively, a very similar character to Derby County manager Jim Smith. He had a tough persona and was someone you didn't ever want to cross. Being completely honest, he scared me. But that was a good thing as I always preferred to play for a manager who I feared a little bit. I didn't want to come in at half time and get shouted at, so it motivated me to go out, give my all, and make the manager happy.

The *Stamford Mercury* covered Deeping's games, so I was able to see my name appear in print for the first time, along with a little write up about a goal I'd scored or a good performance. It was brilliant. Dad cut out all the clippings and added them to a scrapbook he had begun to compile during my school days and continued to update throughout my entire career. He painstakingly kept a record of every game I played, every goal I scored, and where the team sat in the league table. It is not just clippings though, he has kept DVDs, videos, magazines, posters, anything that is related to me. There are at least eight journals that encapsulate every single season of my career. An incredible encyclopedia that I still treasure to this day.

My dad went to every single game – never ever missed one – and when I look back now, I realise how tough that must have been for him, especially as he was holding down a full-time job. His employers were fantastic and allowed him to take time off to follow me. My family were always so supportive of me, and I would never have achieved anything in football if it wasn't for my parents. They were the ones who encouraged me and gave me the drive and determination to succeed.

I never had a conversation with them about wanting to become a footballer, we just never discussed it. The only person I ever told was a careers lady just before I sat my GCSE exams.

"What do you want to do when you leave school?" She asked.

"I want to be a professional footballer," I replied tentatively, as it was the first time that I'd admitted it to anyone.

"That might be what you *want* to be, but what are you *really* going to do?" she responded, totally shattering my dreams in the process. I remember thinking, *Hold on here. I'm allowed to have a dream.*

So, after I passed my GCSEs in 1995, I went to Stamford

College to take my A-levels because that was what everyone else in my school year was doing, and that was what I was expected to do. The college was opposite my house, so it was convenient too, but it didn't take me long to discover that A-levels weren't for me and I didn't want my life to go down that route. I took maths, PE, and art – and hated all three equally.

Art class was just sitting around a table, piled high with junk, and being asked to pick a section and draw it. PE should have been good, but we only did basketball and gymnastics, two of the few sports that I had no interest in.

Maths was even worse. I remember sitting in front of the blackboard with something like $\sin(A + B) = \sin A \cos B + \cos A \sin B$ written in big chalk letters and asking myself, *When am I ever going to use this? What am I doing here?*

A-levels drained the life out of me, but I'm so glad I took them because it forced me to reassess the things that were important to me.

Gavin had just finished a two-year diploma in business and finance which he had really enjoyed. The course covered topics including setting up companies, managing accounts, and leisure and tourism, so I decided to do that, and I loved it. I made some really good friends, it was relaxed, and I had so much fun. It also helped that the course content was exactly the same as Gavin's, so I was able to look at the assignment I had been set, find his coursework, rewrite it with a few tweaks here and there, and then submit it. The biggest challenge was making sure that no one found out. Gavin was awarded a distinction and guess what? So was I!

It was a useful shortcut that allowed me to spend my time playing football, building friendships, and enjoying myself. I had a great social life at college but, the grand sum of £13 a week that I was earning from the paper round I'd held since I was 12 wasn't quite enough, so I applied for a part time job at Somerfield supermarket in Stamford.

I worked as many hours as I could fit into my schedule and was soon earning a couple of hundred pounds a week, mainly working in the dairy section. My parents had instilled a strong work ethic in me, so I made sure that whatever I did, I always gave 100%. I took pride in ensuring that my section was the best in the whole store. My supervisor, Sharon Barnes, liked me because I was always on time, stayed until everything was finished, and I was hard working. She loved my enthusiasm and wanted me to take a trainee management course, but I wasn't sure. For me, the supermarket was just a temporary job to give me some extra spending money while I was at college, not something that I had ever considered as a long-term career.

I was still playing football for Deeping Rangers and harboured distant hopes of one day earning a living from the game that I loved, but there were times when I just didn't think it would ever happen.

One day I was reading the *Stamford Mercury* and saw an advertisement for the local branch of the Manchester United Supporter's Club. There was a coach that picked members up from the Danish Invader pub in Stamford and took them to Old Trafford on match days. I remember showing the advert to my dad and telling him that I'd rather go and watch United than keep playing football. His immediate response was, "Don't do it, Son. Stick to your football and you'll make something of it. I promise."

So, with Dad's encouragement, I decided to give it another season. It proved to be the right decision as I was about to receive an offer that would alter the course of my life, and take me one step closer to turning my dream into reality.

CHAPTER 3
He's turny, he's twisty

In February 1998, as I was leaving the pitch having just scored my 22nd goal of the season for Deeping Rangers, I was approached by a gentleman who introduced himself as Bill Berry, a scout for Nuneaton Borough. "Wow," I said. "They play in the FA Cup."

"Yes," Bill replied. "Nuneaton compete in the Dr Martens Premier League, the sixth tier of English football, and we'd like you to play a game for us so we can see what you can do." I couldn't believe it. A proper scout had spotted me and shown faith in me.

It was a totally random offer as although Nuneaton wasn't a million miles away from Stamford, it wasn't exactly close. Bill, sadly no longer with us, had previously recommended Peterborough-based striker Andy Furnell to Borough, and their manager, Brendan Phillips, had asked him to see if he could find anyone else in the area. Scott Stainsby, a former opponent of mine, had contacted Bill and told him about a young striker named Christie who played for Deeping Rangers. And that was how it all came about.

I was asked to report to Manor Park, Nuneaton's ground, at 6 p.m. on 18th February for my trial, a friendly against Leicester City reserves. I was so excited, and determined to make the best of my audition and show everyone what I could do. But I almost missed out on the opportunity without even kicking a ball.

In those days Dad took me everywhere I needed to be, although he only ever ventured locally. He could get to Peterborough, Stamford, and Market Deeping, but that was about it. Even to this day, if you ask him to drive to somewhere unfamiliar, he will panic.

So on the day of my big trial, we set off on our journey to

Nuneaton with Dad driving, me in the passenger seat and Mum sitting in the back. As we'd never been there before, I had turned on the interior light and was trying to read a map and tell Dad which way to go. The problem was that Dad wasn't great with directions and I'd never read a map before, so we were a bit like the Chuckle Brothers!

We had been driving along the M6 for a while and exited at the junction with a sign post to Nuneaton. So far, so good.

At the end of the slip road we entered a roundabout. Dad was asking me which exit, I was trying to find out from the map and we got flustered, so instead of exiting towards Nuneaton, we missed the turning and ended up back on the M6 heading in the direction we'd just come from! I was reluctant to say anything at the time as I didn't want Dad to get even more stressed, but when I looked at the map again and saw that the next junction was 10 miles away, I knew I had to pluck up the courage.

"Dad, we missed the turning to Nuneaton."

"What! You're joking!" he replied, beginning to worry.

There was nowhere to turn around, so we got off at the next junction and I tried to navigate my dad through the narrow, winding country roads, and before long we realised that we were completely lost. It was comical really.

We were driving on one track roads with no road markings, no lights, and no signs. Dad and I were sat in the front panicking and Mum was in the back shaking her head. By that stage there was no talk of the trial or football, our sole mission was to just get to the ground. My concerns turned from *will we be late?* to *will we even get there?*

The whole journey was so stressful, hardly the best way to prepare for the biggest game of my life, my one chance to impress and make my mark. I'd planned to arrive at the ground nice and early, take in my surroundings and be the first one into the dressing room, so I could introduce myself to the players as they walked in.

We eventually parked at the ground just 35 minutes before kick-off and when I walked into the packed dressing room, everyone stopped what they were doing and stared at me, wondering who I was. I didn't even know what the manager looked like, so I had to ask someone, and then Brendan Phillips came over and said,

"Oh, you must be Malcolm. There's your kit, get yourself ready." Before adding, "Quickly!"

My teammates didn't know me from Adam, so when I joined them on the pitch for the pre-game warm up, they asked me who I was. "Hi, I'm Malcolm Christie," I said, introducing myself, but because of the noise of the crowd, they misheard and thought I'd said my name was Chris, so they started calling me Chrisso. Even though it wasn't my name – or even my nickname – I went along with it as I was just a young lad and didn't feel I could correct these experienced senior players. My dad still laughs about it today and sometimes even calls me Chrisso!

I was named as a substitute – whether that was always the plan or because I was late, I don't know – so I had to bide my time. I knew that arriving late hadn't created the best impression, but I also knew that the only thing that mattered was how I performed out on the pitch.

As I watched the match from the dugout, I looked around the ground and immediately liked what I saw; the terraces with a tunnel for the players to walk down, the vocal supporters in the stand cheering the lads on – I got goosebumps thinking that I might have the opportunity to play here regularly.

Eventually, on the hour mark I replaced Ian King to make my Nuneaton debut against a strong Leicester team that included Steve Walsh and Rob Ullathorne, both vastly experienced Premier League players. The opposition was irrelevant though, this wasn't about them, it was about me. This was my chance, my moment and I was determined to make the most of it. I got such a buzz hearing the fans applause as I stepped over the white line – it was what I'd always wanted.

I felt no pressure at all. Some people freeze in situations like that, but I rose to the occasion, thrived on the challenge, and I found it exciting. I remember at one stage thinking, *Wow I'm playing against professionals here.*

In the 78th minute, I ran with the ball and threaded a pass to Luke Yates who scored what proved to be the only goal of the game. Although I was gutted not to score, I was pleased to have assisted the winning goal.

I was always confident, but I'd be lying if I said I didn't have any doubts before the match.

Am I good enough for this level? Will people be better than me? More technical? Quicker?

My performance that day proved to me that I belonged at that level, and I never doubted myself again.

After the game, Brendan said that he wanted me to train and play a couple more matches before he made a decision. That was fair enough as he'd only seen me play for half an hour and didn't know anything about me.

As I left the ground, my teammates were patting me on the back, congratulating me on my performance. "Well played, Chrisso," they said. I wondered if I'd be stuck with that name forever but during my first training session Brendan called me Mally and everyone else followed suit.

Nuneaton was a world away from what I had been used to and the standard was very high. The dressing room atmosphere was different to Deeping, and I wanted to fit in, so after training, I walked straight into the changing room, took my clothes off and was the first one in the shower. Although it was a daft little thing, it was important for me to feel comfortable in the dressing room and I'd learnt a lot from my experiences at Deeping.

After impressing in matches against West Brom reserves and Rushden and Diamonds, Brendan called me into his office and offered me a semi-professional contract. The fact that the word 'professional' was mentioned was incredible. My head was a bit fuzzy though as I was earning more at Somerfield than the amount Nuneaton were offering, but Brendan was great and promised to beat my wages. When I put pen to paper on my £135 a match contract, complete with goal and promotion bonuses, it felt amazing. It wasn't life changing money – I didn't expect it to be – but the fact that someone wanted to pay me for playing football when I had actually been paying to play for Deeping was a real confidence boost.

I joined Nuneaton at exactly the right time. Brendan Phillips and his assistant Steve Burr, who later became manager, were good, honest people who wanted the best for the club. They saw me as a raw kid with bags of talent and their role was to polish the diamond. Brendan, in particular, took it upon himself to look after me.

I didn't get into the first team straight away, I had to earn my corn playing for the reserves before I finally made my league debut on 28th March 1998, coming on as a second half substitute in a 1-0 defeat at Burton Albion. We travelled on a coach to that game, like proper players, which was another new experience for me.

I did well enough to earn a place in the starting line up the following week, a home match against St Leonards. We drew 1-1 and I scored the goal – my first for Nuneaton – a near post header in the second half. What a feeling that was. There was something addictive about playing in front of a crowd, watching and hearing them cheer for me when the ball hit the back of the net. As I came off the pitch, I knew I'd done my job; first start and first goal. I couldn't wait for the next match when I could do it all over again.

We trained once a week, usually on a Thursday, which meant leaving home around 3 p.m. and not arriving back until 10 p.m. Dad didn't want me driving my C reg Ford Fiesta all the way to Nuneaton and back, so he put me on the insurance of his gold coloured G reg Ford Sierra Estate, a car that I thought was incredibly luxurious. I always felt like royalty driving the Sierra Estate, but looking back now, I probably looked hideous!

Even though I was now under contract with Nuneaton, I couldn't get enough football, so I continued to turn out for my brother's fruit and veg team, Pauley's, in the Peterborough Sunday league. I'd joined them when I was playing for Deeping Rangers and really enjoyed it.

Our manager, Sean Johnson, was a good laugh and never took anything too seriously. Sean was a typical Sunday league manager, who appreciated the fact that players would likely be half cut come match day.

I got off to a great start, scoring a hat trick on my debut. It was a real education, playing Sunday league football, because it was much more physical than I was used to. Getting kicked is one thing, but during one game I got clotheslined by an opponent WWE style! As I went to run past the defender, they held their arm out to the side, smashing it into my neck and flipping me over the top. As I lay crumpled in a painful heap on the ground, I was relieved to see the referee show him a red card. Things like that taught me a lot and helped toughen me up.

Obviously the standard wasn't as high as I was used to, some players were still pissed from the night before for example, but it was great because I often scored three, four, or sometimes even five goals a game which gave me so much confidence that I took into the more competitive games.

It was a good laugh lining up with Gavin and my mates, but when Brendan found out that I was playing for Pauley's he told me I had to stop which was fair enough as I was contracted to Nuneaton, and he didn't want me to get injured. I still went along to cheer the lads on when I could and when they got to the cup final I was asked to play. I couldn't resist. I didn't tell Brendan, of course, but they brought me off the bench and I managed to get on the score sheet which helped us win the trophy.

I scored again in my second start for Borough – a 3-1 defeat to Bromsgrove – and kept my place in the starting line-up for the remaining four league games.

Although we finished the 1997/98 season in 12th place, I knew that we were on the cusp of something special. Brendan made some astute signings during the summer of 1998, and everything just fell into place.

We had a brilliant team with a great set of lads – a mixture of former pros dropping down the divisions, journeymen stalwarts of non-league and then some youngsters, like myself.

One of our new recruits was the veteran full back Steve Prindiville who had played for Leicester City, Chesterfield, Doncaster Rovers, and Mansfield Town, before dropping down to non-league football. I looked up to Prinders because he'd played at a high level and for me to share a pitch with him was massive. He later moved into coaching and was credited for helping in the development of Ben Chilwell.

Another summer signing was the former Fulham defender Terry Angus who became our skipper. Terry was a 100% man, with a big presence, and someone who made you want to give your all in every single game.

Ian Muir, a vastly experienced striker who scored more than 140 goals for Tranmere Rovers, was another new arrival. Ian was great to me. I remember after one game, he pulled me to one side and said, "If you keep doing what you're doing, you'll get a move into league football."

For someone who knew first-hand what it took to say that to me was incredible and another huge confidence boost. Ian's presence kept me on my toes because I knew that he was waiting in the wings, ready to take my place if I didn't perform.

I forged a fantastic strike partnership with Anton Thomas, who'd done the rounds on the non-league circuit. He was a massive help to me. I always enjoyed playing with a big centre forward and we worked well together, developing a little routine where Anton would hold the ball up, I'd spin off behind, and he'd flick the ball on for me to score. Anton was subjected to some vile racist abuse from away fans which really shocked me as I'd never heard anything like that before, but he handled it so well, never losing his temper and getting his own back at the racists by scoring or assisting me.

All these guys were perfect for Nuneaton, and I just slotted in to give the side some youth, energy, and pace. It was the ideal platform for me to express myself, and my teammates couldn't have been more supportive with their constant encouragement.

The pre-season training was a real eye-opener because I'd never had a pre-season before, but I really enjoyed it. As well as improving my fitness, it was the first time I signed an autograph. I'd been substituted in the second half of a friendly, and was standing by the dug out when someone came over with a really scruffy bit of paper and asked, "Can you sign this please?" As I've mentioned, I was a big autograph collector, but mine all had to be pristine: a proper piece of paper or an autograph book and a decent pen. Still, despite the paper quality – or lack of – I put the paper on the palm of my hand (there was nothing to lean on) and scribbled my first autograph. Then, all of a sudden, more people came over and I was signing loads. I loved it and always signed autographs throughout my career. I would never disrespect a fan by saying no. Not every player was as accommodating as I was, but I knew first-hand what it meant to the supporters.

We played friendlies against several professional teams, including Coventry City, Sheffield Wednesday, Tottenham Hotspur, and Aston Villa, and by the start of the season I felt fit, strong, and mentally and I knew that I was ready to go. Brendan had seen enough of me during pre-season to start me in the first game of the new campaign, and I repaid him with the only goal in a 1-0 win over Hastings Town.

During this time, I found myself regularly featured in the local newspapers and it gave me a huge buzz seeing my name in the headlines on the back pages – everything was like a fairy-tale. My dad had an agreement with a Nuneaton newsagent who kept back copies of the *Heartland Evening News* and the *Nuneaton Telegraph* for him to collect at the weekend.

The Borough fans were incredible and took to me immediately. The supporters in the old Cock and Bear stand at Manor Park even created a chant for me:

"He's turny, he's twisty,
his name is Malcolm Christie!"

I don't even know if turny is a word but for me it was heaven to hear fans cheering for me and singing my name. No one else really had a chant but because I was young, and they knew that I was probably going to get snapped up by a bigger team at some stage, they wanted to show their appreciation. After each game, we'd have a drink in the bar and the supporters would be there asking for a photograph, an autograph or just a chat about the match.

It wasn't just the fans who had started to notice me, my performances had also garnered interest from agents. Dad and I were very green and didn't have a clue what was going on around us. After matches, agents would approach me, explaining how they could get me a move to this club or that club. There was one agent that we arranged to meet at a service station McDonalds, and he told me that I was going to be the next big thing. He said all the right things, but something just didn't feel right, so Dad and I walked away thinking that was the end of it. But he began stalking us! He got our phone number from the phone book and was constantly ringing. My dad was on the phone to him until 2 a.m. one morning and another time, he just turned up on our doorstep out of the blue. He was so pushy, and we obviously didn't sign with him. Everything started to get out of hand, and I just wanted to enjoy my football.

We did eventually sign with an agent who was a former professional. He'd played at the highest level and had a good reputation, so we thought he must be alright.

Despite all the attention I was receiving, I never felt nervous before a game. I knew that all I had to do was give it my all and score goals – putting the ball in the back of the net was what had earned me my move to Nuneaton after all. Performances are one thing, but I knew that goals were far more important.

The start of the 1998/99 season was incredible, we went on an amazing run and I couldn't stop scoring – I was on fire! I hit 10 goals in our first 11 games as Borough soared to the top of the league.

And that was when the scouts started to come and watch me.

I first became aware of interest from other clubs because it was in the Nuneaton newspapers. I was the one saleable asset Borough had and they knew that if they moved me on they could receive some valuable money. I think that behind the scenes, Brendan built up some furore around me and created the hype, like agents do nowadays.

Before a game, Brendan would come into the dressing room and hand me a piece of paper that listed all the clubs who were there to watch me. I'd read it and see Leicester, Arsenal, Coventry and think, *Wow.* Some of the lads told him not to put pressure on me, but I didn't see it as pressure – it was inspiration and it made me feel ten feet tall. A different player may have crumbled, not me. I became even more determined to go out there and put on a show.

My first big opportunity came with Tottenham Hotspur. I went to Spurs on a week's trial and was totally out of my comfort zone. I was a real home bird, so I found staying in a hotel in London by myself for five nights very strange and lonely. I was a bit shy and the whole experience just didn't feel right. The Spurs coaches definitely didn't see the best of me, but I didn't really get much of an opportunity either. I was training with the youth and reserve team players, rather than the first teamers like David Ginola and Les Ferdinand. I had trained all week and I was gearing myself up for a reserve game that was due to take place on the Thursday evening. But the first team were struggling, so the manager, Christian Gross, cancelled the match to rest the reserves players in case he needed to call upon them. So, I went home bitterly disappointed, without getting much out of the experience. The only benefit was that the story made the papers – Malcolm Christie is on trial at Tottenham Hotspur – which generated interest from other teams.

Leicester City were the next club to take a look at me. Unlike my trial at Spurs, I was training with the first teamers, players like Ian Marshall and Matt Elliott. Just to be around these professionals and see how they carried themselves was a great experience, but again I felt totally out of my comfort zone, and I didn't perform or train at the same level I did when I was at Nuneaton.

I did play match though, a reserve fixture against Sunderland at Filbert Street which gave me my first experience of playing at a proper ground. I did well, scoring the winning goal and when Martin O'Neill, Leicester's manager, called me into his office after the game, I thought, *Here we go, he's going to sign me.* My heart was going ten to the dozen when he said, "Well done, Son. I thought you had a good game and took your goal well. We'd like to take another look at you."

My heart sank. I'd been doing so well at Nuneaton, had scored in my one game for Leicester and wouldn't have cost a lot of money. I couldn't understand why he wouldn't just take a chance on me. It was a big life lesson and I've since attended job interviews and said, "I don't mind if you don't take me on, but if you don't someone else will and you'll regret it." I wish I'd said that to O'Neill, although I'm not sure how he'd have reacted!

I later discovered that around the time of my trial, Martin was in advanced talks to become Leeds United's new manager, so every transfer deal was put on hold. That was why he didn't sign me for Leicester City, although I didn't know it at the time.

O'Neill was convinced to stay at Filbert Street, but by then I had returned to Nuneaton totally deflated. This was the pivotal moment where I was either going to stay at semi-pro level or become a professional footballer.

Fortunately, there was one club who were willing to give me a chance.

CHAPTER 4
Becoming a Ram

Scouts from Derby County, who were riding high in the Premier League at the time, were in the stands at Filbert Street for my reserve match and they swooped in and invited me to play a game for the Rams. Without even training with them, I turned out for Derby's second string in a reserve tie against Boston United. Unfortunately, I didn't play particularly well. I ran around a lot, held the ball up, but didn't score, and I was substituted in the second half. No one said anything to me after the match and the whole experience felt a bit rushed. As I drove back home with my dad, I remember feeling a bit dejected and wondering if it was ever going to happen for me.

The following day, my agent phoned to say that Derby wanted to sign me on a pro contract. I was shocked, but I think the top and bottom of it was that I wasn't going to cost a lot of money, and they were afraid that if they didn't move quickly someone else would come in for me. The clubs quickly agreed a fee worth £55,000, rising to £130,000 depending on appearances, plus a sell on percentage, so all that was left was for me to take a medical and agree personal terms.

On the journey to Pride Park, my agent explained how things would work.

"They will make the first offer. If I close my briefcase and get up, you follow me," he instructed. My dad and I looked at each other and thought, *This is what must happen then, it's a bit of a game. Great stuff.*

The first challenge was finding the stadium. None of us had been there before and in the pre-sat-nav days, we didn't have clue where abouts in the city it was. We found ourselves in the centre of Derby and decided to ask a passing postman for directions. Now, if you're lost and need to find out where something is, the one person you would expect to know is a postman. Not the one we asked, he was just as clueless as us!

When we eventually found the impressive Pride Park stadium, we were introduced to Keith Loring, the Chief Executive, who sat us down and explained that the plan was to start me off with the reserve team and see how I developed. It was what I expected as I knew I wasn't going to walk straight into the starting line-up of an established Premier League club. He then presented me with a contract, and I was blown away by the numbers. The offer was a three-year deal where I would be paid £800 a week, plus a £30,000 signing on fee and another £30,000 if I was still at Derby at the end of the season – big numbers for a 19-year-old who was earning £135 a match and topping up his wages working in the dairy aisle at Somerfield. I was looking for a pen so I could sign it as quickly as possible when my agent closed his briefcase, stood up and left the room. My dad and I looked at each other perplexed before reluctantly following him out.

When we got outside my agent said, "No way. That's an insult, nowhere near enough." My dad asked him what he was looking for and he replied, "I'm not sure, but more than that. Don't worry, they'll be back in touch."

We got back into the car and drove off and I was scratching my head wondering what we were doing. This was my big chance, and I didn't want it to fall through.

My agent dropped us off at a service station in Leicester, just off the M1, and then Brendan Phillips phoned. He'd already spoken to my agent and was not happy at all with what had happened, so he met us at the service station, drove us back to Pride Park and we signed the contract there and then, without my agent present. I suppose he was used to negotiating big contracts for established pros, but I was different. I'd had a few months playing at non-league level and hadn't achieved anything yet. Becoming a professional was my ultimate dream and I'm so thankful to Brendan for helping us get the deal over the line. My agent wasn't happy at all, although he was happy enough to take his cut of the deal even though he hadn't actually done anything!

I was over the moon at getting my big move, but I was also a little sad to be leaving Borough. Although I wasn't at Nuneaton for very long, they are such a fantastic club with wonderful supporters. It was such a magical experience that I will never forget. In all, I scored 14 goals in 21 appearances for Borough, and I was delighted to see them go on to win the league by 23 points at the end of the 1998/99 season, although I am still waiting for my winner's medal!

Everything happened so quickly. In just a few months, I'd gone from football being something I did at the weekend to seeing the dream lay out before me. The dust was kicked up when I signed for Nuneaton and hadn't really settled by the time I left.

After years of hard work and dedication, I had finally become a professional footballer.

*****

I thought I'd made it before I'd even kicked a ball for the Rams.

At the start of the 1998/99 season, I was desperate to become a professional footballer. If someone had offered me a contract at a League Two side, I'd have signed it immediately. So, to join a Premier League club as a centre forward was the icing on the cake.

I was an unproven, raw talent, who hadn't cost a lot of money which meant there no great expectations on me, so I didn't feel any pressure at all. I'd signed a three-year contract which gave me time to develop and prove that I was worthy of the label 'Premier League footballer'.

There aren't many stories of lads going straight from non-league to the Premier League and staying there. Jamie Vardy is non-league's biggest success story, but he spent two seasons in the Championship before making the step up to the top flight. I hadn't even been part of a professional club's academy, but rather than feeling intimidated, I was excited because I knew that I was on the brink of achieving something special.

The media interest began immediately; newspapers wanted to write the story; readers wanted to read it. Journalists frequently phoned our house looking for a quote or an interview. Dad did most of my talking and that helped alleviate some of the demands on me and my time because, rightly or wrongly, we agreed to everything and anything. I was lapping up the attention – I loved it, although I cringe when I look back at some of the old photos. The *Stamford Mercury* took me back to the Somerfield store where I used to work and I posed for photos behind the deli counter, dressed up in a butcher's hat and apron cutting some ham – crazy as I had never even worked in that section! It was funny because hardly anyone at the supermarket realised that I was a footballer because I never used to talk about it. My job was a nice release from football. The local press hadn't reported my move to Nuneaton, so my colleagues didn't know anything about my goalscoring exploits until they read about them in the newspapers when I moved to Derby.

To go from a supermarket shelf stacker to a Premier League footballer within six months meant my life changed massively. Pro footballers are expected to carry themselves in a certain way, dress a particular way, wear the right trainers. There are things you have to buy, like the houses and the cars. I didn't know any of that. I hadn't been part of that world before, so I did what I thought I was supposed to do. More importantly, I did what I wanted to do at first.

I imagine that nowadays with Facebook, Twitter and Instagram, there is a lot of pressure on the younger players to keep up with the pros because everyone can see what you're wearing, where you go, what car you drive, just from your social media sites. We didn't have that when I started out. We had Myspace and Friends Reunited, so I could lead the life I wanted without having to present a false lifestyle or trying to live up to unrealistic expectations. I led quite an innocent life really.

I always wore a tracksuit to training because that is how I thought footballers were supposed to dress. I couldn't believe it when I saw some of the players arriving to training dressed up like they were going out for dinner. I packed my toiletries in an Umbro washbag, whereas my teammates had Louis Vuitton, Gucci or Prada. At that time, I didn't want to change who I was, I wasn't ready to adapt.

Eventually, reality hits and I thought, *Everyone else is doing this so that must be what I have to do*. I looked around and saw what other people were wearing and doing and the peer pressure meant I began to follow. It's sad when that happened as I lost a little bit of the real me. Whilst getting dressed in the morning I'd analyse my wardrobe asking myself, *What can I wear that people won't take the mickey out of? Can I get away with those ripped jeans?* It becomes a way of life.

It was all new to me though at the start, I'd never stepped foot in a designer shop before I joined Derby – I couldn't afford it for one thing. As soon as I was earning decent money, I was able to go out and buy the things I wanted which was brilliant, but that didn't happen straight away. I didn't sign one day and start shopping at Selfridges and Harrods the next. I had to acclimatise, and it took me a while to get used to the money.

When my signing on fee was paid into my bank, I felt like I'd won the lottery. When you receive a large sum of money, it can go one of two ways; you go on a spending spree and blow the lot, or you don't know what to do with it. I was the latter. I'd seen how hard my parents had worked all their lives, so I understood the value of money. I had – and still have – a Nationwide account that I opened when I was five. I was still living at home and didn't really feel that I needed or wanted anything in particular. Even though I was a man, I felt uncomfortable spending money without gaining my parent's approval because I hadn't ever had to stand on my own two feet or make 'man' decisions before.

The one thing I did buy was my own car because I couldn't keep taking my dad's Ford Sierra Estate to and from training every day as he needed it to get to work, so I went to Motorpoint in Derby to see what kind of bargain I could get. My eyes were instantly drawn to a grey Ford Puma, an Irish import, it was gorgeous. It cost me £10,000. I loved that car.

I went straight from Motorpoint to Pride Park and bought myself a Derby County car sticker for the rear window, and a replica shirt from the club shop. I had been a Manchester United fan all my life, but I knew I needed to switch allegiances in my head in order to make the transition from United to Derby fan. Mum and Dad came with me, and they were like kids in a sweet shop! At Nuneaton you could buy a scarf and that was about it, but Derby's club shop sold all sorts: coats, polo shirts, hats, and even a Rammie the mascot cuddly toy. We were sharing the experience as a family.

We walked to the till with a basket laden with Derby County

goodies and Mum told them that I was a player as we'd discovered that players were entitled to a 20% discount. I was so shy, there was no way I was going to ask, especially as I'd only just signed and hadn't played a game. It was funny because the staff didn't even know who I was!

I was so proud of my new club and I wanted everyone to know I was a Derby player, so I'd wear my replica shirt when I was out and about in Stamford in the hope that someone might recognise me. I must have looked like a right knob but wearing that shirt all the time made it sink in that I was a player. I'd look down and see the badge and think, *Yes, that's my club.* Another part of the transition was taking down all the United posters from my bedroom walls, it was all part of the process of falling in love with Derby County.

My first professional training session was another totally new experience. I hadn't known anyone when I joined Nuneaton, but Derby's side was full of big-name players who I knew by reputation. It was awe inspiring as I walked out onto pitch at the Baseball Ground, alongside people I'd previously only seen on the television.

Igor Stimac was our defensive lynchpin and club captain. He commanded respect and had an aura around him that meant you didn't need to see him to know when he'd walked into the dressing room, you just knew. He dressed well, was an inspired leader and was exactly what you wanted from a skipper.

Darryl Powell was a London-born, Jamaican international, who later became Derby captain. He was unbelievable in training, never gave the ball away and was one of the best trainers I ever saw. I don't know why, but he never quite reached the same levels in a match. Whether it was the crowd or the pressure, I don't know.

Then there was Paolo Wanchope, a Derby legend, who was outstanding in matches but seemed to take it easy in training sessions. I'd requested Paolo's autograph when I was younger, and he was someone I admired greatly. So you can imagine how it felt when I partnered him up front in my first training match. It was surreal. I was also envious of him as he'd previously scored a wonder goal at Old Trafford.

Lee Carsley, an Ireland international midfielder, trained at such a high intensity. I watched him and knew that was the level

I needed to get to. Lee later became the manager of the England Under 21s, inspiring the next generation.

Another Ireland international within our ranks was Rory Delap. A versatile player, we called him the Lash because he could strike the ball so hard. He was a schoolboy javelin champion and is best remembered for his long throws, although we never utilised them at Derby which is a shame. During one session we were doing some patterns of play and rather than cross the ball, Rory threw it 30 metres. Jim remarked that he had a good throw, but we never thought about using it as a weapon, it wasn't our game. When he later moved to Stoke, they started scoring goals from his throw ins and reached the FA Cup Final, and I wondered if we'd missed out.

Our Italian duo, Stefano Eranio and Francesco Baiano, were technically incredible. Stefano was like a magician with the ball. I'd watch on mesmerised as he and Francesco played head tennis for ages without dropping the ball.

The quality of training was a huge step up to what I'd been used to. We did skill drills like chipping the ball to each other from twenty yards, controlling it and passing to someone else while making sure the ball never touched the ground. I'd never done anything like that before in my life. At Nuneaton we'd pass it around on the ground, maybe do a one two and that was it. Now it's a clipped ball in and you have to keep it in the air, so I very quickly learnt that I needed to adapt.

Another thing we did that was different was Rondo possession drills at the start of each session. That's where you have one lad in the centre trying to win the ball back from the others who are passing the ball around in a circle. If you give the ball away, it's your turn to go in the middle. I used to find myself in the centre a bit too often at first. I'd stand on the outside hoping no one passed to me because in my head I thought I'd give the ball away and when I did, I'd think, *Oh my God everyone is looking at me*. It was just a case of adjusting and getting used to the standard required.

I never felt like I was exposed or that I wasn't good enough. The plan was for me to establish myself in the reserves before easing me gently into the first team. Derby had a small squad, so the reserves and seniors trained together which gave me the opportunity to learn from these seasoned pros and international stars. Being around that environment built my confidence and made me feel part of the team from day one.

Derby were the perfect club for me and ticked so many boxes of things that you'd need or want: family club, small squad, short of strikers, down to earth staff and welcoming friendly teammates. Everything just felt right. Spurs and Leicester hadn't felt like this, so I knew everything had worked out the way it should have.

My teammates were fantastic and helped me settle in immediately. There were no embarrassing initiations, and it wasn't a loud or brash dressing room, although I found it very strange hearing so many foreign languages. In my naivety, I thought it was quite rude that not everyone spoke English! The lads had heard my story and they all wanted me to do well. I was so grateful and appreciative of everything that was coming my way and I was respectful of everyone around me.

The only downside was that I was never really myself. I was naturally quiet, a little shy, and developed imposter syndrome because things had happened so quickly. Some players may have thought I was a bit standoffish, but that wasn't me at all. I just never really came out of my shell at Derby, so not many of the lads ever got to know the real me and that's my fault.

On the training pitch, under the watchful eye of Steve McClaren, it was a different matter, and my new teammates respected my strong work ethic. I always gave 100%, although not everyone did. In football, I found that it was quite common for players to save themselves for the games. Not me, I'd chase every ball, was committed in the challenge and trained like I was playing in the FA Cup Final. I was so desperate to impress our manager, Jim Smith.

I'd only met Jim briefly when I played in my trial game, but I knew of his reputation. A hard-as-nails Yorkshireman, Jim had famously taken Oxford United from the Third Division to the top flight during the eighties, and was the manager of Derby when they won promotion to the Premier League in 1996. He was a formidable character, who scared me a little, if I'm honest. Jim loved the fact that I had previously played at a level he called parks football.

"Christie? Yes, he's come from parks football," he often told journalists.

CHAPTER 5
In the big league now

"Why don't you fuck off back to the supermarket?"

That was my first experience of Premier League football!

Jim showed a lot of confidence in me by naming me in the squad for an away match against Liverpool in November 1998, just weeks after signing. Yes, we had a lot of injuries, but he wouldn't have put me on the bench if he didn't think I could do it. I was handed the number 12 shirt, which was great for me as that was the closest number to the traditional 1-11. It was an amazing experience, walking out of the tunnel at Anfield, stepping out onto the pitch for the pre-match warm up and hearing the noise from the 40,000 fans. During the game, I cheered on the lads from the side-lines knowing that one day it would be me out there. To top it off we beat Liverpool 2-1, a fantastic result. However, the experience wasn't all positive.

I watched the first 20 minutes or so from the sub's bench and then I went out to warm up along the touchline, feeling a million dollars. Three months earlier my season had begun against Hastings Town and now I was warming up at Anfield. Everyone I had met on my journey so far had been positive and supportive, so I naively assumed that's how it would continue. I was wrong.

"Why don't you fuck off back to the supermarket?"

"Can't you grow any facial hair?"

"You're fucking shit"

I got absolutely hammered by the Liverpool supporters and I trudged back to the dugout thinking, *Is this what it's really like in the Premier League?*

I'd gone out there excited but didn't want to warm up anymore because I knew I'd get abused. I'd only ever watched Premier

League games on the television where you don't hear the insults, so it was a huge shock to me.

Sadly, I quickly learnt that's just what it was like and it was another thing I had to get used to. Home games were fine, it was all positive, but away stadiums were horrific. It's not nice at all, you just have to stand there are try to ignore it which isn't easy. I'd be thinking, *I wish they'd shut up*. As soon as one person says something and gets a laugh from the crowd, others join in, and you get a barrage of abuse. These are grown men I'm talking about, not kids. I was 19 years-old and some of those hurling insults were old enough to be my dad. In any other walk of life, it is deemed unacceptable to abuse and swear at people, but football tolerates it. I know that there will be people reading this saying, "It's part and parcel of the game. Footballers should just get on with it." But why should we? It's wrong and it has a big impact on players and their mental health. It affected me.

So, my first experience of being a Premier League footballer was more of a negative than positive.

I was frequently included in the squad as an unused substitute, but I felt a million miles away from actually playing in the Premier League. There was never any talk about a loan move – and I certainly didn't push for one – because I was getting match experience playing in the Pontins League for Derby's second string. Reserve games in the nineties were much more competitive than the Under 23 football we have today, because sides featured a mixture of experienced players who were out of favour or returning from injury and hungry youngsters.

My reserve team debut was against Blackburn Rovers, who lined up with their £7,500,000 record signing Kevin Davies and a promising young midfielder named David Dunn. There were always one or two names playing for the opposition and, rather than feeling awestruck, it motivated me.

Reserve football was the ideal transition from non-league to the Premier League. We played our homes at Derby's former home, the Baseball Ground, a stadium full of history, and although it was pretty dilapidated by then, it was still a proper ground which drew supporters. When we played Manchester United's reserves, 2,500 fans turned up to watch. It was the first time I'd played against United at any level and it was an incredible experience. I looked at their line up before the match and spotted David May, Raimond van der Gouw, Jonathan Greening and Mark Wilson on the team sheet. The match was shown live on MUTV, and I rose to the occasion scoring a brace in a 2-2 draw. I could have had a hat trick, but my second half strike was ruled out for offside.

These reserve games did wonders for my confidence, the more I played the more I thought, *You know what, I'm as quick as these, I'm as strong as these. I can score at this level.*

Everything the backroom staff at Derby did was designed to prepare me for the big stage. Steve Round and Billy McEwan played a massive part in my development. Steve used to hold mock interviews with me, setting the scene, he'd say "You've played well, scored a goal and now we're going to interview you." The camera would be running and off we'd go. It was brilliant and got me used to what it's like to have a camera shoved down your throat and questions fired from all directions. Whenever there was a media day, I'd hang around to observe the senior pros to see how they handled the press.

In December 1998, we went away to Dublin, Ireland, for our Christmas party. It was the first time I'd ever been on an airplane, which no one could believe. As we boarded the small propeller plane – not the ideal aircraft for your first ever flight – I was terrified, and the lads were taking the mickey. The actual party is a bit of a blur, but I do remember propping up the bar with Igor and watching in disbelief as he downed shots of whisky while smoking a fag. I felt a little disappointed in him as everything he'd done up until that point had been so professional and I couldn't understand how a top-level footballer could smoke.

The more time I spent around the first team, the more I wanted to be on the pitch with them in an actual match. I just needed a break, someone to be out of form or suffering with a minor injury so I would get picked. Then I could say that I'd played in the Premier League, even if it was just for 30 seconds. It was great training with the lads, being a professional footballer, earning good money and being in the squad, but having come so close it would mean nothing if I didn't actually play. I was just waiting for that opportunity to come and had to make sure that I grabbed it when it eventually presented itself. I didn't ever want to have to look in the mirror and say that I didn't make it.

On 30th January 1999 I got my chance. We were playing away at Sheffield Wednesday, and I spent the bulk of the first half warming up along the touchline, receiving the inevitable abuse. By that stage, I'd become a regular fixture on the bench, had been scoring lots of goals for the reserves and I knew that I was getting closer and closer to achieving my dream. Before every game I wondered if today was going to be the day.

Just before half time, our centre forward, Dean Sturridge, went down and had to receive treatment from our physio, Neil Sillett. When he returned to the bench, Neil turned to me and said, "Deano's done his hamstring so go and get warmed up." My heart started pounding with excitement. I was the only striker on the bench, the score was tied at 0-0 and we were playing well, so I couldn't imagine Jim changing the formation. Dean carried on until the break, but it was clear that he was in a lot of pain as he hobbled down the tunnel.

In the dressing room Neil spent a few minutes with Sturridge, before looking in my direction. As our eyes met, I knew that I was going on.

Jim Smith walked over to me, and I'll never forget what he said, "Your time has come. You're now in the big league, Son." I felt the hairs on the back of my neck stand on end, I was so inspired. Jim was a man of few words, but he didn't need to say much, I'd been waiting for this moment my whole life. The other lads came round to wish me luck. I was a little nervous of course, but I was desperate to get on the pitch and show everyone what I could do.

Spencer Prior popped up with a header to give us the lead in the 54th minute and, two minutes later, I got on the end of a through ball and was running towards the Wednesday goal when their goalkeeper, Pavel Srnicek, came out of the box and karate kicked me in my chest. He was shown the red card and we held on to a 1-0 win. We'd been struggling to win away at the time, so everyone was buzzing after the match – me included. When you're on the bench you never really feel a part of it, and although I hadn't scored, I'd had an impact on the game, so I felt able to celebrate with the lads. I have nothing but fond memories of that day.

It was also a great day for Nuneaton as there was an agreement when I was transferred that meant Derby would have to pay a further £25,000 when I made my debut. It wasn't massive money to Derby but meant a lot to Nuneaton.

That evening watching myself on *Match of the Day* was crazy. It was the first time I'd seen myself play on national television, so I recorded it and watched it over and over again knowing that it didn't matter what else I achieved in my life, no one could ever take that away from me. Playing in the Premier League was my ultimate dream and I had fulfilled it, but I started to crave more. I didn't want that to be the end of the story, I didn't want a 45-minute cameo to define me as a person. I knew that there was even more to come from me.

Not long after the Wednesday game, I went into Derby to do a bit of shopping. As I was strolling around the city centre, I suddenly became aware of a group of lads following me. They weren't acting aggressively or anything like that, but I didn't know how to handle it. After a few more minutes, I noticed that they were still tracking me, so I panicked and walked into the nearest store, which happened to be Specsavers. I didn't wear glasses, but I started trying on different frames, whilst looking at the window to see if the lads were still out there. The staff had noted my odd behaviour and assumed I was with the group of lads outside. They must have thought that I had been sent in to steal something because a security guard came over to ask me what I was doing! Looking back now, I should have just said hello, signed an autograph and then they'd have left me alone, but it was all new to me and I didn't know how to handle the attention.

I made my second and final appearance of the 1998/99 season on 20th March, coming on as a substitute in a 4-1 defeat at Elland Road.

My two Premier League appearances led to another deluge of reporters wanting to speak to me and I loved the attention – who wouldn't? It was the moment my life began to change, and I had to learn to adapt to my new-found fame.

CHAPTER 6
Kicked by Keane

Fame is a funny thing. At the start of my career, I craved the attention and wanted to be recognised everywhere I went. I was proud to be a Premier League footballer and was more than happy to sign autographs and pose for photographs with fans and well-wishers.

But I soon realised that not everyone wanted me to succeed, and I had to contend with the darker side of fame.

Stamford is a small, tight-knit community where everyone knew everyone. I knew that it would be different when I went out into the town with my mates, but I didn't realise how different.

My friends and those who knew me before I signed for Derby treated me the same, but I could sense the resentment from the people I didn't know. They looked at me with disdain: *How dare this lad from the same place as me, who I used to see out and about become a footballer.*

It was crazy and, sadly, it's not unusual. When I speak to Middlesbrough supporters, they tell me that not all Boro fans like players from their area making something of themselves. They dislike people like Jonathan Woodgate and Stewart Downing, the Middlesbrough born players who enjoyed exceptional careers. It's sad, but it's just the way it is. Most young boys dream of becoming a footballer and the reality is that very few actually make it, so there is often a lot of jealousy towards those who have.

The abuse I received on the touchline was one thing, but to receive it on nights out with friends and family was totally out of order. It wasn't my fault that I was doing what others dreamed of. I never became arrogant or got above my station, that was never me. My friends and brother used to keep an eye out for me during nights out to make sure we steered clear of the idiots looking to cause trouble.

I remember one day, watching a Liverpool game with some mates in a bar in Stamford. When Michael Owen scored a goal, someone stood up and shouted, "Now there's a proper English striker, not like the shit that we've got here." I didn't expect any fanfare, I just wanted people to treat me normally, like they had before.

Another time in a bar, I was washing my hands – people always spoke to me in the toilets for some reason – when I was approached by a man who aggressively asked, "What's this I've heard about you burning £20 notes? Who do you fucking think you are?"

"What?" I replied, stunned. "I've never done that. Let's calm down and have a drink."

So, I sat him down, bought him and his mates a round of drinks and by the end of our chat he apologised to me, "Sorry about before. You're a lovely bloke."

*****

After a whirlwind season it was nice to let my hair down in the summer on a holiday in Las Americas, Tenerife, with my brother. We had a great time.

We didn't have phones with internet access in those days, so we had to wait for the fixture list to be printed in one of the English newspapers. The day they were released, I bought a newspaper and took it onto the beach to pour over the fixtures. I looked for our opening game (Leeds), our last (Chelsea) and then the two matches against Manchester United. I spent the rest of the afternoon excited about the season ahead, wondering if I'd get the opportunity to play against the team I had supported as a boy.

I was raring to go when I returned for pre-season training in July 1999, my first as a pro, but it wasn't as difficult as I expected. I actually found that the stuff we had done at Nuneaton was harder; driving out to woodlands, running these ridiculously steep hills with legs feeling like they were on fire!

At Derby, it was more structured and technical, with a lot of ball work and the fitness improvements came from the bleep test. As you'd expect from a group of young lads, it became very competitive, and I prided myself on always being one of the last players to drop out. Darryl Powell was incredibly fit and often won, but I constantly gave him a run for his money.

I've always been a fairly talented athlete, blessed with natural fitness, so training was never an issue for me. In fact, I loved it. Dane Farrell was our strength and conditioning coach and he taught me so many things that I still use today. It was unbelievable really, day to day, one to one training, designed to make me stronger, fitter, and faster. And it worked too.

I'd never been one for pumping weights. Sure, I went through a phase as a kid where my brother, Gavin, and I bought some dumbbells and were convinced that with a few biceps curls we were going to turn into Rocky Balboa!

Dane designed a programme for me where I was in the gym twice a week doing pull ups, sits ups, press ups and weight lifting. Before long I noticed that my physique was changing, and I was developing muscles. Don't get me wrong, I wasn't becoming Arnold Schwarzenegger, but I was beginning to look like an athlete, instead of a skinny, scrawny kid. The sign of a good upper body workout was when my arms were so sore that I struggled to lift them to wash my hair in the shower! It was all geared to getting me ready for the season ahead, so that when the campaign kicked off, I'd be in the best possible physical shape.

The issue I had was that my body wasn't attuned to the stresses and strains that it was being put through; I was pounding my legs running and training everyday which I wasn't used to, and I developed Iliotibial Band Syndrome. The IT band is a big, thick muscle that runs down the side of your leg, mine had tightened and was rubbing against my knee causing swelling and inflammation when I ran. The pain was unreal, it felt like someone was sticking a knife into my knee when I bent it. I'd had the problem for a while, but the club didn't seem to know what was causing the pain until I self-diagnosed – with the help of Google – and explained what I'd found to the physios. When they knew it was the IT band, they put me on a pain management programme, instead of fixing the issue. It was the first example of my body going, *Woah, I'm not sure I like this*. Sadly, it wasn't going to be the last of my injury worries.

IT band aside, the fitness work was great, and I also started receiving proper coaching for the first time. Some of the advice seemed so simple but it was all effective and I passed that information on to the kids that I later coached.

I remember Billy McEwan telling me, ahead of night match under the floodlights, to look at the ground because I'll be able to see the shadow of my opponent. During the game, I looked down and instantly saw where the defender was, so I knew where to make my run.

Billy also said, "If they breathe on you in the penalty area, you go down." So I did, and I won a lot of penalties during my career with that technique. I need to be clear on this, I'm not talking about diving, that's completely different and something I never did, this was about making the most of the contact.

I was lapping it all up and must have been the perfect student. I had no bad habits to unlearn either because I hadn't come through an academy. The Derby lads who'd progressed through the ranks had already been 80% shaped by the time they reached the first team, but I was an open book, a piece of clay ready to be moulded into the player they wanted me to become. I was always willing to learn, took on board everything that was said and never questioned what I was being asked to do. During training, some of the young players would say, "I'm not doing that." I couldn't believe it. *You've got the opportunity of a lifetime here; the coaches are trying to turn you into a pro and you're not putting it in.* I put 100% effort into everything I did for every single minute, whether it was running, technique drills or playing matches, and I never complained once.

There was a lot of optimism for the new campaign. We'd finished 8th at the end of the 1998/99 season, our second successive top ten finish, and there was a good vibe around the training ground. We had turned Pride Park into a bit of a fortress, so opposing teams didn't like coming to us. We always gave the big clubs a run for their money and were capable of getting a result against anyone, so the talk amongst the supporters was about us maintaining that level and maybe making a push for a European spot.

To bolster the squad, Jim Smith paid Crewe £4,000,000 for talented young midfielder Seth Johnson. Seth possessed a sweet left foot, was a really good player, and it was clear that he was destined for bigger and better things. He went on to play for England, but never really fulfilled his potential as injury prematurely ended his career.

Andy Oakes, a goalkeeper who became backup to Mart Poom, was another arrival.

The big problem we faced was that we lost two of our key players, Paolo Wanchope, and Igor Stimac, who both signed for West Ham United. Their departures left two huge gaps in the side, especially Igor who was our captain and leader, the glue that held everything together at the back. We never replaced him.

Jim tried to replace Paolo with Argentine striker Esteban Fuertes, but he didn't stay long. Fuertes held an Italian passport so didn't need a work permit, at least that's what we thought. He came in, scored a couple of goals and everything was hunky dory until we returned from a warm weather training camp in Portugal. As we walked through the airport, we noticed that Esteban was no longer with the group, and someone said he had been detained by customs! I'm not sure what happened – there was talk of his passport being a forgery – but he disappeared after that and never played for us again.

With the exception of Fuertes, there was never any talk of another striker coming in, but even if there had been, I wasn't frightened. I was biding my time, safe in the knowledge that if I kept smashing in goals for the reserves, sooner or later I would get my chance in the starting line up.

It was a frustrating start to the season for Derby and for me personally. We won just two of our first 10 Premier League games and I spent more time warming up the touchlines than I did on the pitch. The only highlight for me was coming on as a substitute for the last 15 minutes against Manchester United on 20th November 1999. To play against Man United at Pride Park was unreal. Although the opponents were idols of mine, some of whom I'd collected autographs, I adopted the attitude that I belonged on the same pitch as them.

This United side had completed an unprecedented treble just a few months earlier and they oozed quality. It wasn't just their technical ability though, I learnt that they were cute too. I went on a little dribble, brought my foot back to cross the ball, and felt a sudden pain in my calf as the ball ran away from me. I turned around and saw Roy Keane giving me a little wink. He knew that I was planning to cross the ball so he'd angled his foot so that when I brought my leg back, my calf would collide with his studs. *I'm in the men's league now,* I thought. It was a very clever tactic as he stopped me without even having to make a tackle.

As we were walking off the pitch, I decided to ask Ryan Giggs for his shirt. I was gutted when he said that they weren't allowed to swap. We lost the game 2-1, but my lasting memory of that game is being kicked by Roy Keane and not getting Ryan Giggs' shirt!

I probably should have gone around the other United players, asking each of them in turn until I got a shirt, but I had to change my mindset from that of a fan to a pro footballer. Having that moment on the pitch with my heroes is something I'll never forget and means more than any shirt would have. However, I did manage to get a little souvenir from the game.

After I'd got changed, I decided to ask Alex Ferguson to sign my programme. I hung around the tunnel area and when I saw him emerge from the visitor's dressing room, I walked over and asked for his autograph. I don't think he knew who I was, probably just assumed I was a fan, but he signed it anyway which was nice. I vowed to make sure that Sir Alex would know all about me one day.

*****

It was around this time that I took the first rung on the property ladder. During the summer, I'd moved out of my parent's house in Stamford, into digs in Derby which had been a huge change for me, one I didn't really enjoy.

Despite being in a house with other lads, I felt lonely and lost. I never felt comfortable living as a guest in someone else's house, not being in charge of my own decisions. Fighting for a seat on the sofa to watch television, but not the programme that I wanted to watch, was alien to me.

One evening, I decided to go to McDonalds for a meal, but when I got back to digs my landlady told me that dinner was on the table. She worked in a café at a local garden centre and used to bring the leftovers home for us. I was full up, but I sat down and ate my dinner out of politeness. I had to force it down though as I was stuffed from my McDonalds. I hardly slept that night as I was suffering badly with indigestion! I knew I couldn't stay there for much longer, so I bought my own house.

I looked at a few properties around Derbyshire before settling on a new-build home in Chellaston, a nice little suburb on the southern outskirts of Derby. The builders were Birch Homes whose chairman, Peter Gadsby, was also a director at Derby County, so he made sure I was well looked after, leaving me a bottle of champagne and a card with his personal telephone number in case I had any problems.

I bought a stunning five-bedroom, detached house for £180,000. I was living on my own, so didn't really need one that size, but I could afford it and thought it would be a good investment for the future.

I didn't have a clue how to furnish a house, so my mum and dad took me to Ikea in Nottingham where I bought some furniture. The only thing I lavished on myself was a conservatory – which was considered a luxury at the time – and a projector with a large screen so I could watch the football in my bedroom.

It was strange being on my own in a big house, but it afforded me the independence that I needed at the time. I had the added responsibility of paying bills, and I quickly went from a boy to a man. My parents often stayed with me the night before a home game which was nice and helped me get into the right frame of mind. We'd play pool, or table football, and just chill out. There was never any talk about football because I always needed to switch off before a match.

The day after a game, all the kids who lived near me would knock on my door and we'd have a kickabout in the back garden. It was a good way of keeping myself grounded and ensured that I didn't lose my love of the game.

CHAPTER 7
This is your moment, Son

By the time December 1999 came around, Derby were sitting in the relegation zone, with just three wins from 17 games. In just a few months our European ambitions were over and our focus had turned to survival.

Jim Smith delved into the transfer market to add some much-needed quality, signing striker Branko Strupar and Scotland international midfielder Craig Burley for £3,000,000 each.

Branko had been a prolific goal scorer in the Belgian league for his previous club, Genk, but rather than see him as another obstacle in my pursuit of becoming a first team regular, I considered him a future strike partner and someone I could learn from on the training ground. He was a target man, a similar player to Anton Thomas, and I always enjoyed playing alongside someone who could hold the ball up and create space for me to exploit.

Craig, a top player, was a big Celtic fan who had also played for them, so when I drew his name out of the hat for the club's secret Santa, I knew exactly what to get him – a Rangers shirt with his name and number on the back! It was all good banter, as were most of the presents given out, but I felt Andy Oakes' gift to me was a little too personal. I've already mentioned that I was a very shy, quiet, lad who had found it difficult to forge friendships in the dressing room, so when I opened my present from Andy and saw that it was a book titled *How to Communicate,* I was hurt. Everyone was laughing when they saw the book, and I joined in, but inside I felt upset. I know it was done in jest, and I enjoyed a joke as much as anyone, but I thought this was too personal. It was something that I was already aware of and anxious about, I didn't need to be told. I certainly didn't need a book!

Rather than make me want to communicate more, I became even more self-conscious and retreated further into my shell. I always found that I was trying to impress people because I desperately wanted to be liked and respected. I spent too much energy trying to be the person I thought people wanted me to be, instead of being my normal self. As a result, my teammates never got to know the real me.

It was a tough time for me; the euphoria of making my debut had died down, I had struggled to forge friendships in the dressing room and was yet to start a match for the first team.

I was biding my time, scoring regularly for the reserves, and had made a handful of substitute appearances, but it's hard to impact a game when you're only getting a few minutes here and there, or sometimes not even coming on at all.

It was equally frustrating for my parents as they attended every match, home and away, even though they knew it was unlikely that I'd play. They travelled in the hope that I would get on for at least a minute. Their support and dedication in following me around the country meant so much to me and I am forever grateful.

There was a village in between Stamford and Derby called Nether Broughton and when we used to drive through it, Dad would joke, "Look, Son, they've named a village after you. Never Brought On!" Thanks, Dad!

I was becoming frustrated, but I never lost faith in my ability. Deep down, I knew that I'd get an opportunity and I didn't ever contemplate knocking on Jim Smith's door demanding to play. Even the experienced players were a little scared of him, so you can imagine how I felt as a young lad! I had to trust that he would start me when he felt the time was right.

There was another young striker in the ranks who was ahead of me in the pecking order at the time, Marvin Robinson. Marvin had made his full debut in the game against Manchester United when Roy Keane kicked me, and he had started a few more games since then. He did OK, but didn't score and as a striker, people expect goals. Still, he was getting rave reviews in the *Derby Telegraph*, and although I was pleased for him, I was also a little envious as I wanted it to be me.

*****

On 14th January 2000, we travelled up to the North East for a crucial match against Middlesbrough. Deon Burton was our only fit senior striker, so I assumed Marvin would partner him up front like he had done previously, and that I'd be on the bench as usual. I was reading the *Derby Telegraph* on the coach up to Middlesbrough and it was all about Marvin.

We stayed overnight at Crathorne Hall Hotel, a beautiful stately home in North Yorkshire, and on the day of the game we went for a stroll around the grounds after our pre-match meal. I was walking with a couple of the lads when Jim Smith approached me and asked for a word. As soon as he said that I knew that I was starting because there was no other reason for him to speak to me on the day of a game.

I'll never forget what he said to me, "This is your moment, Son. You're in the starting line up."

The butterflies – a combination of nerves and excitement – kicked in instantly. I was just glad that he told me after I'd eaten as I wouldn't have been able to manage anything if I'd known earlier. I always struggled to eat before a game anyway because of a mixture of apprehension and anxiety. I'd force a bit of chicken down me whilst wondering how others could shovel a full meal down their necks! Everyone deals with things differently, I suppose.

I walked back to the lads with a huge smile on my face, trying to play it nice and cool even though I was doing cartwheels inside thinking, *Wow, I'm finally playing.* The coaches and my teammates wished me luck, but no one was massively fussed because they had their own games to prepare for. I phoned my parents, and they were over the moon for me, although they didn't go overboard or give me any instructions as they knew that wouldn't help. I didn't need the occasion hyping up, I already knew how big this moment was.

It probably helped me that I hadn't signed and made my debut the next day. I'd spent more than a year thinking about this moment, desperate for an opportunity, and this was it.

This was my chance.

I had earned this.

I reminded myself of everything I had done to get to this moment; working hard, being determined, chasing lost causes and, most importantly, scoring goals. We had Dean Sturridge,

Branko Strupar and Marvin waiting in the wings, so I knew I had to make my mark.

It was the perfect match for me to make my full debut: we were away so I didn't feel the weight of expectation from 30,000 Derby fans, Boro, managed by my childhood hero, Bryan Robson, were struggling in the league and they had an experienced but slow defence.

Walking out onto the pitch at the Riverside was an incredible moment. I knew that my parents, sitting in the stands, were the proudest people inside the stadium and I wanted to repay them for everything they had done for me.

The game couldn't have gone any better from my point of view.

In the eighth minute we won a corner. Seth Johnson's left footed inswinger was flicked on at the near post by Deon Burton, and I, standing unmarked in the six-yard box, headed it into the goal. I heard the cheers from the Derby fans on the other side of the ground and I dropped to my knees in elation. It was a fantastic moment, I knew the feeling of scoring a goal of course, but doing it on the big stage in front of all those people was on a whole other level.

My energy levels, which had dropped during the build up to the game, were now back at full capacity as adrenaline coursed through my veins, and I was raring to go. As I ran back to the centre circle I thought, *Right, I want another one now.*

Early in the second half, Deon Burton doubled our lead, and a few minutes later we scored our third.

Steve Elliott sent a ball over the top of the Middlesbrough defence for me to chase, although it was a lost cause. There was no way that I was going to get there before Mark Schwarzer, the Boro keeper, but at youth level I had learnt that goalkeepers weren't great with their feet and if I ran at them, I would put them under pressure which would occasionally cause them to make a mistake. So I chased Schwarzer, saw him hesitate and that was when I made my move to intercept the ball. He tried to chip it past me, but because of the way I'd positioned my body the ball hit my chest and landed kindly at my feet.

The noise of the crowd faded away and I was transported back to the field opposite Drift Road, where I had spent hours and hours practising scoring from different angles, conditioning my body for this very moment. I didn't need to think about what I was doing, I let my instincts take over.

I dummied the keeper and as soon as I was past Schwarzer I knew that I would score. I didn't even need to look at the goal, I just angled my foot and slotted it into the net before running to the crowd and waving to my parents who were sitting somewhere amongst the jubilant Derby fans. What an incredible moment.

I wanted my hat trick, but I'd put so much into the match that I was suffering with cramp and had to come off just after Middlesbrough pulled a goal back. Still, two goals on my full debut was a pretty good achievement. *It's quite easy this scoring in the Premier League lark,* I thought to myself as I walked off the pitch to a standing ovation from the travelling Derby supporters. Craig Burley scored our fourth right at the end to give us a 4-1 victory – what a match!

In the dressing room, everyone was buzzing and congratulating me. I felt so good, I just wish that I could have bottled up that feeling so I could experience it again. I had an ice bath and then Dane Farrell came over to tell me that everyone wanted to speak to me.

So I got changed, did my bit for *Match of the Day*, and then I met the written press, radio stations, and did another television interview with more cameras shoved in my face – everyone wanted a piece of me. I had worked so hard for this moment, had waited so long, I was determined to enjoy every minute of it. The mock interviews that Steve Round had conducted meant that I felt so comfortable in front of the cameras.

I met up with my parents after the match and they were so happy. All the sacrifices they had made for me had paid off. It was a brilliant, brilliant day, and at the time was the greatest moment of my career. What that day did for my confidence was unreal.

Football is a game of fine margins. Jim had chosen me ahead of Marvin Robinson, and if I hadn't scored, maybe my journey would have been completely different. Maybe Marvin's story would have had a different ending too. Unfortunately for him, he didn't start another game for Derby again.

One of the interviews I gave was with the *Derby Telegraph* and they asked me if there was anything that I would change from the day. I replied that I regretted not having asked for Gary Pallister's shirt. Pallister was another one of my heroes growing up, I used to have his picture on my wall, so to play against him was huge. After the game I was caught up in the moment, dealing with my own emotions and it slipped my mind to ask him. It would have been nice to have a memento from that match, I told them.

I was on cloud nine and returned to training on the Monday with a spring in my step. The Middlesbrough game was our second win on the bounce, so there was a positive atmosphere around the place. When you're winning you can't wait to go in to training and you don't want to leave. It's the total opposite after a loss.

At the Ramarena, where we trained, there was a huge rack where each player had a pigeon hole for fan mail. I had walked past it every day for the last year, and it was obvious who the big players were – Stimac, Wanchope, Eranio, and Baiano – as their pigeon holes were piled high, whereas mine had always remained empty. After the Boro game, I started to receive letters from fans. I went from autograph hunter to the one being hunted, and I loved it. I signed everything and replied personally to all my mail because I knew how much it meant to supporters.

A week later, there was a strange-shaped package waiting for me amongst my fan mail. I opened it and inside was Gary Pallister's Middlesbrough shirt, signed 'To Malcolm.' That was a lovely gesture from Gary, and that shirt still means a lot to me even now. I occasionally bump into Gary now and again, he's a lovely bloke, although he doesn't know I used to idolise him!

Our next match was at home to Coventry, and I was expecting to keep my place in the starting line-up. As a striker, people only want to know you if you are scoring goals, and after my brace against Boro, I thought I'd made it impossible for Jim to leave me out. However, Jim obviously thought differently as when we were doing the passages of play session a few days before the match, I wasn't in the first eleven. Instead, the fit-again Branko Strupar got the nod. I couldn't believe it and Jim never explained why he was dropping me. I respected Jim's decision, but it wasn't the right one in my opinion. I didn't need holding back, I was like a coiled spring.

During the game, I made a point of warming up as often as I could, stretching in front of the bench, reminding Jim that I was ready to go. He left it until the 80th minute before bringing me on and I got a huge ovation from the fans which was amazing. I was desperate to score in front of the home supporters, but ten minutes isn't really enough time to get into the game and make a difference.

We drew 0-0 and all the questions after the match were asking why I hadn't played. I told the journalists that I wasn't injured, that it was a tactical decision from Jim, although even to this day I don't understand why he didn't pick me.

Our next match was another home fixture, this time against struggling Sheffield Wednesday, and I was back in the starting line up.

Wednesday took the lead in the first half through Gilles De Bilde. I had an unbelievable chance to equalise just after half time when I should have headed the ball into the empty net, but I got under it and ended up hitting the bar instead.

The Owls doubled their lead before Branko pulled one back for us with twenty minutes still to play. In the 89th minute, Simon Donnelly made it 3-1 to the visitors and I think everyone assumed that the game was finished.

But Jim and his coaching staff had instilled a never-say-die mentality in us that meant we didn't know when we were beaten. Craig Burley scored from close range a minute later to give us a fighting chance and then we equalised with the last kick of the game.

The ball fell to me in the six-yard box. I whipped in a low cross towards goal, the ball hit a couple of deflections and went in. I tried to celebrate but my leg cramped up, so I just stood in front of the fans, arms aloft, before stiff leg jogging back to the centre circle. It wasn't really my goal, but it was attributed to me, and I certainly wasn't going to come out after the game and say I didn't want it!

Wednesday were devastated to have thrown away a two-goal lead, and I don't think they ever recovered as they were relegated at the end of the season. But from my point of view, it was a great game to be involved in, and a hell of a comeback.

My performances led to Derby offering me a new four-year contract that I was delighted to sign. My agent negotiated the deal and asked me to sign a piece of paper stating that Derby County had included an additional £100,000 in my contract that I needed to pay to my agent. Although I felt it was a lot of money, I was still naive at the time, so I signed the paper and was told to pay him in instalments. It was farcical really when I look back, meeting him in a service station car park and handing over brown envelopes containing £5,000 in cash.

However, what I didn't realise was that my agent had already agreed that Derby would pay his fee directly to him and it is illegal for an agent to take payments from both player and club.

Not long after I paid the first instalment, my dad was talking to an agent from SFX, the biggest sports agency in the UK at the time, and they were shocked when he told them what was happening. SFX said that they'd look into it and would cover any solicitor's costs incurred. It was a no brainer for me; I was going to get my current agent off my back, have the best sports agency firm looking after me, and it wasn't going to cost me a penny.

It took months to resolve and I found the frequent trips to Nottingham to see my solicitor were distracting me at a time when I should have been focussed on my career. The matter was eventually resolved so I didn't have to pay anymore instalments and my agent had his license revoked.

From that moment on, I remained in the team, either as a starter or occasionally a sub, for the rest of the season. I did well too, scoring three more times – against Sunderland, Southampton, and Wimbledon.

I didn't really have a celebration, it was all off the cuff, I just reacted in the moment. Sometimes I'd go crazy, other times, I'd be reserved, but I was always buzzing inside. There is no greater feeling in football than the moment the ball hits the back of the net. The crowd noise, the emotions, the instant adrenaline – it's an amazing feeling.

Despite my personal success, it was a disappointing campaign for the club as we finished in 16th place, just five points above the relegation zone. We had struggled in all honesty. We never had that confidence to play free flowing football and we didn't have a lot of creativity in the team, so most of the goals I scored were from picking up scraps or chasing balls down.

The most creative player at the club was Georgi Kinkladze, he was a wizard with the ball and magnificent to be around. He wasn't the same player who had burst onto the scene with

My first love - Superman.

A rare picture of me and Dad.
He was usually behind the camera!

Me and my brother Gavin, the glory hunter!

Me and Mum.

Say cheese! St George's School, Stamford, football team.

Me and Gavin collecting the Panini stickers, ironically open on the Nottingham Forest page!

Northborough Under 13s in 1992.

My youth manager at Deeping Rangers, Bromley Clarke, taught me so much.

I had the pleasure of playing through the years at Deeping Rangers FC, from boy to man, and loved every minute of it. Here winning the league cup (I am front row, second from right).

The Man United Shrine AKA my bedroom.

The Ryan Giggs look: permed hair, United kit and Reebok boots.

Me, Dad, Mum and Gavin.

Playing for Nuneaton Borough in 1998.

One of my fondest memories after signing for Derby was scoring 2 goals against Man United reserves. Pictured with David May and Raimond van der Gouw (19/01/99).

Scoring in the 8th minute on my first start for Derby in the Premier League was a dream come true. I'd be celebrating a second shortly after half time. (vs Middlesbrough 15/01/00)

Signing my new contract with the gaffer Jim Smith in March 2000.

Winning the Young Player of the Year was reward for my hard work.

I spent all my childhood dreaming of scoring in front of the Stretford End at Old Trafford. The ball was only ever going in one place - past Fabien Barthez (vs Man United 05/05/01).

Relax, relax! I had no idea where I was running, but I was buzzing inside. Left to right: Horacio Carbonari, Paul Boertien and Rory Delap.

No, I haven't fainted! I think the enormity of what I had achieved was sinking in. Andy Cole, one of my childhood heroes is in the foreground.

My favourite picture from my career: fist pump to Jim Smith, ball in the back of the net, with one of my United Heroes, and then England Captain, David Beckham.

Celebrating my first goal for England Under 21s with Jermain Defoe (vs Mexico 24/05/01).

Always a proud moment singing the national anthem (vs Greece 05/06/01)

Securing England's qualification to the 2002 UEFA Under 21 European Championships (vs Greece 05/10/01). The tournament turned out to be a sliding doors moment for me.

Manchester City in 1995, but we saw glimpses of his immense talent, like a drop of the shoulder, a turn of pace, or nutmegging an opponent. When he made his move, I'd make mine, and he assisted the majority of the goals I scored. He is the player I am always asked about by Derby fans which shows he is still held in very high regard.

He was an enigma off the pitch too. One day he'd turn up to training in an old banger, dressed like a homeless person, and the next he'd arrive in a Ferrari wearing an Armani suit! To look at him, you wouldn't think he was a footballer, but that was Georgi.

I finished the season with six goals from 10 starts – not a bad return – and I also made 11 appearances from the bench. It was a huge honour for me to win Derby County's Young Player of the Year award at the end of my breakthrough season. My aim, as I went away on my summer break, was to enjoy a good pre-season before going all guns blazing in the 2000/01 campaign.

Unfortunately, after an unexpected start, my summer turned out to be a total disaster.

CHAPTER 8
Three Lions and a hospital drip

Slovakia wasn't where I had envisaged spending the summer of 2000, but that was exactly where I ended up.

Just days after the season finished, I was lying on the bed in my room at my parent's house when Mum came upstairs, knocked on the door and said, "Howard Wilkinson is on the phone for you." Howard was the manager of England Under 21s, so I was a bit puzzled as there had been no talk or even rumours around me being called up to the international scene. *England managers don't ring people at home,* I thought, wondering if it was a wind up.

"Quick, Malcolm, don't keep him waiting," Mum said in an attempt to hurry me up. So, I went downstairs and, sure enough, Howard Wilkinson was on the phone.

England had qualified for the Under 21 European Championship that were taking place during May and June 2000. Howard explained that although he had already named his squad, he needed a reserve in case there was an injury and he wanted me to fly out to Slovakia to be the 19th man. I was shaking with excitement.

The call came completely out of the blue. It wasn't like I'd been playing regularly, waiting for the squad to be announced or expecting that phone call. This was totally random. The only concern I had was that I was going out as the spare man so I knew that in all likelihood I wouldn't be playing, but I had the conversation with my parents and knew that I couldn't let this opportunity pass me by. I'd broken into the Derby side, scored a couple of goals and the natural progression was to represent my country.

Under 21 football is a cycle and there were a number of players playing in their final tournament because of their age, so I saw it as a chance to get to know Howard and to show the national coaches what I could do.

The way the FA did things for England was perfect. Everything is organised with military precision, and you are treated like a VIP. I was measured up for a Paul Smith suit and given a ton of freebies, including shoes, a wallet, and a watch. A car was sent to pick me up from Stamford, where I was driven to Heathrow and flown first class to Bratislava, the capital of Slovakia, where I met up with the rest of the lads.

We had a strong team featuring Frank Lampard, Jamie Carragher, Ledley King, Paul Robinson and Danny Murphy. My Derby teammate Seth Johnson was also in the squad, so it was nice to see a familiar face. Some of the boys were already top Premier League players and it was a real eye opener for me. The standard of training was at a totally different level to anything I'd done before. During keep ball sessions, the ball was whizzing around, and no one was giving it away which made me feel under pressure to the extent that I didn't want the ball in case I gave it away. When we played a training match, I was on the same team as Lampard, a first team regular with West Ham, and his presence made me raise my game as I didn't want to let him down. It was so competitive; everyone was scrapping for their place, and it gave me the realisation that I'd only come so far and still had a hell of a long way to go.

I'd gotten used to the way we did things at Derby, but I discovered that England's methods were complexly different and much more intense. Howard was very methodical in his approach to football with a big focus on set plays. We spent hour after hour drilling corners and free kicks, learning where to stand in different scenarios. It all became a bit mundane and there was a distinct lack of laughter during the sessions. He didn't have us with him for very long, so I could understand why he took that approach, but it certainly wasn't much fun for a group of young lads who'd endured a gruelling season with our clubs and could have done with a more light hearted approach.

Howard, an old school manager, who had enjoyed success as manager of Leeds United, commanded respect, but he also lived up to his nickname 'Sergeant Wilko' with his regimented approach.

I quickly learnt that I was going to have to fall in line. Everything was scheduled, from what time we ate, to the time we went to sleep, and it all felt too structured to me. If we had a night game, we had to have a nap in the afternoon and the physio would come round to check that our lights were out. It was way too strict, feeling more like a boot camp than a football environment, and I felt a little on edge.

We were a group of youngsters who didn't really know one another, and I feel we should have spent more time mixing as a group and building camaraderie, but we didn't do that. When we arrived at the hotels, we were given our room keys and a detailed itinerary telling us where we had to be and at what time. It was almost like being on a school trip with the teachers telling us what to do all the time! I didn't think it should have been as regimented as that. Yes, I understand that we needed to know the formation and tactics, and we had some really good sessions with the analysts watching videos, but there needed to be a bit more time spent on bonding, making everyone feel comfortable with each other.

The result was that cliques were formed – the London-based lads stuck together, as did teammates from the same club teams – the coaches didn't try to stop it and that obviously trickled through to the senior side in later years.

When he became England manager, Gareth Southgate radically changed the way things are done with the national side and made it a much more inclusive squad which clearly had a massive impact on tournament performances. I think it helps that we have St George's Park, where there are various activities for the players to do together, like swimming, basketball, etc., and you can really see the difference it made to have a good team spirit in the squad. It makes you wonder what England could have won with the so-called Golden Generation without the cliques.

Howard and his coaches should have got us together and encouraged us to have a laugh and a joke, creating a better team spirit. Once you've got the unity there, players enjoying each other's company, that's half the battle. The football side could almost take care of itself at that level as we're talking about top, top players. The majority of that England Under 21 squad were first team regulars of big clubs, with eight of the 11 who started the opening game of the tournament going on to win full England caps.

I don't want this to sound like I am not appreciative of being called up, I was so grateful, and I really enjoyed the experience. I think it was hard for me as I knew I was the spare part, and everyone else also knew that I was the spare part.

Just before our opening game against Italy, Howard took me to one side and told me that I wasn't going to be in the squad as everyone was fit. He gave me the choice of staying with the boys or going home which was a difficult decision. On the one hand, if I stayed, I'd get to experience tournament football first hand, I'd get to know the lads better and have the opportunity to impress Howard in training. On the other hand, I had no chance of playing and I was worried that an injury could affect my preparation for the coming season. I discussed it with Howard, and he told me that if I kept doing well for Derby, he'd call me up to the squad properly, so I decided to fly back home and to get myself in peak physical condition for the start of the new season.

But then I started getting headaches. Severe headaches.

*****

I'd never felt pain like it. After returning from Slovakia, I was staying at my parent's house when I began to feel ill, and they managed to get me an emergency appointment at the doctors where I was told that I had an ear infection. I went straight to bed and when I awoke the following morning, I vomited everywhere. When I closed my eyes, everything was spinning. I felt dizzy and my head was so painful that I was crying. Mum was so worried that she phoned the Derby physio, Peter Melville, who told her to drive me to the Queen's Medical Centre in Nottingham. I was in total agony, my head hurt, my body ached – I didn't have the strength to walk so they had to wheel me into the hospital in a wheelchair.

The doctor took one look at me and rushed me into a room where they put me on a drip and closed the curtains around my bed. I was told that they had to do a lumbar puncture – extracting fluid from my spinal column – and then they put me to sleep.

When I started to come around, I could hear the nurse talking to someone on the phone. "Mr Christie? Yes, he's here. He has contracted viral meningitis."

All I heard was the word 'meningitis' which I knew was a very serious, sometimes fatal condition. Fortunately for me, viral meningitis is less severe than the bacterial version, but it was still horrific. Viral meningitis is basically where the lining of your brain swells, the pressure causes terrible headaches. It completely knocked me for six, I had no energy at all and spent a week in hospital, most of it hooked up to a drip. It highlighted to me just how important my health was and how quickly things can change. Within days, I had gone from a Premier League footballer in the shape of my life, to a bed ridden patient.

I was told to stay at home and rest for a couple of weeks before I could resume light training, so I missed the team's trip to America and the whole of pre-season. I lost all the momentum and fitness that I'd built up in the previous campaign and had to start again from scratch which was so frustrating.

We missed an opportunity to strengthen the squad after our relegation battle and because we didn't replace the quality that departed, we were at risk of going backwards. We lost a trio of experienced defenders: Tony Dorigo, Jacob Laursen and Stefan Schnoor, and replaced them with Danny Higginbotham, Bjorn Otto Bragstad, Youl Mawene and midfielder, Simo Valakari.

Valakari was decent, but not attack minded and we desperately needed some more creativity. Bragstad struggled and wasn't a success, Youl took a while to adjust to the pace of the Premier League. Danny was a good player, but he had only played a handful of games for Manchester United.

The one experienced player we did bring in was the enigmatic Taribo West. When you think of iconic footballers from the nineties, Taribo, with his green dreadlocks, is right up there. He'd won an Olympic Gold medal with Nigeria, the French league and cup with Auxerre, the UEFA Cup, and also represented both Milan clubs, so we knew we were getting a very good player. What we didn't realise was that we'd be getting such a character!

He'd arrive for training wearing either a suit and trainers, or a tracksuit and shoes, never tracksuit and trainers. That's if he turned up at all! We never knew if he was going to arrive for training or a match until he actually got there.

There was one game against Fulham where Jim Smith had to delay the submission of the team sheet as we didn't know if he was actually going to turn up. It was farcical, this was the Premier League, not Sunday league.

Taribo was a devout Christian and before matches he'd get the lads in a huddle and preach to us. It was a bit weird if I'm honest. I have nothing against the church, but he would preach to us in Nigerian and it always felt a bit like he was talking to us in voodoo. Jim Smith was old school and some of the lads didn't really want to do it, but fair play, because everyone did, even though there were some sniggers because not everyone took it seriously. He was a quality player though – when he turned up.

The only positive for me at that time was that Jim didn't bring in another striker, so I knew that I had a chance of getting back into the side when I regained my fitness levels, and that gave me something to work towards.

We didn't start the season particularly well, with two draws and one loss from our first three games, so I was put back on the bench on 6th September 2000 for a home tie against Middlesbrough. Our poor start continued, and we were 3-0 down with just 25 minutes to play, so Jim Smith brought me and Kinkladze on to see what we could do.

I made an instant impact, scoring a header from Seth Johnson's cross to pull it back to 3-1. I then had a goal disallowed for offside, before Branko Strupar made it 3-2 to give us a glimmer of an unexpected comeback.

With just two minutes remaining, I went for a 50/50 ball with Mark Schwarzer, and just got there ahead of him to chip the ball into the back of the net. It was an incredible game and although it finished 3-3, it felt like a win to us and our fans.

When I was hospitalised on a drip, I felt a million miles away from performing in front of thousands of people. Forget fame and fortune, if you haven't got your health, you haven't got anything. It was so good to be back playing and scoring goals.

I scored in our next two games too, which was great for me personally, but we didn't win either match. In fact, we didn't win any of our first 13 Premier League games and the lads were all aware that we were once again in a relegation battle. The deterioration of the squad over the last few seasons was taking its toll on us and we knew we were in for a long old season.

At least my performances had caught the eye of Howard Wilkinson who, true to his word, called me up to the Under 21 squad for the European Championship qualifier double header against Germany and Finland in October 2000.

I found out after training one day when Jim Smith came over to me on the training pitch, tapped me on the shoulder and said, "Congratulations, you're in the England Under 21 squad." That was Jim, very understated. No fanfare, no gathering the rest of the lads around and making a big thing of it. Inside I was absolutely buzzing.

A few days later, I received a letter at my home address, confirming my selection, informing me of the rest of the squad and detailing my itinerary. We didn't have text messages or WhatsApp groups, so you usually found out about international call ups through the post which could sometimes take a while to arrive. There was one occasion I found out I'd been selected when I saw the squad named on television!

My Derby teammates Chris Riggott, Lee Morris and Adam Murray were also named in the squad, as Howard looked to bring in some new faces to replace the players like Danny Murphy, Frank Lampard and Jamie Carragher who were by then too old to represent the Under 21s.

Fortunately, England were blessed with a plethora of talented youngsters, including Michael Carrick and Joe Cole, two standout players who you just knew would go on an achieve great things. Carrick and Cole had competition for their midfield places from Scott Parker, David Dunn and Owen Hargreaves which shows just how much depth we had.

Dunn always liked a laugh and a joke, and he was a good guy to be around, often lightening the mood from the constant seriousness of Howard and the coaches.

Centre back John Terry was usually in the middle of most things that were going on and was another who oozed quality. We could all see he was destined for a successful career in the game.

My England roommate was Paul Robinson, a talented young goalkeeper who was challenging Nigel Martyn to become Leeds United's number one. Paul eventually made 41 appearances for the senior national side.

One of my teammates who did surprise me was Ashley Cole. He wasn't a regular with Arsenal when he came in to the Under 21 squad and although he looked good, there is no way I would have predicted he would go on to achieve what he did. I felt that Jay Bothroyd, the Coventry striker, was at a similar level to Ashley at the time although their careers went on completely different paths. Within a year of his first Under 21 call up, Ashley was Arsenal and England's first choice left back. He used to walk around the hotels in flip flops with his elasticated tracksuit bottoms rolled up to his knees which I always thought was strange, especially when you're representing your country. I always wanted to look the part when on international duty, but then again, he achieved far more in his career than I did in mine, so he can walk around in high heels as far as I'm concerned!

There was fierce competition for the centre forward position.

Darius Vassell, a lightening quick striker playing for Aston Villa was Howard's first choice at the time.

Alan Smith was amazing and training with him was a huge eye opener. We were a similar age, same position and he was also just breaking into his club team, Leeds United.

Oh my God, what a player – strong, quick, could hold the ball up and was a good finisher. He was very comfortable playing with his back to goal and his first touch was incredible, he never gave the ball away when playing keep ball. He went on to have an exceptional career with Leeds and Manchester United.

The best finisher that I've ever seen is Jermain Defoe, another rival for the centre forward place. Of all the players I've played with at any level, he was by far the best goal scorer – he just didn't miss the goal. During finishing training, he was so accurate; left foot, right foot, head – he could do it all and was hard working too. After training, he'd grab a keeper and stay behind to practise shooting from various angles. It was a big cultural change as I'd never come across that before. At Derby when training finished, we all went home. Maybe I should have taken it upon myself to do more, but I was inexperienced so if the coaches told me we'd finished, I thought we must have done enough. People don't realise how hard players like Jermain work. It's no surprise that he made it into the Premier League's 100 club and was still going strong with Sunderland at the ripe age of 39.

Our first game, a friendly against Germany, was held at Pride Park, so the local press were making a big fuss because Chris, Adam, Lee and myself were in the squad. Derby hadn't had too many players in the England set up at any level before, so it was a bit of a novelty for the media, especially as Chris was Derby born and bred, and people always assumed I was from Derby too.

Sadly, despite the hype, I was an unused substitute against the Germans which was disappointing, and I remember feeling that I'd only been called up to add a few numbers to the gate. However, I did come off the bench in our following game, a 2-2 draw away to Finland, making my Under 21 debut. It was a very proud moment for me, and I returned to Derby with a spring in my step.

When I was a kid, I'd read that players who represent England received a cap, but I thought it was figurative rather than an actual cap. I certainly didn't think you got one for playing for the Under 21s which was why I was so surprised when I received a box through the post containing my very own England cap, complete with tassels, the England badge, and the match details embroidered on the peak. It was a work of art, too delicate to ever wear. My wife, Emma, later had my caps framed as a present for me, and I have them all on display at home which is nice and reminds me of what I achieved. I will always be proud to have represented my country in the sport I love.

CHAPTER 9
Super Mal

When Bradford City rocked up at Pride Park on 18th November 2000, the media were describing the game as a relegation six-pointer. The fans had started to become a bit jittery and we needed to get a victory over the so-called lesser teams who were also struggling.

As you'd expect from two sides at the wrong end of the table, it was a tense affair that could have gone either way. Ten minutes after half time I put us in front and as soon as the goal went in, I felt the collective relief from the fans and players.

Rory Delap added a second 15 minutes later to secure a valuable three points. In the dressing room after the match, the general feeling was that our season had finally begun, and the expectation was that we would kick on from there.

And we did, winning three of our next five games, including a 1-0 win at home to Coventry where I scored the winner, prompting the Sky Blue fans to question why their manager, Gordon Strachan, hadn't signed me when I had been playing just a few miles down the road from them in Nuneaton.

But despite our temporary change in fortune, we were always within a few points of the drop zone. There was never a point where I thought we were going to go down, although I knew we'd be there or thereabouts. We were competitive in most games and had to rely on picking up points from our rivals, as we didn't seem to have much luck against the bigger teams.

My scoring streak led to the Derby fans singing my name which was very special:

"Super, super Mal,
Super, super Mal,
Super, super Mal,
Super Malcolm Christie."

The supporters would go through the team, singing the various player's songs during the warm up and the earlier your name was sung, the more in favour you were. I felt a massive buzz when I heard 30,000 fans chanting my name. I'd listen before applauding them – but never too early as they moved on to the next player as soon as you clapped, and I always wanted to make the most of it!

Derby's supporters were incredible during my time at Pride Park, and I enjoyed a special relationship with them. They inspired us greatly and their support naturally meant we raised our games which gave us a huge advantage at home. They really were the 12th man, and the fact that we only lost four of our 19 Premier League matches at Pride Park during the 2000/01 season, tells you a lot.

On the road, though, it was a different matter, as we lost 12 of our 19 away games. Everything about away trips was different; the way we prepared, the unfamiliarity of the stadiums and the hostility of the opposing crowds.

We travelled the length and breadth of the county by coach, so we had a lot of time to fill. Some of the lads listened to music on their iPods, others watched the latest movies on their portable DVD players. I never went anywhere without my laptop and copy of the popular *Championship Manager* game. Seeing myself as a computer game character was another surreal moment, I wasn't a bad player on it either to be fair. There were some young wonderkids who I always signed, players like Tonton Zola Moukoko and Cherno Samba who were both ridiculously good in the game, although never reached the same heights in reality. I often started as the Manchester United manager and, yes, I signed myself, although I played to win, so didn't always pick myself in the starting line up!

Later on, I was a player in the *FIFA* games which was so cool, especially hearing Martin Tyler saying my name. The problem was that I wasn't very quick in the game, even though pace was my biggest asset and that annoyed me a little. With *FIFA*, pace is everything, so I tended to play as Barcelona or Real Madrid, rather than Derby. Being part of a computer game is just a little thing that footballers don't talk about, but it meant a great deal to me because I had played those games as a young fan.

Depending on the opponents, away matches could also mean an overnight stay in a hotel where, like most clubs, I'd share a room with another player. Teams still do it too for whatever reasons – team bonding and financial, I guess – but I always thought it was quite strange for two grown men to have to share a room.

I found it hard to sleep in a hotel because it was an unfamiliar bed with new surroundings, but having someone else sleeping in my room made it even tougher. You didn't get a choice who you roomed with, it's not like you could choose someone you're pally with. You'd literally arrive at the hotel and be handed an envelope containing the room keys, with two names written on the front. I suppose it helps to foster relationships between players, but I always felt more comfortable being in a room on my own.

It's not that I was being anti-social, I just needed to be in a relaxed state of mind and have a good night's sleep before playing in a high-pressure Premier League game in front of thousands of people.

Some wake early, others prefer a lie in, so that's awkward. I've roomed with people who snore which meant I didn't get the sleep I needed. Even things like making phone calls to your family was difficult, so I'd always end up standing in the corridor talking to my loved ones. It was so weird sharing a room and bathroom with another man. I'd wake in the night to go to the toilet – not knowing what I'd find in there – and would worry about waking my roommate. Even though we'd see each other on a daily basis, it was still awkward, and I could never really relax.

We rotated, but there were three people I roomed with more often than others:

Steve Elliott, a Derby-born defender who was a similar age to me, was a good lad, the life and soul of the party. Steve would get in everyone's business and was a good little foil for me as we had totally opposite personalities. I enjoyed rooming with Steve, and we had some good laughs.

Mart Poom, our Estonian goalkeeper was another regular roommate of mine. We all know that goalies are a breed of their own, so that was quite interesting. Poomy spoke good English, much better than my Estonian, but we didn't share that many conversations as we were very different characters. It was just a case of us being put together and getting on with it.

Chris Riggott was the person I roomed with the most for Derby and also occasionally on England duty. Chris was a talented defender who had progressed through the academy, and he became a big part of my story. He was massively into his video games, like *Call of Duty* and was also a sleepwalker.

One night I was in a deep sleep when I heard Chris shout, "Take cover, take cover."

I quickly awoke, jumped out of bed, and as instructed, took cover, wondering what the hell was going on. I peeked over the top of my mattress and saw Chris, crouching by his bed, pointing an imaginary gun at an imaginary enemy. He was acting out his *Call of Duty* dream while sleepwalking!

A few minutes later, he climbed back into bed and fell asleep as if nothing had happened. By that stage I was wide awake and struggled to get back to sleep. Hardly the best preparation ahead of a big game.

In the morning, I asked Chris if he could remember anything from the night. "No. What happened?" he asked.

"You were doing your *Call of Duty* thing."

"You're joking. Sorry Mal, I hope you managed to get back to sleep," he replied.

*****

In February 2001, I made my first start for England Under 21s against Spain at St. Andrews, Birmingham City's ground. The hairs on the back of my neck stood on end as I proudly lined up before the game, singing 'God Save The Queen.' It is one of the highlights of my career. I remembered watching Euro 96 on television and seeing Stuart Pearce, Tony Adams and Alan Shearer passionately belting out the National Anthem, so I made sure that my lips were moving enough to show anyone watching me how passionate I was and how much it meant for me to represent my country. I looked in the stands and saw my proud parents looking on.

It was like a dream . . . until the game started and we were 2-0 down after just 20 minutes! We got absolutely destroyed by a much better side. It wasn't that we played poorly, Spain were just an unbelievable team who went on to beat us 4-0. Pepe Reina, the future Liverpool keeper was in goal for them, and they had a young kid from Barcelona pulling the strings in midfield who was outstanding, everything went through him. His name was Xavi – I wonder what happened to him!

I almost scored a header in my next game for England, which was another home match, this time against Finland. I was asked to play on the right side of midfield in a 3-5-1 formation which was odd as I'd never played there at any level before. I tried to be a tricky winger, taking players on, and getting crosses in, but I was so used to playing as a centre forward that I naturally kept drifting into the middle and almost ended up playing upfront alongside Darius Vassell. Although I was played out of position, after the game I felt that I'd done enough to establish myself as a starting member of the Under 21 team.

CHAPTER 10
Their theatre. My dream

Domestically, it was a tough, long, hard slog of a season and on 28th April 2001, a 2-1 home defeat to Arsenal left us sitting just one place above the relegation zone. We needed three points from our final two games in order to secure our Premier League status. A daunting challenge, especially as first up was a trip to Old Trafford to face the champions Manchester United.

I was on a five-month goal drought at that stage and had began to question if I was doing the right things, living my life in the right way.

The longer I went without a goal, the more I altered, and I wish I hadn't changed anything. I needed to understand that there would be periods in my career where I wouldn't score, but I didn't really know how to deal with that, so I had retreated into my shell a bit and had stopped going out.

I knew I needed to stop the rot, so after the Arsenal game, I went home, got changed, and decided to go out. If I was happy off the pitch, I tended to perform better on it.

I had a really good night and it felt good to blow off some steam, although I did get a bit of stick from a few people who asked me why I had gone out when we'd just been beaten.

Most people were fine though, and the only issue I had was that I was a bit worse for wear when I arrived at the nightclub, Destiny and Elite. I managed to get into the club, but the bouncer wouldn't give me access to the VIP section, an area we readily frequented. I had the relevant pass and my mates were all in there, but the bouncer refused to let me in for some reason. Maybe he was a Forest fan.

There were three steps leading up to the VIP area and I was

standing on the top one trying to argue my case. We got into a bit of a disagreement and then the bouncer pushed me down the stairs. I landed on my left wrist and felt the instant pain. People crowded around me to try and diffuse the situation. I wasn't going to fight him, but I was obviously not happy that he'd pushed me down some steps. I eventually walked away and continued my night in the main section of the club.

When I turned up for training on the following Monday, my wrist was still hurting and the physio bandaged it up. I told him that I'd slept on it funny when he asked how it had happened.

So by the time we faced Manchester United on 5th May 2001, the odds were stacked firmly against us: our away form was poor, we lost our captain, Darryl Powell, through injury on the morning of the game, and our main striker, yours truly, had a sprained wrist and hadn't scored a league goal since December. I always felt that I could finish the majority of chances, but we just didn't create enough as a team, and I wasn't the type of player who created my own chances, I relied on the supply from midfield. To be honest, I probably would have been dropped had we not been suffering from so many injuries that meant we could barely scrape a team together.

We hadn't performed particularly well against the bigger clubs, and we were coming up against the biggest one of all in United, who had thumped us 3-0 at Pride Park earlier in the season.

Everything was against us, and nobody gave us a chance.

But despite us being very much the underdogs, we were fighting for our lives and the huge occasion made us raise our level, so we felt we had a chance of causing an upset. We got a boost when Steve Round put the United team sheet on the dressing room wall, and we saw that Roy Keane, Ryan Giggs and Gary Neville were missing from the starting line-up. Don't get me wrong, it was still a very strong team with David Beckham, Fabien Barthez, Andy Cole and Teddy Sheringham, it just wasn't their strongest team.

Lee Morris had been on loan at Huddersfield Town a month earlier, and was expecting to be on the bench, so when Jim Smith gave him his pre match instructions, Lee was confused, wondering why Jim was telling a sub what to do. He didn't realise he'd be playing until a few minutes before kick off!

Neil bandaged my wrist in the dressing room and it was a huge relief when the manager told me I was starting. For me to get the nod for our biggest match of the season gave me a big lift and I felt quietly confident when we took to the field. *We can win this,* I thought. United were being presented with the Premier League trophy after the game so there was a carnival atmosphere inside the stadium. It was supposed to be their special day, but despite being a Manchester United fan as a kid, I was determined to ruin their party.

You can smell a game early on, and it was clear to everyone that we were up for the match as soon as we kicked off. We were proactive, on the front foot, playing some great attacking football. Stefano Eranio was running the midfield, Georgi Kinkladze was enjoying himself on the ball and Lee Morris was causing United problems on the left-hand side.

This wasn't the Derby side who had struggled all season, this was the team we should have been.

Just after the half hour mark, Eranio chipped the ball in to me. I was standing just inside the United penalty area facing the corner flag, with the United defender Ronnie Wallwork tight on me. I instinctively took a couple of touches with my right foot, turning Wallwork and creating some space. I looked up and saw the whole goal had opened up for me, so I hit the ball with my left foot – more with my laces than I'd intended because I was reaching for it – but I knew straight away that it was going in.

I hadn't woken up that morning thinking that I was going to be the hero because it had been so long since I'd last scored, so when the ball flew into the top corner, I felt shocked more than anything else. I ran – I'm not sure where I was going – and then I heard the delayed cheers from the Derby fans celebrating at the other end of the stadium. Horacio Carbonari pulled me to the ground and said, "Relax, relax." He didn't want us to celebrate too much because there was still almost an hour left to play, but I was thinking, *How can I relax? I've just scored at Old Trafford in a crucial match for Derby.*

The score remained 1-0 at half time, and even though Manchester United had come close a couple of times, there was nothing for us to be too fearful of. There was no talk about playing for a draw during the break, we had come for a victory.

We went out in the second half and, rather than sitting back to defend our lead, we continued to play on the front foot and tried to grab another. I didn't think the scoring had finished at that stage and was convinced that United would get at least one, so we had to maintain our concentration.

I had a great opportunity to double our lead in the 52nd minute, when Kinkladze played a wonderful ball through to Lee Morris who took it past Barthez before squaring to me, unmarked in the six-yard box.

My game was all instinctive, so when the ball landed at my feet, I had all the time in the world to think about it. *Should I hit it first time? Should I control the ball first? Do I place it? Or should I blast it into the net?*

I tied myself in knots by over thinking the situation and unbelievably put the ball wide of the goal when it was much easier for me to score. If I had that chance 100 times, I'd score 99. I was horrified and my immediate thought was, *Can I have that again please?* It was such an easy chance that people still remind me of. The television cameras caught Jim Smith and his reaction, hands on his head in shock said it all. He couldn't believe it, no one could, and I was hoping that my miss wouldn't come back to haunt us.

United brought on Giggs and threw everything at us for the remainder of the game and we rode our luck a few times. I chased every ball, using every ounce of energy in my body, and by the time I came off in the 89th minute, I had nothing else to give. I watched on anxiously from the touchline, desperate for the referee to end the game. When he finally blew the full-time whistle, I ran onto the pitch to celebrate with my teammates and the travelling Derby fans, feeling sheer euphoria.

It was great to see how much our victory meant to the supporters, coaches, and Jim Smith. For us to survive, against all odds, was massive. Every single player gave his all and we thoroughly deserved the victory. Even the United fans applauded us off the pitch, which was incredible, I had to pinch myself. For me to receive a standing ovation at Old Trafford was the icing on the cake. Those 90 minutes were the pinnacle of my career, everything that I had worked towards.

We continued the celebrations in the dressing room, with the lads congratulating me, it was such an incredible feeling, and I didn't want the day to end. I could have gone back into the tunnel to watch United lift the trophy, but it wasn't about them, this was Derby's day, it was about our special moment, and I wanted to celebrate it with my team. At the time I didn't realise the enormity of the situation, but even now, more than twenty years later, people still talk about it as one of the best games and best moments from Derby County's Premier League era.

I was 22 years old, had achieved my childhood dream of scoring at Old Trafford, and had another year of Premier League football to look forward to – I was on cloud nine.

When I returned to Derby later that evening, my parents were waiting for me at my house. My dad gave me a hug on the driveway and he was crying his eyes out. It's the only time I have ever seen him cry and before long, tears were streaming down my face too. It was such an emotional moment for us all.

The day after the Manchester United game, a Sunday, we flew over to Jersey to take part in a friendly match against St Martin's, a local side who were celebrating their centenary.

With our survival guaranteed, Jim Smith decided not to join us, leaving us in the capable hands of Steve Round and our physios, Neil Sillett and John McKeown, or Scouse as we called him.

The trip was a piss up, pure and simple. The drinking began on the flight over and didn't stop until we arrived home a few days later. It was brilliant.

The night before the match, I nearly got into a scuffle with the opposition goalkeeper. I was stood in a nightclub when someone asked me how I thought we'd get on in the match. I was still buzzing from my previous game and had already had a few drinks, so I replied, "It'll be easy. I'll probably get a hat trick."

He went back to the bar and told the St Martin's goalie what I'd said and all of a sudden the goalkeeper stormed over wanting to fight me! The other lads jumped in, trying to diffuse the situation, while I explained that it was just a joke. We ended up sharing a drink together at the bar.

Danny Higginbotham and I were drinking shots of Archers and I've never been so ill from alcohol in all my life! That was the last time I ever drank Archers and to this day I still can't stand the smell of the stuff.

We were all half cut by the time the game kicked off on the

Wednesday evening, I don't know how we managed to play to be honest. My memory of the match is very vague, but I remember Neil and Scouse brought themselves on with ten minutes to go which was hilarious. I also know that I didn't score, but for once I didn't mind. In fact, I was actually trying not to score because I didn't want the goalkeeper to kick me!

The drinking continued after the game, topping up our alcohol levels, and I don't think any of us were sober at any point during the three-day jolly. It was certainly the most pissed I have ever been and I barely made in onto the bus to take us to take us to the airport. I was sick before take off, during the flight, when we landed and again when I got home.

But it was great, one of the best trips I've ever been on and exactly what was needed after a challenging season. It further cemented our bond as a team.

Our final game of the season was against Ipswich Town in front of 33,000 fans – our biggest attendance of the season. When Pride Park was rocking, there was nowhere better to play and the supporters were amazing that day, giving us a hero's welcome.

In the changing room before the game Neil Sillett said, "Give me your hand to bandage up. It worked in the last game, it'll work in this one."

So I gave him my arm and scored my 12th goal of the season in the first half to put us in the lead. I look back now wishing I'd kept my wrist in a bandage for the rest of my career as I might have won a Golden Boot!

Ipswich grabbed an equaliser in the second and the match finished 1-1. The Tractor Boys were flying that season finishing fifth in the league, so a point was a good result for us – especially as we'd been celebrating all week – and it was nice to finish the campaign on a high. Considering I'd started the season hooked up to a drip, lying in a hospital bed, I was pleased to finish the year as Derby's top scorer.

To top it all off, I scored my first goal for England Under 21s just a few weeks later against Mexico at Filbert Street where I partnered Jermain Defoe up front. My role as a striker was to score goals, something I hadn't yet done for my country, so I was putting myself under pressure to find the back of the net.

In the second half, with the score tied at 0-0, Defoe headed the ball towards goal, the Mexican keeper parried it and I slotted it home from six yards. It was another proud moment and my goal set us on our way to a comfortable 3-0 victory.

The work ethic of the England boys and playing and training with so many quality players elevated my game, and I began to put in an extra 5-10% when I returned to Derby as I knew I needed to improve to get to the level I wanted. The national set up was a totally different experience as I constantly felt on trial; every pass, every shot was being scrutinised – I was playing for my place in the next squad. I thrived on the pressure though because I wanted to be the best player I could and to do that I had to compete against the best.

Being part of the Under 21 squad also gave me the experience of being around the senior players as we started to share training bases with them in 2001 when Sven-Goran Eriksson became England manager. Sven had an aura of authority around him when he introduced himself to us at the start of a new era. By mixing the Under 21 and senior players, he made us all feel part of the setup which helped those who made the progression to the senior squad.

I remember one training camp when we stayed with the first team at the Marbella Beach hotel, it was crazy. The fan furore was a whole new experience for me, there were security guards on the entrances, and supporters camped outside, cheering us as we entered and exited the hotel reception.

One day, we were given the afternoon off to sun bathe and chill out by the pool, so I returned to my room, put on my swimming shorts, grabbed a towel, and walked through the hotel wearing a gown and flip flops, before entering the roped off VIP area outside that had been set aside for us. I was thinking, *So this is how we roll when we're with England!*

I found myself a lounger and a few minutes later David Beckham strolled past, with his shaved head and Police sunglasses, before sitting on one of the chairs near me. Bloody David Beckham! He was a legend, the England captain, so I didn't feel that I could talk to him, even though we were in the same group. The cliques were still there, I suppose. It was the first time I'd been star struck since becoming a footballer. Yes, I'd played against him, but I was focussed on my game and not really concentrating on my opponents. Beckham was soon joined by Paul Scholes and Teddy Sheringham, two more Manchester United players, which was nice for me as a United fan to be sunbathing with three of my heroes. I spent the afternoon trying to play it cool as I didn't want to appear too much of a stalker!

At the end of the season, my face was everywhere. Anything that was related to Derby County featured yours truly; newspapers, magazines, posters, trade cards. My dad was lapping it up, buying everything that was written about me.

And then I became a sticker. How cool is that? Forget scoring in the Premier League, that was when I became, in my eyes, a proper footballer.

Collecting stickers was one of those little things that I had done as a kid. Dad would come home from work and play a game where he'd put packets of stickers under the door, while I tried and grab them before he pulled them back. Sometimes he'd be armed with 10 or even 20 packs and I got a huge adrenaline rush. I collected the Premier League stickers every year without fail and if my album was incomplete at the end of the season, I asked my dad to write a cheque so I could send off for the missing stickers. So, for me to have my own sticker and to see myself in the albums was incredible. Best of all, my agent supplied me with boxes of stickers directly from Panini, so my dad didn't have to buy them anymore.

*****

To celebrate another successful season, Gavin, myself and two of our friends, Nick Powell and James Trigg, booked our first proper lads holiday to Ayia Napa, Cyprus, a party town that was popular with footballers in the 2000s.

When we ventured into the bars it was almost like the whole of the Premier League was there; Trevor Benjamin, Robbie Keane, Lee Naylor, Sean Davis – too many to mention.

It was the first time I had been afforded a little bit of celebrity status, as a footballer in a town full of footballers. There were so many girls in the clubs and bars, it was like bees around a honey pot. We were loving the attention.

One evening, I was walking through the dance floor and

knocked into someone, causing them to spill their drink. When he turned round, I recognised him as Jermaine Wright, the Ipswich Town midfielder, so I apologised and said hello. He didn't know who I was and was ready to go for me before his friends intervened and stopped him swinging for me. There is a mutual bond and respect between footballers, so when he realised I played for Derby, we went to the bar and bought each other a drink.

Gavin got very pally with one of Robbie Keane's mates called Matt. He was a big lad, six foot five inches tall, with a broad Brummie accept. He always seemed to know the best places to go to, so we assumed he was a cross between a bodyguard and a holiday rep.

Matt and Gav spent the rest of the holiday organising which clubs we were going to, and we had a fantastic time. I went on the decks with DJ Spoony and was recognised in the street by Allister Whitehead, a famous House DJ who invited us to one of his gigs. I didn't know who he was at the time though, as I wasn't really into House music.

We had an amazing time. When we got home, I was watching a Wolves game and as the teams walked out of the tunnel, I did a double take; Robbie Keane's bodyguard Matt was in actual fact Matt Murray, the Wolves goalkeeper. I rang Gavin straight away to tell him. We'd had no idea that Matt was a footballer.

CHAPTER 11
The managerial merry go round

At the end of the 2000/01 season, Jim Smith had told the media that we couldn't afford to be in the same predicament again. That was music to my ears, and I thought that with a couple of decent signings, we could potentially push on in the 2001/02 campaign.

When I arrived back at the Ramarena for the first day of pre-season training, I was hoping that I'd be greeted by some new arrivals, experienced Premier League players who could help us avoid another relegation battle.

I was delighted when we signed a cracking player in Italian international Fabrizio Ravanelli.

When I read in the newspaper that Rav was rumoured to be joining us, I had goosebumps. He'd won the Champions League, UEFA Cup and Serie A during a trophy laden career, but I didn't feel threatened by his arrival at all, I was looking forward to playing alongside and learning from a legend. Before his first training session, Stefano Eranio introduced me to Rav and told me, "Malcolm, he's here for you. He is here to improve you." That comment was incredibly inspiring.

I was fortunate to play with some amazing footballers, but Rav was the one I enjoyed playing with most. He was the first real superstar that I shared a dressing room with, and although he wasn't the same player he'd been during his heyday at Juventus, he was a fantastic professional, with an unbelievable work ethic that drove me on. Even after everything that he had achieved, he was still working as hard as anyone and it gave me a real insight into what it took to get to the highest level. His diet was spot on, he was always first in and last to leave, putting everything into every single training session.

I can only speak fondly of Rav, although I know that when people reflect on his time at Derby, they think of the later financial troubles at the club where Rav unfairly became the scapegoat. We all knew that he was being paid a fortune – 10-15 times what I was on – but it wasn't his fault that the club were paying him astronomical wages. Although it didn't bother me at the time, when I look back now, I perhaps should have gone in and asked for more money as I was a first team regular and one of the lowest paid centre forwards in the Premier League.

I quickly learnt to adjust my game to play alongside Rav because he played for himself. I don't mean that as a negative, far from it, it was just his style. When I partnered Branko Strupar, he'd often make a run with no intention of receiving the ball, his runs were made to create space for me to exploit. Rav made runs for himself, wanting to get on the end of things. Maybe I should have played my normal game, but I was in awe of him and found myself becoming the secondary striker. Ultimately, Ravanelli played the game the way he'd always played it, and he'd scored a hell of a lot more than I had, so why would he change for me?

Although we worked well together in training, we never really forged a prolific partnership because our styles were too similar. While Rav was approaching the end of his career, I was coming into my own as a player and maybe the coaches should have realised that I was the better long-term investment, but because of his name and stature, they thought he'd score 20 goals, I'd get 10 and that would be OK.

As a result, I didn't score at all during our pre-season friendlies, even though I played in most of the games. I felt a little under pressure because Ravanelli bagged a few goals and I desperately wanted to impress him and show him that I could score goals too. I was probably over thinking things and trying too hard, in all honesty.

Pre-season isn't about results though, it's about fitness and the summer of 2001 was the only time in my career when I enjoyed a full pre-season, and it's no coincidence that the 2001/02 campaign was the only one I played in its entirety without illness or injury.

Jim selected me and Rav as his strikers for the season curtain raiser at home to Blackburn Rovers. Ravanelli opened the scoring on the stroke of half time with a cracking free kick that gave fans a glimpse of what he was capable of, and I doubled our lead in the second half to give us a 2-1 win. We were all buoyed by the victory, but we didn't win again for 10 games as the losing mentality we had developed in the previous season seemed to follow us into the new one.

Rav aside, we didn't do enough in the transfer market and that was the club's biggest mistake. The squad was deteriorating every year, quality players were leaving and being replaced by inferior unknowns. During the early part of the season, we sold Rory Delap, Seth Johnson, and Stefano Eranio for a combined £11,000,000 and we spent just £3,500,000 bringing in Luciano Zavagno and Francois Grenet from French sides Bordeaux and Troyes, respectively. I, like most of my teammates and our supporters, had never heard of them and it was unfair to expect them to come in to the Premier League and hit the ground running from day one. I have nothing against the two lads, I myself had been plucked from obscurity, but they didn't perform and weren't the right type of player that we needed at the time.

In my view, we needed more leaders, players with Premier League experience who possessed a winning mindset. The problem we had was that we didn't have anyone in our squad who was indispensable, no one who could carry or inspire the team when others weren't performing. Our defence was leaking goals, Darryl Powell, our captain, was a regular but he blew hot and cold, and I wasn't scoring 20 – 25 goals a season. We plummeted to the bottom of the season for one very simple reason; we conceded too many and didn't score enough.

Our mindset was too negative so mentally we were beaten before we'd even stepped onto the pitch. Jim Smith and his coaching staff held team meetings where they went through our upcoming fixtures and told us how many points they expected from each game. I don't think that was the right thing to do and it fuelled our negativity. Being told, "It's Arsenal today, we don't expect any points," gave us a free pass really. It was hard to get up for a game when you've effectively been written off by the manager and coaches.

I understand why they did it, because they were trying to take the pressure off us against the big sides and identify the crucial matches we needed to win, but it should have been done in the coaches' room, not in front of the players. We should have set up to try and win every game as on our day, we were capable of beating anyone as we had proved before.

Ivan Toney at the start of the 2021/22 season said his target was for Brentford to win the Premier League and for him to be the division's top scorer. Unrealistic, maybe, but it shows he has a winning mentality. If you have that desire to be the best that should be your target. I'd have preferred our coaches saying, "We've got four games, let's go out and try and get 12 points," rather than, "We should be aiming for three points from the next four games." The coaches' nervousness rubbed off on us and I don't think it was the right approach for that group of players.

The top teams say that winning is a habit, but so is losing – and habits are very difficult to break. Morale was low, team spirit was fading, and we didn't really do much off the pitch to try and address that. Very occasionally, someone would organise something like a team paintballing event to try and boost morale, but it always felt a bit forced because we only did things like that when things weren't going well.

With Derby struggling, it was a relief that I was still involved with the Under 21s under our new manager, David Platt, who had replaced Howard Wilkinson during the summer of 2001.

Platt had been a top player with Arsenal, Juventus, and England, and he immediately changed the regimented training camps that we had endured under Howard to a more modern, technical, almost continental, approach. I scored in his first game in charge, a 4-0 friendly win over a strong Holland team, featuring Dirk Kuyt and Rafael van der Vaart.

Platt's objective was to secure qualification for the 2002 European Championship, and it went down to the wire. On 5th October 2001, we took on Greece in front of almost 30,000 fans at Ewood Park knowing that only a win would do.

I was disappointed not to make the starting line up, so I watched the first half from the bench, cheering on the lads, but also itching to get on. Jermain Defoe gave us a lead after ten minutes to settle the nerves, but the Greeks grew stronger and as the game progressed, they looked increasingly likely to bag an equaliser.

I replaced Jermain in the second half and made an instant

impact, scoring the decisive second goal. It's all very well scoring in a friendly, any goal for me was good of course, but to score such an important goal, so late in a crucial game was very special.

I was full of confidence when I returned to Derby but soon came crashing back down to earth when I heard that Jim Smith had been sacked.

The knives had been out for Jim all summer because of our 16th and 17th place finishes of the last two campaigns, compared to the 8th place we achieved in my first season. The fans could see that we had regressed and for the first time, I could sense their discontent during home games where I heard sections of the crowd chanting for Jim's head. The newspapers were also speculating that his days were numbered.

I was deeply saddened to see Jim leave after all he'd done for the club and for me personally. It was the first time I'd seen someone I was close to sacked, although I knew I had to adapt and just get on with it as best I could.

I suppose it was inevitable really. I had seen the change in Jim's demeanour as the season developed, he became much harsher to the players after a poor result and there were little arguments on the training pitch. Jim's dismissal was instant, as they are in football, so he didn't come and say goodbye to us which was a real shame as I missed the opportunity to shake his hand and thank him for everything he had done for me. I didn't have his phone number, it wasn't the way of the world back then, so I couldn't call him either.

For me, the beginning of the end for Derby County came in January 1999 when Steve McClaren left to join Manchester United as assistant manager. Steve was the glue that held us together, bridging the gap between the old school methods and the more modern approach to football. He was by far the best coach I ever worked under, was progressive in his sessions and was a strong link between the manager and the players. We never replaced him when he left to achieve great things at Old Trafford alongside Sir Alex Ferguson, before starting his own managerial career at Middlesbrough.

Steve Round was another great coach I enjoyed working under, he was very much in the same mould as Steve McClaren, but he left in 2001 to join McClaren at Boro and again he wasn't replaced. Other coaches came in and left without making much of an impression.

Colin Todd was one such coach who had been brought in to help Jim. Colin was a Derby County legend for what he had achieved during his playing days, but he never struck me as a good coach or man manager. The way he operated on the training pitch wasn't what we needed and the sessions he ran just weren't stimulating, so I was shocked when Todd was appointed as our new manager. A very strange decision from the board because if Jim was being blamed for the results, Colin was just as culpable as Jim in my eyes.

Todd was too similar to Jim, and he didn't introduce anything different. He was already running the training sessions his way, so that stayed the same. All he did was swap a few players around. He didn't change the formation, the system or, more importantly, the culture. We had stagnated and we needed something a bit different; we needed freshness, we needed energy. It's not that I didn't get on with Colin, I respected him due to his reputation as a club legend, but he never inspired me as a player or helped me improve my game.

One of the few changes that he did make was dropping me to the subs bench which was a big disappointment as I had been a first team regular until then and felt I was playing OK. It was the first time in football that I had the feeling a manager didn't fancy me as a player, so I rolled my sleeves up, trained harder, kept scoring for the reserves and did everything I could to prove to Todd that I deserved my place in the starting line-up.

In only my third start under Todd, a home match against Bolton, the game remained scoreless going into the last 30 minutes and I looked over to the bench and saw Deon Burton getting stripped. I knew he wouldn't take Ravanelli off, so it had to be me who was being replaced.

Just then, Benito Carbone crossed the ball in, I ran across to the near post and swept it into the back of the net to give us a 1-0 lead. I hadn't played particularly well, but the beauty of being a striker is that you are judged on goals and scoring the winner meant I grabbed the headlines.

After the game, I was asked how I felt about finding myself in and out of the team for the first time in my career. I replied, honestly, that I felt I was good enough to start regularly and that if I wasn't, I might have to consider my future. I didn't want to leave the club, but I needed to play.

Colin responded in public: "That's exactly the reaction I wanted from Malcolm. I want him to have passion and go out there and stake a claim for the first team."

The right thing for him to say but the strange thing was that I was reading it in the newspapers, instead of him sitting me down and having a conversation with me. He wasn't the sort of manager who liked confrontation and he wasn't a big communicator. When I was on the bench, I didn't know if it was because he was resting me or because he thought I wasn't good enough, which is tough. My mind was playing tricks on me, and it knocked my confidence. I wasn't the only player who felt that way either.

Under Jim, we'd always been competitive and although we often lost games, we very rarely got hammered. It was a different story with Colin at the helm – in the space of two months, we conceded five goals in a match three times; to Fulham, Middlesbrough and Manchester United. Within the club we knew that he wasn't going to last very long.

In January we were embarrassingly knocked out of the FA Cup by League Two side Bristol Rovers, and a 2-1 defeat at Aston Villa in the following match was the final straw for the board who sacked Todd on 14th January 2002.

The initial rumour in the newspapers was that Ravanelli could become manager, but that was just paper talk. Then, completely out of the blue, John Gregory resigned as manager of Aston Villa, and he was being linked to the Derby job. Gregory had done a great job at Villa, who were sitting 7th in the Premier League when he departed. He had taken them to the FA Cup Final just 18 months earlier and they were playing regular European football, so I couldn't really see it happening.

But it did.

Gregory had spent three years at the Baseball Ground as a player, was popular with the fans and still held some affinity to the club. I felt that we were lucky to get him, and I was delighted with his appointment.

As soon as he arrived the mood changed as the melancholy that had surrounded the place was lifted. Gregory changed everything he was a breath of fresh air. We needed a change of direction, new energy on the training pitch, a belief in ourselves, and that's what he brought.

On his first day in the hot seat our training levels stepped up a notch. John always turned up at the training ground driving a top of range car, immaculately presented, not a hair out of place. It wasn't that he was arrogant, he had high standards and took pride in his appearance, and that rubbed off onto us. His training sessions were sharp and lively, similar to the sessions McClaren used to run.

He got everyone together at the Baseball Ground, the youth team, reserves, and senior pros, and told us that the slate had been wiped clean. Everyone had the same opportunity which meant that the regulars upped their game, knowing their place in the starting line-up wasn't guaranteed and the fringe players raised theirs as they knew they'd get a chance if they performed in training. My own level jumped by 10%. Yes, it should have always been 100%, but it had dropped under Todd as I didn't know where I stood. Gregory gave us all a much-needed boost.

On his second day, he called us in one by one to introduce himself and tell us his plans. I didn't know much about him other than his reputation as a decent player and that he had done well at Aston Villa, so I wasn't sure what to expect.

"I've managed teams against you, Malcolm, and I rate you as a player," he began, which made me feel better straight away. Then he said, "There's not a lot of difference between you and Michael Owen, you know."

"What?" I replied, totally blown away by the comparison.

"You're very similar players. The difference is that he's got Steven Gerrard behind him providing the ammunition. If we can get people playing for you, creating for you, I can see you achieving what he has."

I couldn't believe it. I'd gone from not knowing if I'd be playing each week to being compared to the Ballon d'Or winner! You can imagine how I felt when I walked out of his office, absolutely brimming with confidence. It was probably all bullshit, but it was very clever, and it elevated me mentally to the next level. I'd have run through a brick wall for him after that meeting.

It wasn't just me who came in from the cold either. Lee Morris, a talented winger/striker had been in and out of the team during both Jim and Colin's reigns, but John picked him for his very first game at home to Tottenham Hotspur. Lee had the potential and ability to change games, but no one had trusted him until Gregory came in. When Lee scored the only goal of the game, John ran down the touchline to celebrate in front of the Derby supporters, showing them that passion that had been missing. It was a remarkable transformation.

John made some astute signings too, bringing in the experienced Warren Barton and Rob Lee. They were fantastic, as people as well as players, and they were exactly what we needed. The problem was that we'd needed them earlier in the season. In fact, we needed them the season before. At 32 and 36 respectively, they were no spring chickens, but they still had their legs, were strong leaders, and they provided invaluable experience, and most importantly some quality.

After the Spurs game, that losing mentality evaporated and we felt competitive in matches, feeling that we had a chance of winning every match.

The question, with more than half the season already gone, was did we have enough time to turn it around?

CHAPTER 12
Is that two?

After a game I'd sometimes go out into Derby, experiencing the vibrant social scene. I don't mind admitting that I enjoyed a few drinks. It's frowned upon for footballers now, but we all did it in those days.

There was a little group of us – Lee Morris, Adam Murray, Lee Grant, and a few of the younger kids – who enjoyed some fantastic nights out in town. I didn't really have any interests other than football, so it was a good way to switch off from the pressures that come from being a professional footballer, and to let off some steam. Saturday nights were great, especially after a win, and we always started in the Pennine Hotel, on the corner of Macklin Street near the city centre. It's since been demolished which isn't surprising as it was run down, a bit of a dive really, back then. I don't know why we chose to meet there, it just became a bit of a tradition. Dougie Smith was the club's 'unofficial' player liaison officer, the most important person on a night out, as he held VIP passes for all the nightclubs in Derby. We'd have a few in the Pennine before deciding where to go.

We had some great laughs and memorable Saturday evenings, but the student nights on a Monday in Zanzibar on London Road, were my favourite. If you'd played on the Saturday, you'd have light training on Monday and Tuesday, if you hadn't it'd be double sessions, so whether or not you'd played dictated how much you could drink. Every now and then someone will contact me through social media to tell me that they used to see me in Zanzibar. We'd enjoy a few drinks, but we never caused any trouble, we just had a laugh like young lads my age were doing all over the country.

Derby County is a true footballing institution, if you're born in the city, you're a Derby County fan. Everywhere I went, whether that was shopping, drinking in a bar, or eating out in a restaurant, I received a positive reaction from people. A big university city, nights out in Derby were fantastic. Walking into a bar, people would look at me – it's a weird sensation that I never quite got used to – and it was only a matter of time before someone came over to ask for a photo or an autograph. As soon as one person came over, it became a free for all and I'd be surrounded. I'd never had to deal with that before – I was a still young lad experiencing nights out for the first time – so I had to quickly adapt and learn to carry myself. It wasn't anywhere near the level of attention that David Beckham or Michael Owen were receiving, but as the club's centre forward, I had a little bit of celebrity status, and although I was often going out to forget about football, I always made time for the supporters. I never heard anything negative when I was out in Derby, but, just a few miles up the road, it was completely different.

On the pitch, Derby County and Nottingham Forest are big rivals, but I didn't realise the level of animosity between the clubs until I went out with some friends for a night out in Nottingham. Standing at the bar, a man approached me and said, "What the fuck are you doing here?" I could barely hear him over the loud music, so I leaned in closer and that was when I saw his fist was clenched. I only just managed to avoid the punch by doing a matrix-style duck, before running out of the club through the fire escape where I met up with my mates and we got a taxi back home.

Not long after that incident, Lee Morris, Adam Murray and I were planning a night out. Lee suggested Nottingham, so I told him about my previous visit and warned them that it wasn't a good idea.

"Don't worry, Malcolm," he said. "Nottingham's a huge city, so the chances of you bumping into that lad again are very slim."

Ironically, as we walked into the first pub of the night, I spotted the lad who had thrown a punch at me sitting at the bar, so I ducked into a booth.

We ended up sneaking out through the back door and got a taxi back to Derby where we enjoyed a good night out. After that, I decided never to go out in Nottingham again.

I had another run in while enjoying a night out in Newcastle. I was having a quiet drink with some friends when I was approached by someone who asked, "What are you doing up here, Malcolm? Are you signing for the Toon?"

"No, just a night out, mate," I replied politely. I continued my conversation and suddenly felt a sharp pain in my calf. The thug had kicked me in the back of my leg. I turned to my friends and said, "Drink up, let's go." It was another weekend ruined.

*****

Two weeks after beating Spurs, we smashed local rivals Leicester City 3-0, so when Manchester United arrived at Pride Park on 3rd March 2002, we felt fearless. We weren't the same team who'd lost 5-0 at Old Trafford earlier in the season, and we knew we had a chance. We were still deep in the relegation mire, but there was a strong belief around the club that a win over United would give us that impetus to push on and achieve survival.

I prepared for that game in exactly the same way I always did. My parents and Gavin stayed at mine the night before to provide a calming influence. By that stage, I'd equipped my house with little things to distract me, things like a pool table, dart board and table football. They knew I didn't want to talk about the match, or I'd get into a state of anxiousness, so they just kept the conversation light. We travelled to the game together, I signed some autographs and posed for photos, and then the stewards escorted me into the ground.

The United game was live on Sky Sports and most people expected us to roll over. The champions lined up with all their star names, but rather than shrinking, it lifted us. The fact that Sir Alex had picked his strongest line up showed how much he respected us. Pride Park was rocking with 33,000 fans packed inside and we were ready to put on a show for them and the viewers at home.

In the 8th minute, I scored the opener. Pierre Ducrocq played a ball into the penalty box to Rav, who got a touch and went to shoot, but I managed to get my foot in front of his and knocked it into the net. The United players looked shell shocked because it was totally against the script, almost like, how dare Derby take the lead. Our supporters were going crazy.

United came back though, as they so often did. Paul Scholes equalised before Juan Sebastian Veron put them in front on the hour mark. A few months earlier, we'd have crumbled and United probably would have gone on to score three or even four, but we kept fighting and got our reward in the 77th minute.

The rejuvenated Lee Morris combined with Luciano Zavagno down the left-hand side. I was over on the right of the penalty area with three defenders in front of me, so I ran across to the near post as I'd been taught during my Deeping Rangers days. The ball from Zavagno was inch perfect, falling straight into my stride, and I just had to angle my foot and send the ball home for the equaliser.

The crowd were going ballistic and so was I. I ran to the supporters counting my fingers as I asked myself, *Is that two?* After the game people claimed that I was being arrogant, but I wasn't. Inside I was absolutely buzzing, and all I was trying to do was calm myself down because there were still 15 minutes left which is a long time against a team like United.

It was such an exciting game to play in and I bet it was fun to watch too. Everyone was probably expecting United to come forward to grab a late winner, but it was us on the front foot. We missed a couple of great chances, and should have had a penalty when Barthez punched me in the back of the head, but the referee waved play on.

In injury time, Rob Lee won a great, crunching tackle, and the ball fell kindly to Branko Strupar who turned and had the goal in his sights. The fans cheered in expectation of the shot, while I was ready to pounce in case the keeper spilled it, even though 99 times out of 100 he wouldn't have.

But Barthez did spill it, and I ran in and kicked the ball into the goal with the outside of my right foot. Once again, the crowd were going crazy, but I was even more reserved with my celebration because I knew it'd be touch and go because I'd challenged the keeper.

I looked expectantly at the referee but instead of pointing to the centre circle to signal a goal, he pointed to Barthez. My heart sank. He'd ruled it out. My first thought was that I was glad I'd tempered my celebration because if I'd slid on my knees to the crowd, Ravanelli style shirt-over-my-head celebration, only to see it disallowed, I'd have made a right fool of myself!

I was gutted to be denied a hat trick. At that time, no one in the Premier League era had ever scored a hat trick against Manchester United, so I'd have been the first.

When the full-time whistle blew, I dropped to my knees, emotionally and physically exhausted. I did a two-fisted salute to the camera before conducting a post-match interview where I was asked about the disallowed goal. Inside I was cursing the ref, it was never a foul, but I had to be diplomatic, so I explained that referees are only human and sometimes make mistakes.

I was named Man of the Match and presented with a bottle of champagne which softened the blow a little.

John Gregory was fuming with the referee, and even Sir Alex Ferguson said that it should have counted. I didn't know whether to laugh or cry! Hearing Sir Alex mention my name in an interview meant so much to me though. When I had asked for him to sign my programme a few years earlier, I'd vowed that one day he'd know who I was – he certainly did now.

We suffered a narrow 1-0 defeat at Arsenal in our next match before beating Bolton, where I was again on the score sheet, to give us a glimmer of hope. I'm convinced that if Gregory had been appointed in October, instead of Colin, we'd have stayed up.

But the damage had already been done during the early part of the season and relegation was confirmed after a 2-0 defeat away at Liverpool on 20th April. If I'm honest, we knew it was coming. We'd been riding our luck for a few seasons, narrowly avoiding the drop, and we had taken too long to make the necessary changes. I was absolutely devastated and I'm not ashamed to admit that I shed a few tears on the Anfield turf. I'd never suffered relegation before, and I didn't know how to react. I didn't even know if I would ever bounce back because I felt hollow and numb.

Having to play the last few matches was horrible. Playing meaningless games really drained the life out of us as we just wanted the season to finish there and then, so we could get away from football to reset and come back stronger the next season.

It was a rollercoaster year for me personally as I started in the team and had a spell out of the side, before winning my place back. I scored nine league goals, the same as Rav, to finish as the club's joint top scorer, so that was pleasing on a personal level. However, as I've already mentioned, the 2001/02 campaign was the only season in my entire career that I played in its entirety, without suffering from illness or injuries – and we got relegated. I don't know what that tells you about my luck in football!

Every interview I did, people kept asking me if I was going to leave. I couldn't very well stand there and admit that if Derby accepted a bid from a Premier League team that I'd be gone. I mean, ultimately, that's exactly what would have happened, but you can't say that in public. I'd learnt by then that you have to say the right things at the right time and not upset anyone

So, I replied with a stock response, "I'm happy at Derby. I'm part of the team who got relegated and I want to be part of the team that wins promotion." I loved Derby and still do, but deep down I considered myself a Premier League player and desperately wanted to stay there. I also knew exactly which club I wanted to join, because I'd already been tapped up and my head had been turned.

Just before the end of the season I'd been called up to the England Under 21 squad for the 2002 European Championship and not long before I joined up with the Three Lions, Steve Round, my former coach, came round to my house. Steve was Steve McClaren's assistant at Middlesbrough, so it wasn't hard for me to put two and two together and I was interested straight away. With the amount of respect I had for the two Steves, I'd have walked to Middlesbrough if I had to.

As it turned out, he drove me up to the North East to meet the Boro manager. McClaren showed me around the training ground, with its world class facilities, he took me to Yarm, a beautiful area, to show me some properties that I could live in, and he took me to the best restaurants in the area in a bid to seduce me and tempt me to join the club. But he didn't really need to. In all honesty, the prospect of signing for Middlesbrough was as enticing as candy to a baby. It was everything I wanted at that stage of my career.

It was an illegal tap up, sure, but it happened in those days, just as I'm sure it still does today.

After being wooed, I sat in McClaren's office, where he told me that he'd already had a £6,000,000 bid for me rejected by Derby who were holding out for £9,000,000 – serious money. I was flattered that he rated me that highly.

"Don't worry about the move, Malcolm," he began. "You go away with England have a good time and we'll sort it when you get back."

We shook hands and as I drove back down the M1 to the Midlands, I was buzzing, knowing that all I needed to do was go to the Euros and set the world alight to prove to McClaren that I was worth the £9,000,000.

It turned out that my excitement was short lived.

CHAPTER 13
The Long Goodbye

Being chosen to represent your country in a major tournament should be the pinnacle of your career. Playing alongside and against the best young players in Europe. There is nothing better, right?

Wrong.

For me, the 2002 European Championship in Switzerland was an absolute nightmare.

Under Howard Wilkinson and David Platt I'd been a regular starter for my country for two years, I scored the goal that secured qualification to the tournament, and I honestly felt that I deserved to be in the first 11 for the Euros. I was included in David Platt's 22-man squad along with my Derby teammate Chris Riggott and we were absolutely buzzing. Platt handed me the number nine shirt too which made me believe I was going to be part of his first 11. After the disappointment of relegation, this was an opportunity for us to be part of a winning team. There were so many scouts in Switzerland, looking for the next big thing, and I felt that it was my time to shine. I already knew that Middlesbrough were keen on me, but there were also rumours that Phil Thompson, Liverpool's assistant manager, was keeping a close eye on me too.

My mum and dad flew out to Zurich with Chris' family to support us and experience the tournament. Chris hadn't played many of the qualifying matches, so he didn't expect to feature, but when the tournament kicked off against the hosts, Chris was named in the starting line up while I only made the bench. Platt selected Peter Crouch up front with Defoe, instead of me which was a big shock as Crouchy had only made two substitute appearances for England at that stage and was yet to score.

Although I felt I should have been the one starting, I really liked Crouchy. He had a good sense of humour, but he hadn't flourished as a player, and was yet to really develop his personality and confidence. The Peter Crouch you see laughing and joking on the television isn't the same guy I played with.

It's the same with another member of the Under 21 squad, Jermaine Jenas. He was a nice, quiet, unassuming lad, and never in a million years did I think he'd become a television presenter but look at him now on *Match of the Day* and *The One Show*. At the time, we were a bunch of hungry young kids, trying to make a name for ourselves. Later on, as your careers develop, once you've got a few games and goals under your belts, you become more confident and your personality changes.

Crouchy justified Platt's decision to start him by scoring the winning goal against the Swiss, so he kept his place for our next match against Italy, the reigning champions.

It was a real sliding doors moment for me as I watched on from the bench, feeling totally helpless as Massimo Maccarone absolutely destroyed us. He gave Chris Riggott a torrid time, turning him inside out, and scoring both goals in a 2-1 win for an Italian side that also featured Andrea Pirlo.

We lost our third and final group match 3-1 to Portugal and that was it, we were out of the tournament, and I hadn't even kicked a ball. It was David Platt's prerogative not to pick me, but I certainly didn't agree with his decision. Fair enough if he'd left me out because we were playing well and winning games, but to be denied a chance to start, or even come on as a substitute when we were struggling, was hard to take.

To make matters worse, Maccarone finished as the tournament's top scorer, one of the stand out players, which earned him an £8,000,000 transfer to Middlesbrough. I was devastated when I heard about the transfer as I knew that was supposed to be my move. Everything was set up for me to take the next step in my career and it all fell through because of that one tournament.

Steve McClaren was very apologetic when he phoned me to explain that they'd decided to go with another target. "Sit tight, Malcolm, and we'll have another look at you in January."

The breakdown of my transfer coincided with the end of my international career as I was too old to be named in any future Under

21 squads. When I reflect back, I enjoyed my time with England. I represented my country 11 times, scoring three goals and I'm proud of that. I improved as a player and evolved as a person, travelling around Europe to places like Finland, Slovenia, and Holland, seeing different cultures and learning more about the world.

I look back now with pride, but at the time my international experience left a bitter taste in my mouth. When you play for England, you are given a full kit for each match; two long sleeve shirts, two short sleeve, shorts, socks, training kits, suits, watches and more, and you are allowed to keep everything. I still have a vast amount of memorabilia from my playing days that I treasure, but my shirts from the 2002 Euros mean absolutely nothing to me.

*****

After the treble disappointment of relegation, not playing in the Euros, and seeing my transfer fall through, I needed to get away from football for a bit, so I booked a mad lad's holiday for myself, Gavin, James, and his older brother Simon. Our destination - Magaluf.

Ahead of the trip, we had the idea to go out there dressed as football players, so I'd ordered some gear from Umbro, who sponsored me at the time.

The day before we were due to fly, I received a package, but it only contained two sets of everything: two t-shirts, two tracksuits, and two pairs of trainers. I phoned my agent who contacted Umbro, and within minutes, they had called me to apologise and explained to me they'd send the other box of clothes straight away. Three hours later, there was a knock on the door of my parent's house. It was a taxi driver who had driven all the way down from Manchester to Stamford to deliver the rest of our gear. Umbro were fantastic, even paying the taxi fare of £450.

We flew from East Midland's Airport and landed in Magaluf, wearing identical tracksuits. We thought we were so cool, although in reality we probably looked like Will, Jay, Simon, and Neil from the *Inbetweeners* in their Pussay Patrol t-shirts! As if the matching clothes weren't bad enough, just before we left England I'd had my hair dyed with blonde tips!

Gavin was a real worrier. The minute we arrived up at the hotel, Simon, James, and I wanted to go straight out and get on it, but Gavin was looking at the reps board to see what time we were being picked up for the flight home! We ended up calling him Brian, after the 400m runner named Brian Whittle, because he kept whittling on. Whenever he whittled we sang the song Delilah to him, changing the word Delilah to Brian.

To be fair to Gav, he was playing the role of protective big brother, never getting too drunk so he could keep an eye out for any trouble.

However, one day we decided to play a little trick on him. We told Gavin that we were going to have a big night, so would be starting the drinking early. I went to the bar and ordered three shots of water for Simon, James, and myself, and one shot of vodka for Gavin. We were on the fifth round of shots before he finally cottoned on to what we were doing. While Gav was feeling a bit worse for wear, we were all stone cold sober. It lightened the mood for him and he enjoyed the night a lot more as a result.

Gavin wasn't a ladies man, but he met a girl on the holiday and we were all taking the piss, saying that he was in love. Gav had arranged to meet this girl at the beach and rather than let him get on with it, we all decided to tag along. They hired a pedalo, so we hired one too.

We could see that Gavin was sweating a bit, a combination of nerves and the blistering heat, so I decided to offer him a drink of my water. However, before I did so, I poured my water over the side of the boat and refilled the bottle with sea water. I screwed the cap back on before pedalling over to Gav.

"It's hot isn't it? Here you go, have some of my water to keep yourself hydrated," I said while handing him my bottle.

Simon and I were trying not to laugh as Gavin drank the water. As soon as he tasted the sea water it came straight out his nose and mouth, all down his top. The girl was horrified and we were in stitches. After that we pedalled back to the beach and left them to enjoy the rest of their date.

There weren't nearly as many footballers in Magaluf as there had been in Ayia Napa, but one evening we bumped into my former England Under 21 teammate David Dunn in a bar. We said hello and Dunny offered to buy us a drink. Someone in the bar heard him and said, "Why don't you buy us one?"

So he did. Dunny bought a round of drinks for everyone in the bar! I thought that was a really nice gesture, but I certainly didn't feel any pressure to get my round in, that's for sure.

I got recognised in a few places and the lads were loving the attention. Simon was a really good footballer who had signed a professional contract at West Brom before a bad knee injury ended his career before it had even begun.

Simon thought it would be a good idea if we stood on the beach doing some keepy uppies with a football. There was a crowd watching us and Simon loved the attention as people assumed he was a footballer too. He went along with it, although he had to say he played for a reserve team because if anyone followed football closely they'd be able to call his bluff.

I'd bought myself a pair of Police fashion sunglasses to take on the trip. With their clear lenses, they reminded me of the pairs I'd tried on in Specsavers a few years earlier. I remembered David Beckham wearing his Police sunglasses in Marbella, so I decided to buy them even though I wasn't sure if I could pull it off.

I had some designer clothes at the time, including some white linen Prada trousers, and Simon was forever rummaging through my wardrobe looking to see what clothes he could borrow. As soon as he saw the Police glasses he was convinced that they'd suit him, so he spent the rest of the holiday wearing the sunglasses, thinking he was Beckham! He loved them so much that when we got home, he even bought himself a pair.

It was a fantastic holiday and exactly what I needed at the time.

*****

I returned to England feeling refreshed, but my head was still all over the place following the breakdown of my move, and things were about to get even worse.

I want to make it clear that I didn't ever approach Middlesbrough, they came to me. It wasn't that I wanted to leave Derby, it more a case of me wanting to stay in the Premier League. I didn't push for a move, and I didn't hand in a transfer request. There was no way I would do that to the club after all they had done for me. As soon as I knew that the Boro move was off and that I was staying, I was 100% committed to Derby and our promotion charge.

There had been rumours for months that the club was struggling financially. During the 2001/02 season we'd spent just £3,500,000 on transfers, despite selling stars for a total £11,000,000. To be fair, the rest had probably gone on Rav's wages!

As soon as we returned for pre-season training, the truth came out, and we discovered the true extent of the financial crisis – it was much worse than we thought. Derby had no money; in fact, we were reportedly £30,000,000 in debt.

I had a clause in my contract that reduced my wages by 25% in the event of relegation. I imagine others had the same clause, but I don't know for sure as it's an unwritten rule in football that you don't talk about your contract with your teammates. I can't say I was happy to take a pay cut – who would be? – but you take the rough with the smooth and I understood that it was necessary for the club to survive.

But when we were told that we might have to defer our wages, that caused a massive split in the dressing room.

So, we've had two horrendous seasons, three managers, a relegation, you've just turned down a bid of £6,000,000 for me, and now you're telling us we might not get paid?

It was absurd.

Warren Barton was the club captain and our PFA rep, and he wanted us to take the deferral and do what was right for the club, but others disagreed. Danny Higginbotham took it to heart and handed in his resignation. He told us that we had the power because we were assets with a value to the club, so they had a choice – pay our wages or sell us.

Money is an emotive subject and the topic of a wage deferral understandably caused divisions; some players lived within their means, others were frivolous. Some earned extortionate money, while the younger lads were paid a small wage. There weren't many millionaires in that dressing room, so most of us were affected.

All credit to Warren who was the right person to try and sort it out. He was respectful of everyone's viewpoint, and it certainly wasn't an easy task. There were factions and things got a little heated at times. There weren't any scraps in the car park or anything like that, but it clearly caused disdain amongst teammates between those who wanted to defer and those who didn't.

I was one of the many players who agreed to a wage deferral

because I felt it was the right thing to do for the club. Nobody likes to take a pay cut, but when you see hard working people within the club losing their jobs because of the financial mismanagement from the board, I couldn't say no.

It was a toxic situation that meant we spent far too much time in meetings talking about the dire financial situation when our focus should have been on mounting a promotion charge. It was a distraction that we didn't need.

The media were tipping us for an instant return to the top flight. When you look at our first eleven on paper, we were as good as anyone else, and we got off to a fantastic start, beating Reading 3-0 at home with goals from Rob Lee, Ravanelli, and yours truly.

Then we went to Gillingham, and I learnt what the Championship was all about.

Four years earlier, I'd have loved to play at somewhere like Gillingham, but I had become accustomed to Old Trafford, Anfield, and the other top-class stadiums with luxurious facilities. Gillingham was a world away from the Premier League. We got abuse getting off the bus, abuse coming out for the warm up. The dressing rooms were portacabins, so tiny that you had to try not to knock the person next to you while you were getting changed. It was a rude awakening.

It was different on the pitch too. I found that I got less time on the ball, the defenders weren't afraid to kick me, and the crowd was much more intense. We were one of the biggest clubs in the division, which meant we were there to be shot at.

As the centre forward, one of Derby's danger men, I had a target on my back. In the second half, I fouled someone and then kicked the ball away in frustration. All of the sudden, the whole crowd went mad, chanting, "Malcolm Christie, what a wanker!" We lost 1-0 which was another shock, as most people, including us if I'm honest, had expected us to sail through. I'm sure that if we'd got a good result at Gillingham, it would have set us up for a cracking season.

Relegation, coupled with the financial crisis, badly affected morale and the biggest issue we had was switching from a losing mentality to a winning one, which isn't easy without an injection of fresh blood. We obviously had no money, so Gregory couldn't bring in any new signings.

The other challenge was changing our mindset as we were going into most matches as the favourites, whereas previously we'd always been the underdogs. Pride Park was one of the best stadiums in the division and everyone wanted to come to us. We were the team to beat, and everyone raised their games against us.

In our fourth match of the season, we faced Wolves, our big promotion rivals, at Pride Park. They battered us 4-1, that was a humbling experience, and sent out a message to the rest of the league that we were there for the taking.

We couldn't deal with adversity, so if we went behind in a game, we crumbled, never able to get back into games or turn it around. The fight we'd had in those stunning comebacks against Sheffield Wednesday and Middlesbrough had long since left us.

Rotherham beat us in the match after the Wolves defeat and our season never got going. The games were coming thick and fast, and we just rolled from one poor performance to another. It was a nightmare, and we soon became embroiled in yet another relegation battle. Despite this, I can't recollect many team meetings or anyone doing anything to fix it.

I've sung John Gregory's praises for the impact he made when he arrived, but I saw him change during his second season. His team talks were always about how bad our opponents were. "Don't worry today, Malcolm," he'd say. "Their defender is slow and won't be able to catch you."

When you've spent all week hearing the manager dismissing our opponents as rubbish, it's a big shock when the game kicks off and you realise that they aren't. His team talks should have been about how much the other team wanted it, how the crowd would be against us. He should have created a siege mentality and built the games up. His assumption was that we were better players, so should win, but football isn't that simple. That desire to go out and perform on a cold night at Bradford wasn't there. Motivation became a huge problem and that was part of our downfall. We were built up to feel that we were better than everyone else, so we became complacent and fell into the trap of believing our own hype while opponents were raising their games.

I think John found it hard when people questioned or challenged him because he wanted to be everyone's mate, so he tried to force himself to be more of an authoritarian, but it was ridiculous. From the arm around the shoulder type manager, he started falling out with people left, right, and centre.

Craig Burley was out injured and Gregory wasn't happy with the way Craig was managing his injury which caused a bust up that resulted in Burley telling the media that he wouldn't play for Gregory again.

Ravanelli was still earning mega bucks, and Gregory told him that he had no future at the club and made him train with the youth team to try and force him out of the club. That didn't sit right with me, we're paying him all that money, we should have been playing him. It didn't make sense to me at all because for everything people thought he was, when Rav crossed that white line, he gave his all. He wasn't a shirker, although his legs had gone by that stage.

Several players felt the wrath of Gregory, with some lads having their names removed from the back of the match day programme, others were told they weren't allowed to park their cars at the stadium on match days.

Gregory even had a little dig at me, handing me a £50 fine for littering the car park with a McDonalds cup! He didn't even tell me face to face, he sent me a letter! I was so incensed that I went to see Ross MacLaren, Gregory's assistant. "I've got this fine, Ross, but it's wrong. There is no way I would wind my window down and throw a cup on the ground. And I can't even remember the last time I went to McDonalds."

"No, it's definitely you," he replied. "We've caught you on CCTV."

I demanded to be shown the footage and when I saw it, I realised that it was Luciano Zavagno who'd littered, and he had the same car as me. I was fuming, if you're going to go to the trouble of typing a letter and fining someone £50, at least get the right player! Gregory didn't even apologise to me.

These petty little incidents were daft and increased the negative feeling surrounding the club. He was nit-picking, looking for any opportunity to have a go at the players.

In mid-November, I received the first and only red card of my career. We were away at Brighton who were playing their home matches in an athletics stadium, called the Withdean. In the 34th minute, I went in for a 50/50 challenge with their goalkeeper,

Michel Kuipers. My studs were up a little bit, but it wasn't a malicious tackle. Yes, it was a foul, but the fans were screaming like mad which twisted the referee's arm and he booked me, even though it was never a yellow. After that incident, the Brighton supporters took pleasure jeering me and getting on my back every time I went near the ball. It was the only time I ever let the crowd get to me.

Early in the second half, I tripped an opponent, and the referee gave Brighton a free kick. They put the ball down, but it was no where near where the foul had occurred, so I kicked it back to where the free kick should have been taken from. The Brighton crowd erupted, yelling at the ref. The referee hadn't seen the incident, but as he turned towards me, he saw the ball rolling away and assumed I'd kicked the ball away. I think he wanted to be a bit of a hero, so he put his hand into his pocket and showed me a second yellow, followed by a red. It was a tame sending off for two very soft bookings.

Maybe it was a bit of frustration on my part because it was certainly out of character for me to be in trouble with a referee. I can count the number of yellow cards I received in my whole career on one hand, so to get sent off was devastating. I felt the referee was very poor that day and allowed himself to be influenced by the home supporters. The crowd were venomous as I trudged off the pitch towards the dressing rooms which were like little cow sheds.

It was strange sitting in an empty changing room. I didn't know what I was supposed to do. *Do I sit down, or stand up? Can I get changed or do I wait for the others?* The weirdest part was the dressing rooms were underneath the home supporters, so they were hurling abuse at me. I couldn't figure out why the noise was so loud until I noticed that the window was open! I soon got up and closed it.

Even though I didn't deserve to be sent off, I felt that I'd let my teammates down and I sat there, feeling helpless, listening to the crowd, staring at my watch, counting down the minutes to full time. My nightmare afternoon was complete in the 89th minute when I heard the Brighton fans celebrating Kerry Mayo's late goal which gave them a 1-0 victory.

When the lads walked in, their heads were down, and they

were gutted that we'd lost in the last minute. I felt awful, it was one of the worst moments of my career, and I apologised to everyone. To their credit, no one pointed the finger at me or attributed any blame.

After getting showered and changed, we got abused again boarding the team coach for the long trip back to the Midlands

The following day at training, I was given another typed letter from Gregory, and another fine.

For the first time in my career, I began to question myself and my own performances, but I always came back to the fact that if the chances were there I'd score. Yes, I missed the odd chance, but not many people would say I was a bad finisher. If the opportunity was there, I'd make the keeper work. I'd scored seven goals in the first half of the season, so was on target for 15 to 20 goals which would have been a decent return, I suppose.

I remember Lee Morris telling me that I needed to play with better players if I wanted to develop. That was the first time a fellow player had said that to me, but it made sense. I knew that if I played with better players, they would be capable of finding me if I made the right run.

As the January transfer window approached, I knew that my days at Pride Park were coming to an end as the club desperately needed all the money they could get, especially as we knew we wouldn't be making an instant return to the Premier League. It was a real shame as nothing would have given me greater pleasure than seeing Derby win promotion. If we had been challenging for the play offs or in the upper echelons of the division, I wouldn't have left the club when I did.

I loved Derby, still do, but I didn't want to be languishing in mid table in the Championship. I had ambitions of scoring goals in the Premier League and playing for England, so it was the natural time to move on. I'd been at Derby for four and a half years by then and I felt that I was ready for a fresh challenge, ready to write a new chapter in my career.

I always gave 100% for Derby. Yes, I had games where I didn't score or could have played better, but I never came off the pitch thinking I hadn't given it my all. It is one of my biggest regrets that I didn't play in a successful Derby County team.

I don't think I was the only one who had one eye on the exit door and maybe that was our problem. We weren't pulling in the same direction because players knew the club were desperate to sell them, so their focus was on finding themselves a new club.

We'd already said goodbye to Bjorn Otto Bragstad, Darryl Powell, and Horacio Carbonari. Deon Burton was next to leave, closely followed by Mart Poom. Danny Higginbotham got his move back to the Premier League, joining Southampton for a cut-price £1,500,000. There were a few clubs who got some good bargains in the Pride Park January sales!

So I knew that I was leaving, the question was *where* was I going? Bolton and West Brom were reportedly interested and there were rumours that Leeds United's manager, Terry Venables, wanted me to replace Robbie Fowler, who had moved to Manchester City.

But Steve McClaren's Middlesbrough was my most likely destination. Ever since our summer courtship, I'd wanted to join the North East club and had been keeping a keen eye on their progress over the season. I knew that McClaren still wanted to sign me, so I made sure I kept playing well and put myself in the shop window.

On 18th January 2003, we took on Stoke City at the Britannia Stadium in the final match before the transfer window closed. I knew that in all likelihood, it was going to be my last game for the Derby County, and I wanted to sign off with a goal.

I did.

Georgi Kinkladze swung in a corner that evaded everyone as the ball headed in my direction. I did a sort of bicycle kick, caught it sweet as a nut and the ball flew into the back of the net, almost taking the keeper's head off in the process! It's one of my favourite goals and was the perfect way to bow out.

I ran over to our fans, kissing the badge to show them my respect and to thank them for all the support they had given me. We went on to win the game 3-1 and I applauded the supporters as I left the pitch at the final whistle. A very special, and emotional moment.

On 31st January 2003, transfer deadline day, Middlesbrough made a joint bid for me and my teammate, Chris Riggott. We shared an agent, Paul Martin, who told us to go and wait by the phone.

After four and half years, I was leaving Pride Park.

CHAPTER 14
Deadline day drama

As soon as the clubs have agreed a transfer fee, the agents take over the negotiations and us players rarely hear from the clubs or their managers until the deal has been finalised.

As instructed, Chris and I were sitting together staring at the phone for what seemed an eternity before Paul Martin, our agent, finally rang and told us to go to the Ramarena to grab our boots.

The move was on.

We drove to the training ground to pack up our belongings and were shocked when we were denied access.

"Sorry, lads. John Gregory's told me not to let you in," the kit man explained.

How petty can you get? We'd come to collect our boots, shin pads, and other items that *we* owned – they didn't belong to the club – and there was no way we were leaving without them. We told the kit man not to be ridiculous before walking into the changing rooms and emptying the contents of our lockers and stuffing our possessions into bin liners as quickly as we could. The training ground was quiet as the lads had a day off, so we only managed to say a few goodbyes to those who were there, like the receptionists, Derby legend Archie Gemmill, and a few others.

I took a moment to gather my thoughts and reflect on what I'd achieved since walking into Derby County for the first time as an unknown, naïve, wide-eyed kid, back in October 1998. Now, after making 129 appearances and scoring 36 goals, I commanded a seven-figure transfer fee.

I was expecting to feel a tinge of sadness, but because of the way we were initially denied entry to the training ground, I wasn't emotional at all. In fact, the experience left a bitter taste in my mouth. Neither Chris nor I had asked to leave. Yes, we were happy to be returning to the Premier League, but Derby were desperate for the money, so we had no choice about going anyway. We had both been good servants to the club – Chris was a lifelong Derby fan for crying out loud – and I felt we deserved to be treated with a bit more respect. Even a quick, "Thanks for your service, boys. Good luck for the future," from Gregory would have been nice. Football is like that, though, there is no room for sentiment.

After leaving the Ramarena for the final time, we travelled up to the North East, where we met with Paul and Keith Lamb, Middlesbrough's Chief Executive, at Blackwell Grange, a beautiful country house just outside Darlington. The clubs had already agreed a fee of £3,000,000 for the pair of us, a bargain considering Derby had rejected a bid of £6,000,000 for me alone just six months earlier. Another example of their financial mismanagement.

One aspect of the transfer that did work in Derby's favour was when it came to splitting the transfer fee between myself and Chris. The biggest chunk was assigned to Chris, with a much smaller proportion attributed to me, even though I was arguably the bigger signing. The reason for this was simple; Nuneaton were due a percentage of any sell on fee, so the lower my transfer fee, the less Derby would have to pay them. I wasn't happy about it, I guess it made sense from Derby's point of view, but it didn't sit right with me that Nuneaton got shafted in the deal.

Another little bit of uncertainty was around whether one of us was initially joining Boro on loan. As it turned out, I was signing on the dotted line, with Chris going to Middlesbrough on loan until the end of the season when his move would be made permanent.

Paul and Keith were in a separate room negotiating our contracts while Chris and I sat chatting in the hotel reception. After a few minutes, Paul appeared and said, "Right boys, we're off." Chris and I looked at each other before following him out of Blackwell Grange and into his car. As we drove away, Paul explained that Middlesbrough's initial contract offer was for less than I was being paid by Derby. I couldn't get my head around that as I was on £3,000 a week at the time, peanuts for a Premier League striker, so I completely understand why Paul was reluctant for me to sign for a reduced wage.

"Don't worry, boys, they'll be on the phone soon. The fact that they've agreed a transfer fee means that they won't walk away after the first offer. We've got to hold firm and get the best possible deal for you both," he reassured us. The situation was reminiscent of my first contract negotiation with Derby, although the big difference was that Paul was an experienced agent and knew what he was doing, whereas my first agent didn't! We trusted him and it was exciting as we drove around the North East countryside, waiting for the phone to ring.

Sure enough, it didn't take long for Steve McClaren to call. "Where are you, Paul?" he asked.

"We've left," Paul replied. "We're not even close to signing a contract."

"Turn the car around and come back please," Steve said.

So we returned to Blackwell Grange and the second round of negotiations went much smoother than the first. Keith Lamb was renowned for low balling his first offer on the off chance that you say yes straight away. To be fair, we'd probably all do the same in his position, but Paul was wise to the game and knew what we were worth.

Second time around they offered us something that was acceptable, and I was happy to put pen to paper on a four-and-a-half-year contract, starting on £5,000 a week, which would rise each year, with a £3,000 appearance bonus, and £1,000 a goal. Not a huge contract by Premier League standards, but the length of the deal gave me long term security and time to develop which was ideal for me.

After signing the necessary paperwork, Chris and I travelled back to Derby to pack some clothes and other essential items before returning to the North East the following morning. Blackwell Grange was to become our home for the next month until we found more permanent accommodation.

It was an exciting time, but I didn't realise how much the stresses and strains of the prolonged transfer was taking out of me mentally. Moving clubs is a big thing; new surroundings, new teammates, living in a hotel – it was mentally exhausting.

Derby County meant so much to me and Chris, they always will. They were the club who gave me my big break and I am eternally grateful to them. Leaving midway through the season with the

Rams struggling in the Championship didn't sit particularly well with me because I had genuinely wanted to win promotion back to the Premier League. But ultimately, a footballer's career is short – as I would soon discover – and I had to do what was right for me.

Chris was a Derby fan who, as a kid, went to the Baseball Ground with his dad, so it was a big wrench for him too. But we were both ambitious and harboured dreams of becoming Premier League regulars and full internationals. Middlesbrough ticked all the right boxes for us; up and coming club, performing well in the league, a bright young manager, and a team littered with internationals.

I'd had an affinity towards Middlesbrough since I made my full debut at the Riverside three years earlier, and I'd followed their results when Bryan Robson, my hero, had managed them in the nineties. I had so much respect for Steve McClaren and his assistant Steve Round, having worked with them both before at Derby, and their stadium was almost a carbon copy of Pride Park. I also knew how passionate the Boro fans were.

I was all hyped up to be the marquee signing until I found out that McClaren had signed another striker on deadline day – Michael Ricketts.

Mention his name today and it won't mean a lot, but in January 2003, he was a big name after his goals for Bolton Wanderers had earned him a call up to the England squad. I didn't know whether he was being brought in to play alongside me or to provide competition, but I was a bit disappointed, and it took the shine off the move a little. If I'd signed the previous summer, I could have been the club's record signing and now I was having to play second fiddle.

Ricketts didn't turn out to be the club's greatest signing, I wasn't either, to be fair, but high hopes were placed upon his shoulders because he'd achieved relative success with Bolton, and he certainly didn't live up to the big expectations in any way, shape, or form.

Of all the people I've trained and played with, Michael was probably one of the most laid-back, giving me the impression that he didn't really want to be a footballer and didn't enjoy it. He was always one of the last in and among the first to leave, which isn't a problem if you're putting in the effort and going 100 miles an hour while you're there, but he wasn't doing that.

Michael's wages rocketed when he joined Boro and I don't think he ever had the desire to step up to the next level. I don't know if he'd had that hunger at Bolton, I can't comment on that, I can only say what I saw, and in my view, he just didn't ever seem interested. I couldn't work out what motivated him. At the time, he was someone I looked up to because he'd achieved a little bit more than I had, and I thought we could've formed a decent partnership.

I had worn the number 12 shirt during my first few seasons at Derby, before Gregory swapped me to number 10 when we were relegated. At Boro, I was handed the squad number 19, but I took 11 in the summer of 2003, after Alen Boksic departed. It didn't really matter to me what number I wore on the back of my shirt, although some players can be very superstitious about squad numbers.

Arriving at the training ground for the first time reiterated the fact that I had joined a big club who were going places. The dressing rooms were huge and luxurious, and I had my own station, containing a locker, mirror, wardrobe, and a comfy, cushioned seat. I sat next to Ugo Ehiogu – God bless him – and it was nice to have a senior player nearby helping me to settle in.

The standard of football was much higher than I had been used to, so I knew I'd have to raise my game another level. The training was excellent, as you'd expect from two Steves, arguably amongst the best coaches in the game, and I immediately felt at home on the pitch.

You talk to any of the Manchester United or England players of the 1990s and 2000s and ask them to name the best coach they've worked under, and I guarantee that Steve McClaren will be in the top three, without a doubt. He was an unbelievable coach, so was Steve Round, their sessions were brilliant, fun, and lively. Whether it was fitness, shooting, or passing drills, you'd always get something out of the session. It was impossible not to improve as a player with that level of coaching.

There was a third Steve on the coaching staff, Steve Harrison, or Harry as everyone called him. His dad was a comedian, so it's no surprise that he was an absolute joker; a funny, quick witted guy who was great around the place. Everyone loved him.

Harry, a full back during his playing days, was an outstanding defensive coach who had learned his trade at Aston Villa under Graham Taylor, before coaching England when Taylor was appointed national team manager in 1990.

Everywhere we went, he'd be cracking jokes, making us laugh. Harry often led you into a joke and it would take a few seconds to catch on. On one occasion, he was sitting with a newspaper laid out on the table in front of him, opened on the crossword page. "Nine across, contents of a postman's sack."

"How many letters, Harry?" I asked, naively.

"Hundreds!" he responded bursting into laughter before moving on and doing the same joke to another player.

Harry had learnt how to fall down stairs without hurting himself and that became his little party piece. I remember the first time I saw him do it. We were standing around in a hotel foyer with several people milling about. Harry nudged one of us and said, "Watch this." He then climbed to the top of the stairs before throwing himself down them all the way from top to bottom. When he landed, several hotel guests and staff rushed over to see how he was, while we were all trying hard not to laugh! He was hilarious and was great at lightening the mood.

He gave me a new nickname too, 'The Doc.' He was the only person in football who ever called me anything other than Mally, apart from my trial match at Nuneaton where I was known as Chrisso, of course. When I asked him why me called me The Doc, he replied, "There was a serial killer in the 1940s and 1950s called Doctor Christie." Bizarre!

People would ask, "Why does he call you Doc?"

I'd reply, "Oh, it's after a serial killer!"

The dressing room was vocal and full of people you could trust. We'd lacked leaders at Derby, but when I looked around my new teammates, I saw people who meant business. Everything felt different. I was part of a squad of players who really cared, who would challenge each other, with good camaraderie. We had a good blend of youth and experience, English lads, and foreigners.

McClaren wanted his team first and foremost to be solid at the back. Football was different in those days, so the defenders didn't necessarily have to be good on the ball, their primary role was to defend. We didn't play out from the back, the defender's job was to win the ball back before clearing it from danger, allowing the midfielders to get it under control and create chances for the attackers.

In the summer before I joined, McClaren had moved on some of the old guard, players like Paul Ince, Robbie Mustoe, and Phil Stamp, as he started to assemble a more dynamic team, a side that was built on a blend of youth, experience, quality, and pace.

Mark Schwarzer was our goalkeeper, very reliable and a solid base, and although he did make the odd mistake – you can argue which goalkeeper doesn't – he also made some outstanding saves.

Ugo Ehiogu was a very strong, underrated defender who'd played for Villa during a successful period where he won two League Cups, played in an FA Cup Final, and represented England. I'd written to him when I was younger and still have his signed picture in my loft.

Colin Cooper, a Boro legend, was another experienced solid defender, another former England international, and another whose autograph was in my collection. I obviously didn't tell anyone that I'd written to them as a fan.

At the heart of our defence was Gareth Southgate, a guy I idolised. Gareth was our captain, a true leader of men, who went out of his way to welcome me and Chris to the club.

In the canteen after our first training session, we collected our food and found an empty table to sit together as we didn't know anyone else. Gareth came over to introduce himself and ate his lunch with us, taking the time to get to know us and explaining how the club worked. He was a really nice bloke and put me at ease straight away which certainly helped the transition.

In midfield we had Geremi, who was on loan from Real Madrid having won two consecutive Champions League trophies with the Spanish giants. What shocked me about Geremi is that he looked awful in training. He constantly gave the ball away and was tripping over himself during small-sided games. When we did crossing and shooting drills his balls would end up in the next field. I couldn't believe it, he was terrible.

But come match day, when he stepped onto the pitch, he was the total opposite; he rarely gave the ball away, was committed in the tackle, and he passed the ball with pin point accuracy. What a player. He was truly world class. Some people are like that, they save themselves for the games, whereas I always trained like I was playing in a match.

Alongside Geremi in the middle of the park, providing some grit, was George Boateng. I admired George having watched and played against him when he was at Coventry and Aston Villa. He was reliable, with a good work ethic, and he'd run through walls for the team. A great, funny guy, who always took time out of his day to see how I was.

Jonathan Greening and Mark Wilson were two young lads who had joined us from Manchester United and were trying to assert themselves in the side. McClaren had worked with them both during his spell at Old Trafford.

Alen Boksic, the Croatian striker who had partnered Fabrizio Ravanelli up front in Juventus' 1993 Champions League winning team, was a huge name, and I was hoping I'd have the opportunity to play alongside him. I saw him in the gym but didn't speak to him, and I was disappointed when he was released the day after I signed, meaning I didn't even got the chance to train with him.

Speaking of legendary players, the undoubted star in the Middlesbrough side was Juninho. He was enjoying his second spell at the club and was a superstar, a wonderful magician of a player. I'd watched him on television when he won the World Cup with Brazil just six months earlier and he was a dream to play with. It was very similar to the situation with Kinkladze at Derby; a flair player everyone loved, but he wasn't quite at the peak of his powers by the time I linked up with him. He was suffering with a knee injury, so I only saw glimpses of what he was capable of.

Two moments stand out to me: in my fourth game for Boro, he scored a cracking goal from outside the box against Leeds at Elland Road to help us on our way to a 3-2 victory against a very strong Leeds side.

A few games later, against West Brom, he hit the crossbar from a stunning bicycle kick that left me in awe, thinking, *Wow, this player is amazing.*

Juninho was held in such high esteem by the Boro fans, they worshipped him like a God. At Derby, I was one of the bigger name players, but it didn't take long for me to realise that I was in the bottom three at Middlesbrough, which was actually quite refreshing. We had a lot of supporters who came to watch us train and they waited around afterwards collecting autographs. Juninho, George, and Gareth were the signatures the fans sought, not necessarily mine, so I could just go about my business in the normal way.

Having left a side that had been struggling in the Championship, it was a complete change to join a team who were on the up and enjoying their football. At Derby we had a team capable of giving the big teams a good game, at Middlesbrough we went into every game thinking we could win because of the players we had.

I couldn't wait to pull on the red and white shirt and get started.

CHAPTER 15

A dream start

I was supposed to make my debut on 1st February 2003, in a match against Newcastle United, but the game was postponed because of a snowstorm.

The adverse weather meant that we spent the week training in the indoor hall which contained a full sized pitch. At the end of one session Steve McClaren lined us all up on the half way line and told us we had to score a goal from there without the ball touching the floor. As soon as we achieved the task we could go in and have some lunch.

For me, when I was feeling a bit anxious about my move, that goal might as well have been the size of a postage stamp. One by one, the lads completed the challenge and headed to the canteen and eventually there was only me and the manager still in the hall. By then, even McClaren had hit the target.

If I'd still been at Derby, I'd have done it first time, but as his new signing I felt under immense pressure and just couldn't do it. I was scuffing them, hitting them too high, too low, and in the end, Steve told me to pick my ball up and go in.

That had a big impact on my confidence because as the team's centre forward, I should have been hitting it in first time. I walked into the canteen while the rest of the lads were eating their desert and they asked me if I'd done it. "Yeah, of course," I said, even though I hadn't.

I made my debut away at Liverpool on 8th February, replacing Joseph-Desire Job at half time. It was nice to be involved in Premier League football again, especially at Anfield, one of my top three stadiums to play at, a place that always generates a fantastic atmosphere. We drew 1-1 which was a good result, but it was perhaps a sign of things to come that I came off towards the end of the game as I suffered a dead leg.

My full debut, two weeks later, came at the Stadium of Light against local rivals Sunderland. Middlesbrough fans call it a derby, but as far as Sunderland are concerned, their only derby match is against Newcastle. Still, it was an important game for both teams and a chance for me to endear myself in front of the supporters who made the short trip up the A19. There was a huge away following, as usual. The Boro fans are real die-hards, and their travelling support is second to none.

We took the lead through an unlikely source, Chris Riggott, who smashed the ball in from four yards after just 20 minutes. Seven minutes later, Chris was on the score sheet again to double our lead. He scored just seven times in 100 appearances for Derby, so for him to bag a brace in only his second game for Middlesbrough was unbelievable.

Kevin Phillips pulled one back for Sunderland early in the second half, and then I scored my first goal for Boro, latching on to a poor back pass before calmly slotting the ball past Thomas Sorensen into the net. I ran over to the Boro fans and kissed the badge to show them how happy I was to be at the club, while my new teammates jumped on my back to congratulate me. It was the perfect way for me to introduce myself to the supporters.

To score so soon into my Middlesbrough career was a huge relief. If I'd gone three or four games without scoring, I'd have felt the pressure. As it was, a goal on my first start was fantastic, as was the 3-1 victory that accompanied it. It was the best I'd felt for a long, long time, as I'd been struggling with my mental health for a while.

There is a lot of banter within the dressing room, it's part and parcel of the game, but I took it to heart more than anyone else because I didn't want anyone to think badly of me. Not outwardly, but inside I let it get to me.

Why don't people like me?

Why didn't I get invited out?

They were some of the thoughts going through my head from day one at Middlesbrough. I kept myself to myself and I think people saw me as standoffish. I wish I could have relaxed more and shown people the real me as I'd have played better, trained better and, ultimately, felt much happier. I occasionally showed glimpses of the real me which surprised people. I played a lot of golf with Franck Queudrue, and he once told me "You're pretty funny. Not like you are at the club."

My personality in the dressing room was someone who was very quiet, which isn't necessarily who I was as a person, it was who I became in football. I went into the pro game as a naïve kid who never came out of my shell, and I learnt to suppress the real me. I tried to tell myself that I could become me when I transferred to a new club, but it didn't happen because I moved with Chris, who knew me from Derby, so I couldn't very well go to Middlesbrough and be someone completely different. Instead, I continued to be the person Chris expected me to be.

It's hard to admit, but I was never my true self throughout my entire football career and it saddens me to think that I spent all those years pretending to be someone else. I made myself introverted and that doesn't work well in a dressing room packed full of big characters and jokers. If you're quiet, you're being a weirdo, basically. A group of athletes, full of testosterone, isn't the kind of place where you can go out and say, "I feel a bit down."

I didn't want the next few years to be like the previous four at Derby where I struggled to connect with teammates, so I got a bit panicky. And when I felt anxious, I retreated back into my shell. I was trapped in a vicious circle. Once I lost myself, it became crippling, and it started to chip away at my mental health. My mind became a very busy place, I found myself constantly over thinking things which is a dangerous thing to do.

I'd been having these battles off the pitch for a while and football was my release, the one time I could actually switch off my mind and be myself. My problems escalated when my mental health started to affect me on the football pitch.

My anxiety levels had been increasing at an alarming rate since the 2002 Euros, and by the time I eventually joined Middlesbrough, I was no longer able to suppress it and I began to suffer with bouts of double vision. One day I was driving and had to stop and pull over as I was struggling to see the road ahead of me. My vision returned to normal after a few minutes, so I was able to continue my journey.

It happened a few more times, but I tried to ignore it and just put it down to one of those things, until my third Boro match, a home game against Everton, when I suffered from double vision during the game. I couldn't see what was going on, it was horrible. The ball was coming over to me, but I could see two and didn't know which one to go for. I was substituted at half time because there was no way I could continue playing like that. I felt strange and began to worry that something was wrong with me, so I told the physios what had happened, and they sent me off to some specialists to get checked out.

I was sent to the opticians, but everything was fine with my eyes. I was sent for brain scans, but everything was fine there too. I took every kind of test you can imagine, but no one found anything that could be causing my double vision.

Never once did anyone consider that it might have been stress related. In those days, people didn't really think about athletes suffering from stress and anxiety like they do today, it was taboo and certainly never spoken about in football. *Why would a young man, playing football, earning a decent wage suffer from stress? What could we possibly have to be stressed about?* That was the thinking, and no one ever took the time to ask me how I was actually feeling.

The pressure had been mounting, and it took just one trigger for all that accumulated stress to be released. That trigger was my move to Middlesbrough.

I don't know how I did it, but I managed to pull myself through it and I only missed one game due to stress. Had I been diagnosed at that stage, and got the help I needed, things would have been massively different for me. There was such a stigma attached to mental health that if the club had known I was suffering from stress, they'd have had to say I'd pulled my hamstring or something like that.

Most people nowadays are aware of the importance of the mental side of the game and the fact that footballers are normal people who are just as susceptible to depression and stress as anyone else, but during the early 2000s, there was a total lack of awareness. You only have to look at how Glenn Hoddle was ridiculed for bringing Eileen Drewery in to work with the England boys to see why it was so difficult to speak out.

Steve McClaren was a progressive coach and he worked closely with Bill Beswick. Bill was great, a brilliant sports psychologist, someone you could speak to if you needed to and, with hindsight, I should have gone to him as he would have probably been able to help. But I didn't know I was suffering from stress, so I didn't feel I needed to speak to him. I knew I didn't feel right, but I had no idea what was making me feel that way.

By the time we faced Leeds in the middle of March, I was feeling a little more settled, having moved out of the hotel into a nice flat, just off Yarm High Street, that I was renting from my boyhood hero Bryan Robson. I was back in the starting line-up and played 85 minutes in the fantastic 3-2 victory where Juninho scored his wonder goal. We had a good team, and I was pleased with my performance, even though I didn't manage to get on the score sheet.

I did score in our next game, however, a 1-1 draw with Charlton, and the one after, a 3-0 win at home to West Brom, winning Man of the Match in both games. When I look back now, that was the time when I was at the peak of my powers on the pitch and if I could take myself back to somewhere and be that the player for my whole career, that was the moment. I was scoring goals, playing in a very good team, the crowd were behind me and my performances on the pitch meant I could forget about my mental health issues for a while.

Steve McClaren was part of the England set up and he told me that if I kept my performances high and, most importantly, continued to score goals, I would give Sven-Goran Eriksson a headache and maybe even earn a call up to the senior squad. Although there was a lot of competition for the centre forward position for England, with players like Michael Owen, Emile Heskey, Jermain Defoe, and Peter Crouch, I knew I was only an injury or two away from a call up.

After the West Brom game, the newspapers were speculating that I was on the verge of making the squad, but it didn't ever happen. I honestly believe that had I continued to perform like I had started my Middlesbrough career, I would have achieved another dream and represented my county at the senior level, but I began to suffer with injuries.

It's hard for me to look back and see players like David Nugent, Michael Ricketts, Francis Jeffers, and Jay Bothroyd who all played for England instead of me, because I felt I was at least as good as any of them.

Although I didn't know it at the time, I tore my groin in our next match, away at Manchester City. I felt a really sharp pain in my groin and every time I turned, it felt like someone was sticking a knife into it. The physio thought it was just wear and tear, so the agreement was for me to play the last few games of the season and then get it looked at properly in the summer. So I played the rest of the campaign, although I was nowhere near 100%. I did manage to score one more goal that season, in a stunning 5-1 victory at home to Spurs, but I struggled to play my normal game because of my groin.

The difficult thing from my perspective was that I knew I wasn't right, the club knew I wasn't right, but the supporters didn't, so they were probably wondering why I wasn't running about as much, and I heard a little bit of discontent from them.

At the end of the season, we finished 11th in the league, just two points away from Manchester City who qualified for Europe. I scored a total of 13 goals, nine for Derby and four for Boro, so it wasn't a bad year all round.

With the season over, I could finally get my groin looked at, so I attended a consultation with Dr Gilmore, a specialist in groin injuries who had the injury Gilmore's Groin named after him. In order to diagnose me, he placed his little finger deep into my groin and asked if it hurt. *Bloody hell. Yes, it hurt!*

Dr Gilmore explained that I had the Gilmore's Groin injury which would need surgery because my groin had completely severed from the bone and was as bad as you could get. No wonder I'd been in so much pain!

Over the years, I'd suffered from recurring sore throats and swollen glands, and had been advised that it would be best to have my tonsils removed at some stage in the future, but I'd delayed it because I didn't want an operation to interrupt my football career. The club decided that because I was going to be out of action for a while recovering from my groin op that I might as well have my tonsils out, so I could recover from both at the same time.

Just before my operations the club suggested I go away for a short break, so I flew out to Cyprus for a relaxing week in the sun with Gavin and his friend Ashley Wilcox.

After returning from a luxurious hotel in Cyprus, my brother drove me down to London for a less glamorous overnight stay in the Harley Street clinic.

It was crazy really. After my groin operation, I was kept in overnight for observation and Gavin picked me up the following day and drove me back up to the North East for my second op. The car ride was so uncomfortable, my groin was in agony and I still felt groggy from the general anaesthetic.

We didn't go home first, Gavin took me straight to the next hospital. I met the consultant ahead of my tonsillectomy, they asked if I'd had general anaesthetic in the last six months. "I had one yesterday!" I replied.

It can be highly dangerous to have two doses of anaesthetic in a short period of time, so they contacted the club to check that it was OK to go ahead and then I had to sign a disclaimer, basically waiving my rights if anything went wrong.

I had my tonsils removed the following day, just 72 hours after the surgery on my groin.

After the double op, I felt so sore and disorientated for a few days because of the effects of the general anaesthetic. I couldn't move, couldn't talk, and couldn't eat. In fact, there wasn't much I could do!

After a brief stay in the hospital, I spent the rest of the summer of 2003 resting at home. It was a horrendous ordeal and a huge setback in my career as I missed the bulk of pre-season, so was playing catch up when the new season began.

That was the beginning of the end for me. Sadly, I was never the same player again after my groin injury.

CHAPTER 16
Treading treacle

Pre-season is so important to make sure that you are physically and mentally right for the start of the new season. You want to tick all the boxes; you've done all the running you're supposed to do, you've met the standards set by the fitness coach, you've learnt the strengths and weaknesses of your new teammates, and built rapport. Unfortunately, I can't remember many seasons as a professional where I went into the new campaign feeling fresh and sharp. In fact, I can only recall two summers in my entire career where I wasn't either injured or ill. Preseason is vital, so I always felt that I was playing catch up.

The double operation hit me much harder than expected, completely obliterating my fitness levels. I hadn't had an operation as an adult before and the general anaesthetic totally wiped me out. I was very fortunate to be a Premier League footballer as it meant I was well looked after. Harley Street was a place I'd heard about and as far as hospitals go, it was pretty luxurious, and I felt safe that I had the best people looking after me.

As I recovered at home, and later at the training ground, I was excited to see McClaren sign a host of legendary footballers approaching the end of their careers. It was the recruitment policy at the time to sign experienced, quality players to play alongside the fantastic youngsters the academy was producing.

It was an unbelievable time to be at Boro and the fans must have been licking their lips when Bolo Zenden, Gaizka Mendieta, and Danny Mills joined us.

When someone has PSV, Barcelona, Chelsea, and Holland on their CV, you know they must be a fantastic player, and Zenden certainly didn't disappoint. I'd played against him when he was at Chelsea, so I knew he was a top player, but I didn't know how strong his work ethic was. He was so professional and set a great example to the kids. This is what it takes to get to the top.

Mendieta, a Spanish international who had played in two Champions League finals and was at one time the sixth most expensive footballer in the world, was the same. A good person, dedicated, hard working, and someone who made you increase your own intensity.

When you are training with superstars every single day, you can't help but raise your level and improve as a footballer. It was a joy to be surrounded by so many quality players.

Danny Mills was an experienced right back who had played for England during the 2002 World Cup. He liked to talk a good game, during training and matches, and he was one of the more vocal members of the dressing room. If things weren't going well, he would be one of the first to shout up.

Behind the scenes the academy was beginning to produce the next generation of Boro stars; Stuart Parnaby, James Morrison, and Andrew Davies all broke through into the first team. But the real standout young player was Middlesbrough born Stewart Downing.

Stewy became a first team regular during the 2003/04 season and looked the part straight away. I remember the first time I saw him in training, as an 18-year-old kid whipping in inch perfect crosses with his left foot. *Wow, this kid is good*, I thought. Then he did the same with his right!

As soon as the first young player made it into the team, it showed the other youngsters that the pathway was there if they continued to work hard. Over the next few seasons there was a conveyor belt of youth teamers progressing to the first team which culminated in us fielding the youngest ever team in Premier League history. We'll come to that later.

Our season kicked off against Fulham and, despite the fact that I had missed the bulk of pre-season, I was included in the starting line-up. It showed that the manager had faith in me, although I was still feeling tired. My game was about twisting and turning, getting away from players and finding that extra yard of space, but my groin was holding me back because I was worried the pain would return. In all honesty, I returned too early, although I would have been disappointed if I hadn't played.

I'll never forget the game, played at Loftus Road as Fulham's ground, Craven Cottage, was being redeveloped, because it was the first and only time of my professional career that I took a penalty.

I had been the penalty taker for my school team, Northborough, Deeping Rangers, Pauley's, and Nuneaton, but not at Derby for some reason, probably because I was young. At Middlesbrough we didn't have a designated penalty taker, Steve McClaren left it to us to sort out on the pitch. So I didn't expect to be taking one, and therefore hadn't practised many. If I'd known before the game, maybe my mindset would have been different as I'd have spent time visualising how I would take it.

Joseph-Desire Job was fouled in the area and Juninho handed me the ball while saying, "Go on, Malcolm, you take it."

I took the ball and placed it on the spot. Although I wasn't prepared, I still backed myself to score. Penalties look easy, but I can assure you they aren't. Most of the chances I had during a game were instinctive, I had no time to think about what I was doing, I just let my body take over. With a penalty you have all the time in the world to think about what you're going to do. Time seemed to slow down, and I became aware of the enormity of the situation. Fulham were leading 2-1, so I was expected to bring the scores level.

Edwin van der Sar, all six feet six inches of him, was Fulham's goalkeeper, and as I focussed on the goal, deciding which way to go, all I could think was, *Bloody hell, he fills that goal well!*

When you're not 100% confident, you go to your preferred side which for me was my left, van der Sar's right. I hit the ball well, but it was the perfect height and power for the goalkeeper who guessed correctly and saved it.

I was gutted, absolutely gutted. van der Sar later saved the deciding spot kick in the 2008 Champions League final, so I'm not the only to have missed one against him, but I still felt devastated.

We lost the game 3-2 which made me feel low, really low, like you wouldn't believe. I'd never missed a penalty before at any level, so I hadn't experienced that feeling before. I just felt like I'd let everyone down.

We flew back to Teesside from London, and I sat by myself in the airport convinced that no one wanted to talk to me because

I'd cost us the game. The experience of that short sharp burst of emotion led me to sink deeper into my hole. I wasn't the type of person who could forget it and just move on. I couldn't act like Mr Bubbly and say who cares? I cared and it hurt me. I couldn't even think, *It's OK, I'll score the next one,* because I knew I wouldn't get another chance. My record as a professional was one penalty taken, one missed. I couldn't very well tell McClaren to trust me again because I'd score a few spot kicks for Northborough Under 13s!

I knew that I'd never take another penalty again which in some ways was a relief, but I would have loved to do a Stuart Pearce and redeemed myself. My miss wasn't huge in the grand scheme of things, it didn't cost us the league title or send us crashing out of a cup competition, but I felt like I'd missed the deciding penalty in the World Cup Final.

Maybe I wanted an arm around me from someone like Gareth, our captain, who had experienced missing a penalty in an important game, but no one said anything to me. I suppose it's difficult because no one wanted to mention the miss. If you score a goal everyone congratulates you, but when you make a mistake no one says a thing, which is how it is in football, but silence for me meant I had my internal torture. It certainly wasn't up to anyone else to make me feel better, that was up to me, but the way I was at the time and the way I handled things, the worst thing I could do was over think. Maybe if I'd realised how much a miss would have affected me, I would have told Juninho, "No thanks, mate. You take it."

Part of the devastation was that my over thinking mind was reflecting on what would have happened if I had scored. I'd have enjoyed the adulation from the fans and my teammates, we may have won the game, my confidence would have been sky high and I'd likely take the next penalty. I realise now that my mental health was so fragile, and I was at the stage where I could go one way or the other. Unfortunately, I fell towards the darkness.

I returned to the training ground on the Monday, carrying the negativity with me, still convinced that I'd let everyone down.

I played in our next match, a 4-0 drubbing at home to Arsenal and then I found myself on the bench which further dented my confidence.

*****

People often talk about footballers living celebrity lifestyles, but that wasn't really true of me. My nights out were pretty similar to most lads of my age, and centred around the clubs and bars of Stamford, Derby and Middlesbrough.

However, one night Gavin, myself, Simon, and James decided to venture down to London for a 'proper' night out.

Our evening began at Titanic, a bar that had been beautifully decorated in the style of the ill-fated liner. From there we went to the nightclub Trap, a famous celebrity hangout in Soho. My agent had got us added to the guest list which was great. We were a bunch of normal young lads from Stamford, excited at the prospect of rubbing shoulders with the rich and famous.

As we stood there, taking in our surroundings, I spotted Martin from *Eastenders* strolling across the dance floor. "Look, lads," I shouted to my mates, excited to have spotted someone. Our eyes followed Martin as he disappeared into another area of the club.

"Of course," said Simon. "There must be a VIP area here."

"How can we get in there?" asked James.

As I've mentioned, I'm not the most confident of lads and the whole 'do you know who I am thing' was never my style, so I wasn't going to go over there and ask the bouncer for entry. Simon told us to leave it with him and off he went. A few minutes later he appeared and proudly declared that we were allowed into the VIP section.

Oh my God, it was amazing. Myleene Klass, of the band Hear'Say, was standing at the bar, and as I looked around, I saw the room was full of soap stars, pop stars and footballers. I had a chat with Anthony Gardner, the Spurs defender who I'd played with for England Under 21s. There was an *Eastenders* table, a *Coronation Street* table, and another for *Emmerdale* actors. We'd never been in this sort of environment before and were all absolutely loving it.

Then we heard a commotion caused by the entrance of the boy band Blue, who were huge at the time. As they walked past, Simon Webbe, a member of the band, spotted me and said, "Malcolm, how are you doing?"

Bloody hell, he's recognised me, I thought. We had a chat and it turned out that he'd played football with Michael Ricketts when they were younger. Simon told me that they were celebrating the birthday of Antony Costa, another member of Blue, in a roped off area towards the back of the back of the club, almost like a VVIP section, and he asked if we wanted to join them.

So, Gavin, Simon, James, and I spent the night surrounded by beautiful women, drinking champagne with Blue. It was a bit comical as the VVIP area was right next to the VIP section, separated only by rope, so we could still talk to people on the other side.

It was one of the best nights ever, a world away from our previous evenings out that typically began at the Pennine Hotel, Derby, and ended at the Zanzibar nightclub!

I can understand why so many young footballers want to play for the London clubs because the nightlife in the capital is unbelievable.

*****

I was disappointed not to return to the starting line-up for the League Cup tie against Championship side Brighton, so when I came on in the second half, I was determined to make an impact. The game finished 0-0 which meant extra time. I was terrified that if we didn't score, the game would go to penalties, so I knew I needed to grab a goal and settle it in additional time. There is no way I wanted to take another penalty so soon after the Fulham game, so I had extra motivation.

In the first half of extra time, Jon Greening hit in a first time cross from the left-hand side, and I put the ball into the back of the net with an improvised, back heel, scorpion type kick. I had no idea what I'd done until I watched the video back afterwards. Good goal scorers play off the cuff like that, it's not like I was thinking about it, I was just trying to adjust my body so I could get something on it, which I did.

That goal at the Riverside, in front of 10,500 fans on a Wednesday night, is what Boro supporters fondly remember me for. They probably won't remember anything else I did at the club, but that goal was the start of an incredible journey for Middlesbrough.

Scoring the winner was the spark I needed, and I was recalled to the starting line-up for our next game, which was away at Southampton. I scored again, a decent goal with my left foot just inside the penalty area to give us another 1-0 win.

I started the next three games and came on as a half time substitute on 1st November 2003 against Wolves with the scores tied 0-0. Mendieta and Juninho both scored in the second half to give us a 2-0 victory and although I didn't score, I played well.

The first few months of the season were like treading through treacle as I was battling my mental demons and still trying to recover physically from my double operation, but I felt that I was turning a corner. I was starting to feel a little bit more like myself, had scored a couple of goals, was gaining confidence and felt happy with the knowledge that I had done my job for the team.

And then it all went horribly, horribly wrong.

CHAPTER 17

Remember, remember the 4th of November

I will never forget the 4th November 2003. It was the day my life changed forever. It was the day my football career ended. It's as simple as that.

The day began the same as any other. I arrived at our Rockliffe Park training ground in the morning and enjoyed a bit of good-natured banter with the lads while getting changed, before heading out on to the training pitch. After a warm up we were split into groups for a defenders versus attackers drill, and that's when it happened.

The ball was played in to me, I knocked it round the corner and Chris Riggott came in for the challenge. The ball was there to be won, and I just nicked it ahead of him, chipping the ball over his leg with my right foot. My right leg was still swinging when he came to clear the ball, but he cleared my leg instead.

It was a shin on shin collision and I heard a loud cracking noise, almost like the sound of a tree branch snapping, before I fell to the floor. When I looked over and saw that Chris was also lying in a heap on the ground, I instantly knew that one of us had broken a leg, I just didn't know who. It was only when I looked at my sock and saw a big indentation in my shin that I realised it was me. I went straight into shock mode, and I grabbed hold of Colin Cooper and Bolo Zenden's boots, squeezing their feet as hard as I could as the pain washed over me.

A golf cart type tractor drove onto the grass, and I was carried into the trailer, driven off the pitch, before being taken, by ambulance, to the Memorial Hospital in Darlington. Upon arrival, the pain had subsided, so I was hoping that meant my injury wasn't too bad. They put me in a lower leg cast with crutches and told me to report back to the hospital in a couple of days for a full X-ray. That was when I would find out the full extent of my break and the surgeons would decide whether or not to operate.

I was driven back to the training ground and the lads all asked me how I was. Chris was in tears and came over to apologise to me even though it wasn't his fault. Chris and I were really close, he was a big part of my journey, and it was hard to see him so upset. I've since heard him speak on podcasts and say that he hopes I don't hold any malice towards him. *Chris – if you're reading this, I don't.*

The situation probably hit him as hard as it did me because we'd been through so much together. It was a freak accident, and I don't attribute any blame whatsoever to Chris; you don't see that many injuries sustained in training, and you certainly don't get many leg breaks.

One of my biggest regrets is not wearing shinpads during training. That lesson will never leave me and now, as a coach, my players will always wear shinpads in training. I think it's a vanity thing in some respects. If I'd put shin pads on before a training session, people would have taken the piss, "Are you playing cricket, Mal?"

When I joined the professional scene at Derby, the foreign players like Lars Bohinen, Jacob Laursen and Stefan Schnoor, always wore shin pads, but the English lads didn't so I didn't either. I followed the crowd and couldn't understand why the foreigners were going out onto the training pitch dressed for combat.

Had I been wearing shin pads, there is a good chance that I wouldn't have broken my leg in that challenge, and my whole life would have been completely different. It was a sliding doors moment. You can imagine how I feel when I see people like Emile Smith Rowe and Jack Grealish wearing postage-sized shin pads. What happened to me is very rare, I know that, but as a footballer, your legs are your livelihood, and we should be forced to protect them. I later had some carbon fibre pads made for me, they fit the shape of my leg perfectly and offered me the best possible protection, but it was too late by then. The damage had already been done.

I later found out that the defenders had been instructed to go in hard on the attackers during the session. Massimo Maccarone was struggling to adapt to the physicality of the English game, going down too easily in matches, and the coaches thought a hard session would toughen him up and get him used to the Premier League.

Chris told me that he wouldn't have gone in for that tackle if they hadn't been instructed to go in hard. I know that he didn't go in to hurt me, he wasn't that sort of player and I'm sure that if we could go back in time, we'd both change it.

When you've just suffered an injury, the first question you ask is, how long until I can play again? Grant Downie, the Middlesbrough physio, explained that he needed advice on whether or not I needed an operation before he could give me a definite date. "If you're back playing in four months, we'll be doing well," he said. "You're the first leg break I've had since Ally McCoist when I was at Rangers."

Bloody hell, McCoist's leg break was twenty years ago, I thought, hoping he knew what he was doing.

A few days after the break, Grant and I went to see a consultant at the Friarage Hospital in Northallerton. After taking some X-rays, the consultant told me that we should treat it conservatively which meant I didn't need an operation. "The reason we'll treat it this way is because it'll the best thing to do in the long run. The bone will heal better without an operation," he added.

I was looking at the X-ray myself focussing on the displaced fracture, thinking, *It looks like it needs an operation to me, but you're the expert, you deal with trauma injuries all the time, so you must know best.*

"First of all, we need to straighten it, so we'll put you in a full leg plaster cast for six weeks," the consultant said. "Then we'll give you a knee joint with two casts, one top and one bottom, for three weeks. Then we'll get rid of the knee joint and just have the lower leg in plaster."

I was adding up the weeks in my head, thinking, *That seems like a long time.*

"How will you get the bone back in line?" I asked.

"Good question," he replied. "Once you're in plaster, we'll saw some bits out and insert some wooden wedges to align it. We'll X-ray your leg every week to see how the alignment is going and make any adjustments as necessary."

This doesn't sound right, I thought, beginning to feel a little uneasy.

The consultant told me he predominantly dealt with amateur rugby players and he'd treated a break this way recently, I wasn't an amateur rugby player, though, and I wasn't 100% convinced that they were doing the right thing, but I had to trust that they were going to give me the best possible treatment to get me back playing in the shortest possible time.

I left the hospital with my whole leg in plaster and all I can say is that it was an absolute nightmare. The plaster cast started at the very top of my groin and continued all the way down past my foot. I know there are worse things that can happen in life, but I wouldn't wish a full leg plaster cast on anyone. I couldn't climb stairs, but luckily by then I'd left the flat in Yarm and moved into a house in Wynyard, so I set up camp downstairs in the lounge.

My brother Gavin was between jobs at the time, so he came to stay with me for a bit which was nice, but also a little uncomfortable as he was more like a live-in-home-helper than a brother. I needed someone to help me with little things like going upstairs to get my clothes and preparing my food, so I'd have been completely stuck without him. Mum came to stay for a bit too and she had to help me have a wash in the kitchen sink, it was like being a child again.

And the pain, oh my God, the pain! When I initially broke my leg, it didn't hurt too much, but with the full cast on, whenever I tried to move or put any weight on my leg, it bloody hurt like anything, and even the strong painkillers I'd been prescribed did little to ease the pain.

Those first six weeks were incredibly hard. Although I visited the training ground occasionally – lying lengthways across the back seats of my brother's car, which took forever to get in and out of – I was pretty much housebound and because of my lack of mobility I was practically bed ridden and even developed bed sores.

My teammates George Boateng, Frank Queudrue, and Michael Ricketts visited me at home one day. Mum was staying with me at the time and when she walked into the lounge-cum-bedroom to announce that some friends had come to see me, I felt so uncomfortable. I was lying on the sofa bed, sitting in my underwear – I obviously couldn't wear shorts or trousers because of the cast – and I hadn't shaved or washed as I couldn't get in the shower. They came in and had a chat, and I don't think they could get out of there quick enough when they saw the state of me. I would have been the same; I had a simple leg break but looked like a car crash victim. I felt so embarrassed and pretty much cut myself off from the outside world after that.

When I returned to the Friarage Hospital a few weeks later to have the full cast removed, I looked down at my thigh and it made my stomach sick. All the muscle had disintegrated, when I lifted my leg up, I could see my thigh bone. When I told Steve Round about it, he replied that it would never be the same size as my left leg. He was right, even to this day I have one leg bigger than the other despite the efforts I've made to try and rebuild that muscle. And believe me, I've battered that leg with weights.

The upper cast went back on very tight, then they added a knee brace before recasting my lower leg and hammering in some more wedges to keep it straight. I was still in incredible pain, but the brace gave me some movement in my leg so at least I could move about a bit with the help of crutches.

The next few months were absolute hell. I was going back to the hospital on a regular basis for X-rays. The bone didn't appear to be healing the way they'd expected, so each week, while I was going in expecting to be taken out of cast, I'd be told that they wanted to leave it on for another week. Before I left the hospital, they agonisingly whacked more wedges into my lower cast before telling me they'd see me next week. It was soul destroying.

After 12 weeks, which was when I was supposed to be back playing, or at least training, my leg was still in plaster. I was still seeing the same consultant who had made the original decision not to operate, although by now I'm sure he was having doubts whether that had been the right thing to do. I certainly was, but the decision had already been made.

I was relieved when the cast was finally removed, although by now my calf muscle had wasted away as well, and I was able to begin a rehab programme, although that was horrendous as I literally had to relearn how to walk. I'd spent that much time on crutches, putting all the weight on my left, foot that it had altered my gait.

As I began walking, I could feel where I'd broken my leg, and when I began jogging, I was limping because it hurt so much. I walked with a limp, jogged with a limp, ran with a limp, which meant that my left leg was having to take the majority of my body weight.

I told Grant Downie about the pain I was experiencing, and he replied, "Malcolm, it will always hurt you. You will always feel it." I felt I was being dismissed. I understood that I would likely feel it now and again, but this wasn't a little feeling, it was real pain. I think Grant thought I was making more of it than it was and being a bit weak.

In March 2004, Andrew Davies, a young Middlesbrough defender broke his leg while playing in a reserve game. *Poor lad, what a nightmare for him. He's going to have to go through all this,* I thought.

The next day, I heard that he was going in for an operation and I was shocked. Even more so when I heard Grant say this on the radio, "We hope that the operation to pin the fracture will lead to him making a quicker recovery than if it had been put in plaster."

It was a very similar break to mine, I know it was, although Grant explained that it was slightly different, as Dava had fractured his fibula also, and that was why he was having an op when I didn't. It knocked me for six as I'm sure by now they realised they'd made the wrong choice to treat my leg conservatively and didn't want to make the same mistake twice.

So Andrew had his operation and returned to the training ground pretty quickly; no plaster cast, no bed rest, no loss of muscle definition. He spent just three weeks on crutches before beginning his rehabilitation programme, so even though he broke his leg almost six months after I broke mine, we did our rehab together at the same time. It was nice to have a buddy – I liked Dava, a good lad – but it didn't sit right with me because I couldn't help wondering if I'd have been playing by now had I been operated on.

When we were jogging, I told him that every time I put my foot down it was like someone was stabbing me with a knife and asked if he felt the same. "No, Mal, I don't feel a thing," he replied.

Straight away I knew that something wasn't right with my leg, so I went back to see Grant. "Everything is fine, Malcolm. You will feel it, stop worrying."

So, I continued, both mentally and physically, to muddle on through.

When you're an injured player and the team is struggling, you feel helpless, cheering on the lads from the stands, wishing you were on the pitch able to make a difference. The fans are desperate for you to return – "Come on, Christie. We need you out on that pitch," – the manager is desperate for you to comeback, and you know your place in the team is assured as soon as you're fit.

It's so much harder when your injury coincides with the most successful period in the club's history.

CHAPTER 18
A goal but no medal

Since its formation in 1876, Middlesbrough Football Club has spent the majority of its existence bouncing between the top two divisions. When I joined Boro in 2003, they had never been crowned champions of England and the closest they had come to achieving cup success was FA Cup runners up in 1997 and League Cup runners up in 1997 and 1998. Middlesbrough had also never competed in Europe before.

But under Steve McClaren, that was about to change.

Our 2003/04 League Cup run began in September with the game against Brighton at the Riverside when I scored the only goal of the game. Victories over Wigan, Everton, Tottenham, and Arsenal followed as Boro progressed to the final where we met Bolton Wanderers. The final was being staged at the Millennium Stadium, Cardiff, because Wembley was being rebuilt.

Every footballer wants to be involved in a successful team – it was why I joined Middlesbrough, after all – and I sort of was, but then again, I wasn't. I was witnessing it all from afar, watching all the glory, but not feeling part of it. Training on my own in the gym while the rest of the lads were out on the training pitch, laughing and joking and enjoying the adulation of the fans. There was an incredible buzz around the place, the whole town, in fact, and I felt like an outsider.

I'd only just had the plaster removed from my leg by the time the League Cup Final came around on 29th February 2004, so I knew there was no chance at all that I'd make the squad, but I was still looking forward to being around the team during the preparation for the big game.

Like most football fans, I always enjoyed watching cup finals.

The players dressed in their suits, the lengthy television coverage showing extended footage of the teams in their hotels and their journey to the stadium before kick off. I couldn't play, but the next best thing was being there with my teammates to saviour the moment and experience the occasion.

You can understand my disappointment when I found out that the club had decided that the injured players would not travel to Cardiff with the rest of the squad, we'd travel down with club officials, effectively cut off and hidden away from everyone else. I was absolutely devastated.

I saw so many cup finals where you see injured or suspended players celebrating on the pitch after the game, some with crutches, others, like John Terry, wearing a full kit, sharing the glory as a squad of players.

It's not like there were 50 of us, there were only a couple of players injured and what an experience it would have been to involve us all. What an incentive for us to get back to full fitness. How motivating and inspiring it would have been for us to be there enjoying the moment with the lads. Instead, we were isolated, treated like lepers and cut off from the celebrations. I was recovering from a broken leg, not an infectious disease.

I flew from Teesside to Cardiff with a mixture of injured players, former players, supporters, and club officials. On our arrival in Wales, we travelled by bus to our hotel, a different one to the hotel the squad were staying at. I'm not complaining about the quality of travel or accommodation, we had a nice meal, the hotel was lovely, and we were well looked after. It's just that we weren't dignitaries or club officials, we were players.

On the day of the match, we walked the half a mile route from the hotel to the Millennium Stadium, through the thousands of Boro supporters who did a double take when they saw me and asked, "Why aren't you with the rest of the squad, Christie?"

Good question!

Our seats were high up in the stands and the walk up the stairs combined with the journey from the hotel meant that my leg was throbbing by the time I finally sat down.

Middlesbrough got off to a dream start, taking the lead in the second minute when Joseph-Desire Job knocked in Bolo Zenden's cross.

Zenden got on to the score sheet himself five minutes later, smashing home a penalty.

Kevin Davies pulled one back for Bolton, capitalising on a rare mistake from the normally reliable Mark Schwarzer, but we held on to win the match 2-1, sparking unbelievable scenes on the pitch.

It was an amazing day for Middlesbrough, winning the first major trophy in the club's history, a real underdog story. I was torn between wanting to cheer and wanting to cry. I wanted Boro to win, of course I did, they were my team, and I was delighted for the lads and, especially, the supporters. But a part of me hated every single moment of the day, it was horrible. As I watched my teammates take turns lifting the famous three-handled trophy, I was waiting for Jim Bowen from *Bullseye* to jump out and say, "Here's what you could have won!"

After the game, while the Boro players were celebrating in the dressing room ahead of what I'm sure was going to be a huge party, myself and the other cast-offs, including Carlo Nash, and Stuart Parnaby, were boarding a coach that took us back to the airport, again missing out on a once in a lifetime opportunity.

Stuart, like myself, had played in the earlier rounds of the League Cup, we'd contributed to the success, and I still, to this day, cannot understand why we were kept away from the celebrations on and off the pitch. Brad Jones, our reserve goalkeeper, didn't even kick a ball in the competition, but he was named on the subs' bench for the final, so he got his hands on a medal and enjoyed the jubilation. I'm not having a go at Brad, but did he really contribute more than me?

Frank Queudrue phoned me from the changing rooms and said, "Mally, I know you're not here, but I wanted to send my best wishes because you were part of this journey. We wouldn't be here now without your goal in the second round." I will never forget that. For all the euphoria he must have been feeling at that moment, for him to take a moment to call and involve me meant so much. George Boateng spoke to me too. A lovely gesture from two really nice guys. I congratulated them on their success.

A couple of nights later, the club arranged a celebratory meal for everyone – players, staff, officials, to celebrate the victory. The whole experience had left me not wanting to go.

I explained my reasoning to Bill Beswick, "I can't go, Bill. I'm not right mentally. I wasn't wanted on the day, you didn't want me to be part of the squad before, this feels like an afterthought."

Some people may read this and say that I should have swallowed my pride and attended the dinner, put on a brave face, and celebrated with the lads. But I couldn't, my mind was in an awful place. I was hurting inside. I was excluded from the travelling squad because I was injured, not because I had done anything wrong.

Bill knew that I felt very strongly about it and told me he'd let Steve know that I wouldn't be attending. He also explained that it was the first time as a management team that they had been involved in a cup final and they did what they thought was best. I understand that, but I didn't think it was the right way to treat people.

So I didn't attend the dinner and I don't regret it at all. I did the right thing for me and for my mental health and it sent a strong message to the club that you can't treat someone that way.

When it was time for the open top bus parade through the town, Steve McClaren came to me and said, "I know you don't feel we did the right thing with you injured players. I understand your feelings, but I really want you to come along on the bus tour. You've been a big part of our success, please come and join in the celebrations and give the fans an opportunity to show their appreciation."

I really appreciated Steve taking the time out to speak to me like that. I felt that I'd made my point and I didn't want to cut my nose off to spite my face, so I agreed to join the team on the bus tour.

I still felt a bit weird and detached standing on the top of that bus, but seeing the 150,000 Middlesbrough fans lining the street, cheering us on, and looking so happy, was amazing. It's a really fond memory that I look back at with joy, not because of me, but because of what it meant to those supporters. I've said it before – the Boro fans are incredible; the whole town was behind us.

We arrived back at the Riverside Stadium, and it was incredible; the car park and streets were packed with a sea of red and white, everywhere I looked I could see people. Some were crying, others singing and dancing.

Before McClaren and our captain, Gareth Southgate, said a few words to the fans, they passed me the trophy first. I held it aloft and the noise was deafening. That was a special moment as I knew that the Boro supporters appreciated my contribution.

I've since been contacted by fans who have told me that true Middlesbrough supporters will never forget that it was my goal that started our journey to the cup final and I appreciate that. I know that I've got my little piece of history, but I still find it hard to look back with any kind of pride because my overriding memory is the way I was treated for the final. I couldn't help it, but it affected me in a big way, more than I thought it would have.

I didn't receive a winner's medal for playing in the earlier rounds. You only got one if you were involved in the final itself which I think is a crazy rule. Instead, the club had some embroidered cup winners jerseys made that they gave to all the players and staff. I had mine signed by all the squad which is nice, and it's at my parent's house, although if I'm honest, it doesn't mean a great deal to me.

The cup win meant that we had qualified for Europe for the first time in the club's history, so I set myself a target of building up my fitness and returning for the start of the new season. I couldn't let another opportunity pass me by.

CHAPTER 19
Don't call it a comeback

Once again, Steve McClaren used the summer of 2004 to bring in another batch of legends.

Dutch international right back Michael Reiziger was the first arrival, joining us from Spanish giants Barcelona. He carried a big name alongside a big reputation, but things didn't really work out for him at Middlesbrough for one reason or another. The pace of the Premier League was much quicker than La Liga and while he was used to bombing forward at Barca, we needed him to play in a more defensive role which I don't think he particularly enjoyed.

Ray Parlour was another winner, joining from Arsenal where he'd won pretty much everything. He became the court jester, a really funny guy who loved messing about and having a laugh. He was nearing the end of his career and didn't want to bog himself down with tactics or anything too serious, he just wanted to enjoy his twilight years, so he sat with the younger lads, involving himself in most of the banter. Ray was still good enough to get into the Arsenal side, but I think he wanted a fresh challenge and a new start after he'd suffered a bad experience in his personal life with a high-profile divorce.

When I saw how Ray was in the dressing room, I could see how instrumental he must have been behind the scenes during his successful years at Arsenal. The younger players loved him, looked up to him and he thrived on that. Ray was just fun to be around, and I sometimes tagged along for a night out in Yarm. I think we both needed that release at that stage of our careers.

Two other arrivals sent alarm bells ringing in my head – Jimmy Floyd Hasselbaink and Mark Viduka. They were both quality strikers, proven goal scorers. On the one hand I was impressed that we'd signed two top players, on the other hand I wondered if I'd be able to get back in the side when I got fit.

Although I was still in constant pain with my leg, I was able to join in the pre-season training where I got the opportunity to witness their quality first hand.

I knew straight away that I would be able to forge a great partnership with Viduka, his style of play was a perfect match to mine. He reminded me of John McHattie who I'd played with at Deeping Rangers. Viduka held the ball up well, attracted defenders, and I'd make runs off the back of that. He was such an unselfish player and I know he'd have played for me and helped me score a lot of goals.

Jimmy was a different type of player, a born winner who was very selfish in front of goal, like most prolific goal scorers. I didn't have a problem with that because he was such a good finisher. All Jimmy wanted to do was to score goals and win, it didn't matter if he was training or playing, he wanted to be on the winning team. If the ball wasn't played into him, he'd have no problem letting you know about it!

Training alongside Mark and Jimmy gave me a different perspective of being around the upper echelon strikers. I learnt a lot from them and improved as a player mentally, although physically I struggled because I wasn't 100% fit. It is a regret of mine that I never earned their full respect because the only way I could have done that was by showing them what I could do on the pitch. I wanted them to see me as a good player who could score goals, but if you ask them what they thought of me as a striker, they will probably reply, "I don't know because he was never fit." It's still nice for me to be able to reminisce of a time when I did actually train and play with these big-name players.

The fans were in dreamland with the progress we'd made under Steve McClaren. We were improving as a team, regularly finishing in the middle or top half of the league, had won a trophy, and were signing these amazing players. It was exciting, but I think we probably got a little ahead of ourselves. We had quite an old squad and we were playing for the now. It was hard to see what would happen in a few seasons when the big-name players eventually left.

Although our youth team was very strong – Middlesbrough

won the 2004 FA Youth Cup – and a good number of youngsters progressed to the first team, only Stewart Downing, Lee Cattermole, Adam Johnson, and James Morrison really went on to forge careers at the highest level.

We always had a group of hungry young players waiting in the wings and it was a pleasure to be around them. They made you feel young and lively and when we were playing away matches, the general mood was light hearted because of the constant banter. David Wheater never took himself too seriously and was always in the middle of the jokes, even if most of them were against him. It was all in good fun and helped foster a good team spirit.

I played in a couple of pre-season friendlies and started the season with the reserves, desperately hoping that I'd soon get back into the first team. The problem was that it was agonisingly painful every time I put any weight on my leg or whenever I kicked a ball. It was horrendous and I wondered if I'd really have to play through the pain barrier for the rest of my career.

I told Grant Downie that I was struggling, and he prescribed me some co-codamol tablets that I took before every training session and game to try and mask the pain, which they did, but they were so strong and made me feel light headed and dizzy. I felt spaced out during the pre-training meetings and always felt weird when I took to the field. I managed to muddle on through and did OK actually, scoring three goals in the first five reserve games which meant I was recalled to the squad for our UEFA Cup tie away at Banik Ostrava on 30th September 2004.

Flying out to the Czech Republic was a new experience for me at club level and it reminded me of my England Under 21 days. We did some light training at the stadium the day before the game to familiarise ourselves with the arena. The facilities weren't as good as those we were used to in England, but it was still a brilliant experience.

As I walked out of the tunnel before kick-off, almost 11 months since my last match, I heard the roar of the crowd, and got an instant adrenaline rush. *I've missed this so much,* I thought as I took my seat on the substitutes' bench.

In the 83rd minute, with Boro a goal down, Bill Beswick called me over and told me I was going on. "When you get on that pitch, just keep closing down the full backs. We need you to chase the ball down," he instructed.

I can do that, I thought. My game was all about chasing. If I didn't have the ball, I wouldn't stand around waiting for it, I'd go and get it. As I took to the field, I ticked 'play European football' off the checklist in my head.

I'd always been taught that your body position dictates where the ball will go, so if I showed my body on the outside, the full back would naturally pass it inside to the centre half. I wanted the ball to be played up the line, so I positioned myself between the full back and the centre back, effectively cutting off that passing route, forcing the defender to play it forward.

I chased everything, I ran like I'd never ran before, in the hope of something dropping for me. Those seven minutes felt like 90, I didn't stop moving.

In injury time, George Boateng played through James Morrison who put it into the back of the net for his first ever senior goal. It was such a great moment and although I hadn't scored, I rushed over to James to celebrate his goal as I knew what it would mean to him. I always liked to be amongst the celebrations, it was the next best thing to actually scoring myself.

We held on for a 1-1 draw which was enough to take us through to the next round. It was only a cameo appearance in the UEFA Cup, but no one can ever take it away from me.

A couple of days later, I was selected for the reserves for a game against Manchester United's second string. I played well, but towards the end of the match, I went in for a 50/50 block tackle and won the ball, but. . . Oh my God, the pain. It felt like it had when I broke my leg. I could barely walk, so I signalled to the bench that I needed to come off.

I had some doubts in my mind when I went in for that challenge, but I was always a committed player, and if I was to return to my old self, I needed to play my normal game. As I limped off the pitch, Chris Moseley, one of the Boro physios, gave me a pat on the back and said, "What a test that was for your leg. Well done, Mal."

I was still in pain the next day when I found out I'd been called up to the first team squad for our next Premier League match, a visit to Old Trafford. Although I was desperate to play against United, I knew deep down that my leg still wasn't right , so I told Grant that I couldn't play. Normally, the physio is the one responsible for informing the manager when a player is unavailable, and it's usually the physio who gets it in the neck. I think by this stage, Grant had had enough of me, and he washed his hands of me, telling me to let McClaren know myself.

I was a bag of nerves as I knocked on Steve's office door and asked for a word. "I know you've put me in the squad and I'm grateful for that, but I'm not right. My leg hasn't healed, something is not right with it, and I've been saying it for a long time. The physios say I'm ready, but I'm not," I explained.

Steve was great. "Thank you for coming to see me, Mal. You stay here then and instead of an X-ray, we'll get you a CT scan so they can look right in on the bone and figure out what's causing the pain. We'll get you back to full fitness soon." I think Steve respected me for going to see him and we shook hands before I wished him luck. As I left his office, I was both relieved and gutted that I wasn't playing.

The original consultant who had made the decision not to operate on me had retired, so I met with a new one, Mr Van Niekerk. He took a CT scan and somberly told me that I had a stress fracture along the original break line. Basically, I'd been playing and training with a broken leg the whole time – no wonder I was in so much pain!

The consultant asked me if I'd been running on it much.

"Running? I've played a UEFA Cup match and 85 minutes for the reserves this week," I replied, telling him about the block tackle.

"You're very lucky then," he said, before adding. "Your leg could have snapped in half."

I couldn't believe it. While I was frustrated to find out that I was still injured, I also felt vindicated; everyone was doubting me, thinking I was making it up, being weak, making a meal out of it, and I wasn't. I had a broken leg.

I never had the conversation with the physios, but I felt I was owed an apology. *Sorry for not listening to you. Sorry for not believing you when you said you were in pain.* I didn't get one.

Mr Van Niekerk then explained that the callus hadn't grown strong enough, it hadn't fully healed because of the angle of the break. In short, I needed an op. "I'm surprised you didn't have an operation before," he told me.

My heart sank. I'd missed nearly a year of football and I was back to square one. While I was going into hospital for my operation, Andrew Davies was back playing football again six months after his op. All I could do was focus on the positives and hope that this time they'd get it right.

To finally fix my leg, they cut my knee, pulled my knee cap over, drilled down the bone and inserted a metal rod that was clamped to the bone. As soon as I had the operation, they were keen to get me back on my feet straight away and I was left wondering why this hadn't happened 12 months earlier.

I couldn't believe it when I finally walked again – there was no pain at all. It was an incredible feeling and I remained pain free when I began running and training.

So physically, I felt better, but my personal life was becoming a mess.

I felt isolated at times when I moved to the North East. When I lived in Derby, there was a group of us who went out together socially, but at Middlesbrough most of the senior players were married with kids so there was rarely anyone interested in a night out. Franck Queudrue and Massimo Maccarone came out occasionally, but not too often, so I convinced myself that I needed to find someone to start a family with. I was trying to become the stereotypical footballer so of course I had to have a stereotypical footballer's wife on my arm.

I met someone in the gym and we began dating. She knew me as Malcolm Christie the Premier League striker, not Malcolm the person. I don't feel we shared the same values and were very different people who wanted different things from life. I wanted a strong family unit, to look after my money and make the right decisions. We weren't compatible, but I'd almost convinced myself that I needed to settle down with the first girl who came along.

My life changed and suddenly it was all about the latest designer handbags, cosmetic surgery, where we were going to live, what holidays we were going to have, what car we should drive.

Although I was living in a beautiful house when we met, before long we'd sold that and bought another one. However, rather than moving straight in, we rented a different property for 10 months while we carried out some renovations.

Stupidly, I agreed to spend £400,000 on 'home improvements', changing the layout and totally gutting what was already a lovely house. It was ridiculous really as I'd saved that money over the years by overpaying on my mortgage and it was wiped out in less than a year. I had very little involvement as I was trying to get myself fit again.

I had always been conservative with my money, but in some ways it was a relief to let someone else take the reigns. It was the first time I had ever lived with someone, and I was doing what I thought I needed to do to keep her happy, so I just went along with it.

The problem was the money wasn't being invested wisely, if at all, it was almost like the film *Brewster's Millions* where Brewster has to spend all his cash without having anything to show for it. The money was going out quicker than it was coming in – it was a distraction that I didn't need at the time. That was not what I was about and in quite a short space of time, I changed as a person.

My parents, who could see what was happening, tried to warn me, but I didn't listen and that put an enormous strain on our relationship. I alienated the people who had been on the journey with me, the people who wanted the best for me. I eventually pushed away my parents and friends; they regrettably became casualties of my relationship.

I should have been stronger, I know that, but mentally I was really struggling.

*****

Middlesbrough were exceeding expectations in the league, eventually finishing the 2004/05 season in seventh place, only three points behind a Champions League qualification spot.

The worst part of being a footballer is being injured. All anyone wanted to talk to me about was my injury and they always looked at my leg while they spoke, which made me even more aware of it.

I did my rehab away from the bulk of the squad and at a different time, so socially, I was cut off and at times, I was grateful for that because whenever I saw anyone it was the same old questions:

How's the leg, Mal?

When are you coming back?

It's nice that people care and it's natural that they want to know about your injury, but when you're faced with the same questions over and over, it becomes exhausting. Teammates, friends, relatives, journalists all wanted to talk about the same thing – my injury started to define me as a person.

If you're injured for a short spell and return it's fine, but my injury went on and on, and it was hard to deal with. I really wish I'd gotten help with my mental health because I was trying to get through it on my own, battling the negativity. There was nothing positive at all at that time.

People will say that at least I was being well paid. Yes, I was, but you ask anyone in any field to go into work and watch someone else do the job that you love – hour after hour, day after day, month after month, year after year. Every time you think you're going to get a chance to work again, you're told you've got another month or two of watching again. You tell me that doesn't grind you down, regardless of your pay packet. Money doesn't come into it. I got zero job satisfaction.

I think my teammates found it difficult to be around me too because I was a reminder that anyone could suffer with an injury, it could quite easily have happened to any one of them.

I eventually returned to action on 1st February 2005, starting in a Premier League fixture away at Portsmouth. It was my first start for 15 months and I opened the scoring after half an hour. Ray Parlour's long range shot was parried by David James, the Pompey keeper, and because I'd chased down the goalie, like I always did, the ball landed kindly for me and I smashed the ball home. It was a great moment and a huge relief for me personally, although we lost the game 2-1.

I started the next match too, at home to Blackburn Rovers, but I came off injured in the 69th minute. Brad Friedel, the Blackburn goalkeeper had the ball, so I ran to close him down. As I pushed off my left leg, I felt an intense pain in the outside of my foot and I knew straight away that something was wrong.

I went to the hospital for another X-ray and discovered that I had a stress fracture of my fifth metatarsal and that meant I needed another operation, this time to put a pin into my foot. All those months I'd spent in plaster and on crutches had altered my gait and the balance of my body. The pain I'd felt whilst training and playing with a broken leg meant that I'd naturally put more weight on my left-hand side and that ultimately caused my stress fracture.

It was yet another bitter blow, and I was in tears when I was told that my season was over again. With the first few injuries, I knew that I'd back, but now I started to doubt myself, wondering if I'd ever be fit. I was only 25.

You'd expect that an injured player at a Premier League club would have structure; do this for week one, this for week two, etc. But there was nothing like that for me. I honestly don't think the physios knew what to do with me. Weeks after my foot operation, I was put in a weighted jacket and made to climb up and down the stairs at our training ground at Rockliffe. The canteen was on the top floor, so while I was climbing up the stairs, others were coming down, I had every Tom, Dick and Harry asking what I was doing. I wish I knew myself!

I'm not sure who thought it was a good idea because it just put more stress on my foot, so I told the physio's I didn't want to do it and they got me to walk around the perimeter of the training ground on my own for two hours instead, still wearing the weighted vest. It was a farce really.

One of the biggest problems I had was that I had too much time on my hands and with nothing to do the boredom became unbearable. Away from football, I had developed a keen interest in golf, and I used to play a lot at Wynyard Golf Club with others like Frank Queudrue, although I had to put my hobby on hold while I was injured as golf uses a lot of muscles.

So I spent a lot of time watching television, in particular the four *Superman* movies which rekindled my passion for the Man of Steel. I purchased some large posters of Superman to put on the wall of my study. I was looking for a bit of inspiration and trying to recreate those happy memories from my childhood.

Superman II is my favourite film, and as I watched it again as an injured footballer, I saw parallels between myself and Superman.

In the movie, Superman meets Lois Lane and decides to change direction. He loses his powers and becomes a normal man, but when he gets beaten up by a trucker in a diner and sees his own blood for the first time, he realises he's made a terrible mistake.

I always felt that my football talent was my superpower and with my injuries, I felt that I too had lost my powers.

Superman goes to his home, the Fortress of Solitude, to try and regain his powers. He calls out to his parents, "Father? Mother? I really wish you could hear me because I need you. See, I, I, I failed."

Superman's father helps him find a green crystal that restores his powers and allows him to save the world from General Zod, Ursa, and Non.

Like Superman, I desperately needed my mum and dad. I needed their help to find the strength to regain my powers. I wanted that green crystal to light up for me.

But I couldn't go to the Fortress of Solitude because I'd pushed my parents away. I'd never felt so alone and powerless in all my life.

The club encouraged me to go on holiday, so I ended up travelling the world to exotic destinations such as Las Vegas and Dubai, a week here and there. They were lovely trips, but I longed for the days of the lads holidays I'd previously enjoyed with Gavin, Simon, and James. It did help me switch off and get away for a bit, but it also made me feel a little bit worthless, almost like they were happy to get rid of me for a bit.

Then I was sent to Lilleshall, near Telford, a place for injured soldiers and lower league players whose clubs didn't have a decent medical facility. At the time I thought it was another way of the club getting me out of their hair, so they didn't have to keep putting up with me.

I felt like a fake footballer; I was paid the wages, I spent time around the training ground and stadium, but I didn't actual play football. I'd missed pretty much two seasons through injury, and as we approached the start of the 2005/06 season, I was praying I wouldn't miss a third.

CHAPTER 20
Always chew your food

Our 7th place finish meant that we had qualified for the UEFA Cup for the second successive season and Steve McClaren continued with his transfer policy of signing quality, experienced players.

First in was Austrian defender Emanuel Pogatetz, or Mad Dog Pogatetz as we called him because he took no prisoners. He loved nothing more than flying into a challenge with a snarl on his face. The coaches were always telling him to calm down so he didn't hurt anyone. That was just in training, so you can imagine what he was like in matches!

Mad Dog was so committed, never afraid to go in for a tackle, often putting his head in the way which meant he frequently ended up covered in cuts. He even finished one game wearing a blood-stained bandage. Although his technical ability let him down a little at times, he was a real heart on the sleeve player. He gave everything for the team, so whether you were a teammate or a supporter, you couldn't help but love him. Opponents may have a different opinion!

Midfielder Fabio Rochemback joined us from Barcelona, although he'd spent the previous two seasons on loan at Sporting Lisbon. He was another player who struggled to adapt to the Premier League because he was used to having more time on the ball and lacked the aggression needed to succeed in England.

One player who was suited to the Premier League was Abel Xavier, another summer signing, who joined us from Roma. He was such a funny bloke and as mad as a box of frogs. With his bleached blonde hair and beard, he was one of the most recognisable footballers during the 2000s. Abel had already turned out for a whole host of big clubs across Europe, and he spent a lot of time in the gym working out. He worked out for hours after training, lifting weights, working on his abs, chest, legs – his body was like an Adonis.

One thing I always found strange at Boro was after training, while the rest of the lads were eating lunch in the canteen, the majority of the foreign boys went off to find an Italian restaurant. Not Abel though, he always stayed at the training ground. A lot of us had our regular seats in the canteen, but he'd sit anywhere and with anyone. I remember the first time I ate lunch with him, it was bizarre.

Quite a few players, myself included, didn't eat a lot before training, preferring to play on an empty stomach, so you can imagine how ravenous we were by lunchtime, often wolfing down our meal. Abel sat there and watched us for a few minutes before saying, "Lads, lads. You need to chew your food for 30 seconds to break it down and help your body digest it. And the taste will improve too as the flavours come out."

Every single one of us immediately slowed down our eating, and you could see the cogs working in our minds as we silently counted to 30. Even now when I'm eating my dinner, I'll sometimes hear Abel Xavier in my head saying, "Don't forget to chew for 30 seconds." I've no idea if it works or not, but we all did it!

Our final summer arrival was Yakubu, a striker who signed for £7,500,000 from Portsmouth. Our paths had crossed before a few years earlier when he had been on trial at Derby. He trained with us for a couple of weeks, and we partnered each other up front in a behind closed doors match. He was powerful, strong and a very good player.

One night a group of us went out into Derby for a few drinks and Yak just turned up out of the blue. I'm not sure how he knew where we were, but he did, and he joined us on our tour around the bars. He certainly enjoyed a night out!

Unfortunately, although Jim Smith wanted to sign him, he couldn't get a work permit at the time. He married a Portuguese lass and turned up at Portsmouth a few years later where he began banging in goals left, right and centre.

When I saw Yak on his first day at Middlesbrough, I asked him if he remembered that night out and we had a laugh reminiscing.

He was another big name, another goal scorer. He wasn't

happy if he wasn't in the team and was prone to sulking, but he knew where the back of the net was, and I admired him for that. It wasn't about the link up play for him, like it was Mark Viduka, he was all about scoring goals. He could have a terrible game, but grab the winner and he'd be happy, a bit like me really.

We had a very eclectic mix of personalities in the dressing room, and while the big-name arrivals added bundles of quality, it was Gareth Southgate, Ugo Ehiogu and Mark Schwarzer who were the glue that held us together. They kept us true to who we were as a club and were vital to the manager's philosophy.

Unfortunately for me, a week before the season began, I was back in hospital for yet another operation.

During pre-season training, I developed a pain in my knee while running so I was sent for another X-ray. That is when they discovered that the metal rod that had been inserted when I had my first op for the broken leg hadn't been placed down far enough, so whenever I bent my knee, the rod was rubbing against the my knee ligaments. I couldn't believe it, everything else was great, the bone had healed well, it was just the rod. The good news was that it was only going to set me back a few weeks, rather than months.

The bad news was that because I had been battering the bottom of my feet, I developed Morton's Neuroma, a condition where the nerves in your feet become trapped, causing pain whenever you walk or run. So, that led to another operation, my sixth in two and a half years, to remove the nerve endings under my feet.

I was soon back in rehab, but instead of resting my feet and giving them chance to recover, the physios had me doing box steps, box jumps, more walking with a weighted vest, lots of things that were constantly pounding my feet. I think the idea was to rehab it to the point that I wouldn't get injured again, but it backfired and in October 2005, I re-fractured my foot due to over training. It was so unbelievable, if it hadn't actually happened to me, I don't think I'd have believed it.

Mentally at this point I was gone. I stopped considering myself a footballer because I wasn't training with the lads, didn't play in any games and I spent more time in the operating room than I did in the dressing room. I'd forgotten the feeling of stepping out on to the pitch and whenever I saw any videos of my previous games, it felt like I was watching someone else. On the few occasions where

I did train, I felt like an imposter; it wasn't *my* body running around, it wasn't *my* foot kicking the ball. I was there, yet not there at the same time.

You ask anyone with a knowledge of football from the 2000s about me and they will likely say, "Injury prone, couldn't keep fit." A fair assessment, I suppose, but they don't know what I went through. I've never gone into this much detail before

It was almost comical, the unprofessional approach towards me. They got it so wrong in so many ways. Maybe I should have been stronger and listened to my body. Maybe I should have had the confidence to say no, I'm not doing that. But I was surrounded by professionals, people who had studied for years and obtained all the necessary qualifications, I trusted them.

All injured players were expected to watch all the home matches from the Director's Box. I got a totally different perspective sitting high up in the stands; I almost become a better player in my head. You can read the game better and I was spotting all the runs I would have made.

The fans sat around us, so when a striker missed, they'd say, "You would have scored that, Christie." And I'd think, *Yeah, I would.*

I learnt a lot about football watching from the stands, and I could see first hand what it meant to the supporters.

It was a novelty at the start as I hadn't been to many games as a kid, and I suppose watching from the Director's Box was the next best thing to playing, but after a while it became harder and harder because I missed it so much. I felt distanced and eventually morphed from player to supporter.

Sometimes I found it difficult to leave my house and travel to the Riverside, it became a real struggle putting on a brave face and answering all the questions about when I'd be back, especially after I'd been hit by yet another injury blow.

My injuries coincided with the best period in Middlesbrough's history, so it wasn't like I was sitting there knowing the team desperately needed me. I sort of lost that focus because deep down, I questioned whether I would even be able to get back in the side when I was fit.

Season after season, we signed quality strikers and competition was fierce. I wasn't worried about Joseph-Desire Job or Szilard

Nemeth; Michael Ricketts hadn't been a threat either, and I could tell that Massimo Maccarone wasn't going to become a top centre forward, so I felt I'd get the nod over him if I was fit.

I never had that fear factor until we signed Jimmy Floyd Hasselbaink, Mark Viduka, and Yakubu, three very good goal scorers. I wanted to be the one out there, holding my arms aloft, hearing the crowd cheering for me. It was so hard watching them doing what I loved and doing it so well.

Middlesbrough's league form during the 2005/06 season wasn't great, but we excelled in the cup competitions, reaching the quarter final of the League Cup, the semi-final of the FA Cup, and the UEFA Cup Final. The fact that the club were doing so well was a negative to me because I was missing out. People talk to me about those days and say it must have been amazing to have been there on the inside.

It wasn't. It was horrible, one of the hardest things I've ever gone through.

If the team is struggling, it's tough because you feel helpless, but it's also a bit of an ego boost because the fans keep telling you they wish you were fit. When Boro were winning games, I didn't feel wanted because I knew the team didn't need me. While I was sat in the stands watching these unbelievable performances, memorable games, and historic moments, I was experiencing it all as a supporter, instead of with the players. It was impossible not to feel a tinge of sadness, mixed in with the excitement of knowing that *my* team were achieving success.

Occasionally I left early to beat the traffic. As I walked back to my car, I'd sometimes hear an eruption as we scored and although I was pleased for the players and fans, part of me was glad that I hadn't been there to see the goal.

My sole purpose in life had been to play football and score goals, but that was all put into question with my injuries, and I felt like I was stealing a living. When I first broke through at Derby County, I craved the attention, but by this stage, getting recognised was the last thing I wanted.

In January 2006, Middlesbrough were drawn against Nuneaton Borough in the third round of the FA Cup. I was shocked as it was only the third time in their history that Nuneaton had reached the third round. It was bittersweet – as most things were for me in those days – as although I was looking forward to returning to Manor Park, I wouldn't be able to play.

Steve McClaren, aware of the significance of the tie, included me as part of the squad that travelled down to Warwickshire which was a nice gesture. I was back doing a bit of light training at the time, so I went out on to the pitch with the team for the pre-game warm up. That was a very special moment, presenting me with an opportunity to applaud the Borough supporters and thank them for their support. Nuneaton was the launching pad for my career and still holds a special place in my heart.

Manor Park was packed to the rafters with close to 6,000 fans, including 1,000 who had made the long journey down from Middlesbrough. The game panned out perfectly.

We took an early lead through a Gaizka Mendieta free kick, before Nuneaton levelled the score with a late penalty, sending the tie to a replay. It was a fantastic result for the non-league side and their fans were going crazy in the old Cock and Bear stand.

Middlesbrough won the replay a few days later which was the right result really. I didn't want us to lose as Boro were my team, but it was great that Nuneaton had a day out at a Premier League stadium and also benefited financially from the additional television revenue.

Those two games brought me back into the media spotlight and it was a good opportunity for me to see some familiar faces, like Terry Angus, a former teammate of mine, who was still playing for Borough. Overall, it was a special occasion, but tinged with regret as it was yet another moment that passed me by.

Gareth Southgate was approaching the end of his career and had become quite susceptible to injuries, so I did a lot of my rehab with him. It can be very monotonous in the gym, with endless hours spent on the cross trainer, treadmill, and exercise bike, and it's so much easier when you have someone else alongside you, sharing in the banter and competing with each other.

I remember one occasion when Gareth, Andrew Davies and I were grinding away in the gym. To try and relieve the boredom, we decided to have a little forfeit for the person who did the fewest pull ups. Andrew lost so he had to pull his shorts down, while me and Gareth slapped him on his bare arse, leaving massive red hand marks on both cheeks!

I managed to get myself almost fit by the middle of April 2006 and made a couple of cameo appearances in Premier League games against Portsmouth and West Ham. It was good to be back.

Confidence was sky high around the squad, we were riding the crest of a wave. The matches were coming thick and fast because we were still competing in the FA Cup and UEFA Cup, so my return was a huge boost to McClaren as it allowed him to rest the main strikers for the cup ties.

The UEFA Cup run in particular was very exciting. Travelling to different countries, learning about different cultures – who doesn't love a European match under the lights on a Thursday night? We played against big-name teams in some fantastic stadiums, but most importantly, we kept finding a way to get through each round. It didn't really come as any great surprise to me as Middlesbrough ticked all the right boxes at the time; top notch coaching, the recruitment was spot on, and our chairman, Steve Gibson, backed McClaren to the hilt.

Gibson was a wonderful chairman, probably because he was a fan too and he must have been in dreamland. It was such a marvellous period for the club, something that the fans can look back on and reflect on the various comeback victories where all the odds were stacked against us.

Although I was nothing more than a supporter during the UEFA Cup run, I remember jumping up and cheering when Maccarone scored *that* late diving header in the last minute of the semi-final against Steaua Bucharest, to send Boro into the final. I was desperate to be out there on the pitch of course, but I got caught up with the excitement of what the team were achieving. For a club the size of Middlesbrough to reach a European final was incredible, a once in a lifetime achievement.

Three days before the UEFA Cup Final, I started my third game of the season as part of an historic line-up. With McClaren keen to rest the regular first teamers, he took the opportunity to showcase some of the talent that had graduated from our youth academy and he fielded the youngest ever Premier League side with an average age of just 20 years and 182 days. It is a record that will, in my opinion, never be broken. For me, aged 27, to be the elder statesman in the team, helping and advising the talented youngsters is a very proud moment. To go one step further, in the second half

I was replaced with Josh Walker as McClaren wanted everyone on the field to have been born within a certain radius of the Riverside. I was a bit disappointed as I felt fit enough to play the full 90 minutes, but I accept that I was brought off to create history.

We flew out to Eindhoven the following day to prepare for the final. Unlike the League Cup Final two years earlier, this time I travelled out with the squad, so I had the opportunity to experience it all first-hand. There were four strikers ahead of me, so unless someone twisted an ankle on the morning of the game I knew I wouldn't be involved, although deep down I would have loved to sneak onto the bench. Everyone wanted to be involved.

It was an unbelievable stadium, and we were facing a very strong team in Sevilla, who lined up with Dani Alves and Jesus Navas. I'm not saying that we underestimated them, but I think we had a little too much confidence going into the match and maybe that hindered us. Before each game, the coaches gave us an information pack that included details about the opposition, but I always found them to be more of a confidence booster than anything useful. The dossier focussed on your opponent's weaknesses, rather than strengths, so we didn't always realise how good they were.

Sevilla took the lead just before the half hour mark, but we created some good chances and were unlucky not to snatch an equaliser. Fatigue kicked in late in the game which resulted in Sevilla scoring three late goals to give them a 4-0 win. On paper, it looks like a drubbing, but the score line flattered them, it was a much closer game than that.

I honestly thought we were going to win the final; I know the fans thought so too and I felt really sorry for them. They had been magnificent and deserved to see their side lift the trophy. Steve Gibson came into the dressing room after the match to tell everyone how proud he was of them. That was a nice touch considering how deflated the players were, and that gesture says a lot about him.

Overall, it was another good season for Middlesbrough. I played in six matches towards the end of the campaign and felt that with a good run of games, I would be able to get my sharpness back. Things were starting to look up a bit, but then I was dealt another bombshell – Steve McClaren left Middlesbrough to become the new manager of England.

CHAPTER 21
Please play me

I was proud of Steve McClaren when he became England manager. He did a fantastic job for Middlesbrough, and he deserved an opportunity in the biggest job of them all.

On a personal level, Steve had given me the opportunity to sign for Boro and I learnt a lot from him. He didn't always see eye to eye with everyone – I know the situation between Steve and Mendieta wasn't great, although I don't know the ins and outs because I was witnessing it from afar – but he was always fair with me. We didn't talk a great deal because I spent most of my time with the physios, but all I was concerned about was, did he rate me as a player? Yes. Did he pick me when I was fit? Yes. Did he improve me as a player? Yes. Could he have developed me to the stage that I could have played for England? Absolutely. In fact, part of me felt that if I could get a good run of games under my belt, he might give me an opportunity for the national team.

Just like when Jim Smith left Derby, I didn't have an opportunity to say goodbye to Steve and thank him for everything he did for me. I felt a little sad that I hadn't repaid the faith he'd shown in me on the pitch because of my injuries. He'd tracked me for so long, I just didn't get the opportunity to show him the player I should have been.

McClaren appointed Steve Round as his assistant at England. Roundy stayed at Middlesbrough in a dual role until December 2006, when he left us to focus on his national team duties. Steve had played under Brendan Phillips at Nuneaton, so he had been there for pretty much all of my journey. It was like the end of an era.

Unfortunately, it didn't work out for McClaren at England. That transition from coach to manager isn't as easy as people naturally assume it should be. I think he found it difficult to go from being the arm around the shoulders coach to push away manager. The situation with David Beckham, where Steve initially dropped the England captain before restoring him to the squad, certainly didn't do him any favours. You live and die by your decisions.

McClaren always used to talk to us about defining moments.

"There will be one defining moment in the game, make sure we take it. Whether it's a chance in front of goal, or a block tackle at the other end, make sure we take it," he would tell us before a match.

At the next training session after a game, we'd watch the match on video and Steve would pause it at the defining moment. It could be a save from Schwarzer or a last-ditch tackle from Ugo and five minutes later Viduka or Jimmy would score. "The goal is not the defining moment," he'd say. "That tackle was, because if that had gone in, we wouldn't have had the opportunity to score."

Sadly, the defining moments for England didn't go his way.

*****

McClaren's successor was a familiar face; Gareth Southgate retired from playing to become the new Boro manager.

Gareth didn't hold the necessary qualifications to manage a Premier League club, so his appointment was on an initial 12-week basis. In November he was given special dispensation to continue in the role providing he completed his coaching badges by the end of the 2006/07 season.

His second challenge was to transform himself from teammate to manager and that wasn't easy. Gareth was a highly respected figure at the club, and a fantastic guy. He was the best captain I ever played under. He led the club to silverware, was brilliant on and off the pitch, a true leader. I only ever saw him lose his head two or three times and when he did, you listened. He was very quick witted and always involved in the banter, and my opinion is that the Middlesbrough job came too soon for him. He tried to change too much too quickly, instead of relying on his relationships with the players and asking them to help him make the transition.

It was so strange when he stood in front of us – players,

coaches, physios – for his first meeting as manager. I couldn't help thinking, *Wow, a few months ago I was playing slap arse with you in the gym and now you're my boss!* We all found it a bit weird.

Ray Parlour tells a funny story in his autobiography *The Romford Pele*. During that first team meeting, we were all a little nervous, and I could tell he was nervous too. It was the first time he'd addressed us, and it was awkward. He explained that now he was the manager he wanted us to call him boss or gaffer. Ray Parlour piped up and said, "What about big nose?"

I was trying hard not to laugh, and when I looked around the room, I could see that everyone else was also trying to suppress their smiles. We all turned to Ray thinking, *Why did you say that?*

Gareth just ignored him and carried on talking, but there was a definite tension in the air, and I realised at that moment that he didn't yet have the same kind of respect from us that Steve McClaren had. He had good coaches around him, Steve Harrison was still there, and Malcolm Crosby had come in too. But Gareth had to stamp his authority and he eventually sold Parlour to Hull City.

I always knew that Gareth would do well as a manager, he commanded respect, knew a lot about the game, and had a very methodical approach. I just don't think Middlesbrough was the right club for him at that time. Certainly not with the transition from player to manager, and certainly not following in Steve McClaren's footsteps on the back of the most successful period in the club's history.

It hasn't surprised me to see the success that Gareth has enjoyed as England manager. His England squad only know him as a manager, not as a mate, and his achievements in the game have earned him their respect. International management suits him better as he doesn't have to deal with the day to day work that club managers are expected to do. I still have bags of respect for him and am proud to say that I played with him and for him.

I don't think Gareth's appointment was the right one at that time for me, even though he knew me well, and I think he rated me as a player. The problem was that I had the stigma of 'injured player'. For the last three years, he'd seen me in the gym, doing rehab, rather than on the football pitch, and I think that weighed heavily on his mind. He probably didn't trust that I could get myself in a position where I was fit enough to play a run of games. If a new manager had come in, I might have been given more of an opportunity to prove myself.

Southgate's retirement left a huge gap in the side. He wasn't just a talented player, he was a leader on the pitch too. Colin Cooper also retired, with Doriva, Jimmy Floyd Hasselbaink, Joseph-Desire Job, and Franck Queudrue all moving on to new clubs.

The recruitment policy under McClaren was very much centred around bringing in experienced, quality players to play alongside the emerging young talent, and that changed when Gareth took over, as we tried to become a team who developed young players, rather than bringing in big name players as a quick fix. I'm not sure if that was Gareth's idea, or whether he was following instructions from the board, but without being disrespectful to those who came in, with a only a few exceptions, they weren't the players we needed to push us on to the next level.

Herold Goulon, a young French midfielder, came in from Lyon. There was a lot of hype surrounding him, but he found the move to England a challenge and he left two years later without playing a single minute of first team football for Boro.

Julio Arca made the short journey from Sunderland to Middlesbrough. Julio was a good player, but I don't think he was any better than Queudrue, the man he replaced.

No-nonsense defender Robert Huth joined us from Chelsea. Although he wasn't a first team regular at Stamford Bridge, he had won two Premier League titles and was a full German international. I'm often asked, who is the hardest player I've ever played against. My answer: Robert Huth, even though I only played against him in training!

Like Pogatetz, he would fly into challenges, but Huth was nasty with it too. I remember one of his early training sessions when I was lining up against him, he just kicked me. I didn't even have the ball, so I turned around and said, "What are you doing? This is training." He didn't reply. He just stared at me, without any emotion on his face and I realised that he was completely in the zone, fully focussed on the game. It didn't matter to him that it was just a practise match at the end of training, he had a deep desire to win.

It suddenly dawned on me – that is what makes a top player.

At Chelsea he'd played alongside John Terry and JT was the same, they both hated losing. Robert was a winner as he proved 10 years later when he won his third Premier League winner's medal as part of Leicester City's fairy-tale success.

Another top defender who joined us was Jonathan Woodgate, the Middlesbrough-born defender who signed on loan from Real Madrid. Woody didn't mind kicking you in training either! He had played at the highest level and if you're training against him every day, you are only ever going to improve as a player.

To be competing against defenders like Huth, Southgate, and Woody, and learning from Jimmy and Mark Viduka in training was amazing. That was a dream for every player. I just wish that I'd had the opportunity to take those lessons I learnt and put them into practise in matches.

Jason Euell, an experienced, steady Eddie striker was our final summer signing. Jason was a decent player, but nowhere near the standard of Jimmy Floyd Hasselbaink, so in my opinion we began the 2006/07 campaign with a weaker squad than we'd had the season before.

I made my first appearance of the season in our third game, replacing Mark Viduka in the second half of a 4-0 defeat at home to Portsmouth. A disappointing result, but even more so for me because I tore my ankle ligament, shortly followed by a groin strain. It was so frustrating. My bones had healed and now I was developing muscular injuries. People began to question me and I even started questioning myself.

I got myself fit again and started the match against Aston Villa on 25th November 2006. I felt that I had a point to prove and made my mark just before half time, turning inside the six-yard box to score my first goal in 21 months.

That was a huge moment for me, although it shouldn't really have counted because I was a mile offside. As soon as the ball hit the back of the net, I looked over at the linesman and didn't see the flag, so I ran over to our fans to celebrate. It had been a while since my last goal, so I decided to carry on my celebration until I heard the referee's whistle, but it never came. Maybe I deserved that bit of luck. My teammates were great, taking it in turns to congratulate me. That meant so much, as did the relief I felt as I ran back to the half way line for the restart.

I chased every ball, making some dangerous runs, and even though I was substituted in the second half, I won the Man of the Match award.

I started our next game, a 2-1 defeat at home to Manchester United. Although I didn't score, I did manage to walk away with a souvenir. The first time I played against United, I'd asked Ryan Giggs for his shirt, and he said no. I'd asked Paul Scholes after another match, but the answer was the same. This time, I realised that it could be the last time I played against them, so as the players were walking off the pitch, I approached Rio Ferdinand and asked if we could swap shirts.

"No problem," he replied. "I'll give it to you in the tunnel." I couldn't get in to the tunnel fast enough! I gave Rio's shirt to my brother as a gift.

As Christmas approached, I started to think about my future because my contract was up at the end of the season. I was getting my fitness back, but I needed a good run of games to become fully match fit to either win a new contract at Boro or convince a new club that I was worth taking a chance on, so I went to see Gareth.

"I've got to think about getting my career back on track and I need to play games. If you're only planning to give me a few minutes here and there, please let me go on loan so I can prove my fitness," I pleaded.

Gareth replied, "You've done brilliantly to get back into first team contention and you should be very proud of yourself. The Christmas and New Year period is very busy, so you'll get your chance."

That was all I needed to hear, but then, on transfer deadline day, we signed another striker, Lee Dong Gook, from a South Korean team. Lee had a brilliant goalscoring record before and after his time at Middlesbrough, but he wasn't a brilliant player for us, either in training or matches. That frustrated me because this was a guy who was preventing me from playing. He didn't score a single goal in his first season and only two in his second before he returned to South Korea. He was a nice enough guy, I think – he didn't speak a word of English and needed a translator, so we rarely spoke – but he just wasn't up to speed. He was a really strange signing; no one had heard of him before and he certainly didn't set the world alight. After games, I'd go home in disbelief that he'd got the nod ahead of me. I guess the problem was that Southgate felt he had to play Lee because he was his signing.

Could I stay fit? That question hung over my head during the latter stage of my career. Any footballer will tell you that you need to have a run of five or six games to get your sharpness back, get up to speed, and return to full fitness. I was training every day behind the scenes, but nothing can replicate a first team football environment. That just increased my frustration. Finally, after all those years of injury hell, I was fit and available for selection and I wasn't being picked.

I wasn't even selected for the reserve team because the squad was thin on the ground, so I missed out on the opportunity to put myself in the shop window. After all those hours on the treadmill, all those hours of rehab, I just wanted to play.

It was crazy really. There was a match against Arsenal on 3rd February 2007 where Gareth had me warming up for the whole of the second half before bringing me on in stoppage time. He had people sitting up in the stands, relaying information to him, and he was a little gun shy in his substitutions during those early days of management.

We were drawing 1-1, it wasn't necessarily a case of stick or twist, but it seemed that Gareth was worried about changing anything in case Arsenal took the lead. I felt we could win the game and was desperate to get on. I saw myself as a potential game changer, someone who could run at the defence, chase the balls and, hopefully, get on the end of something. He called me over a couple of times before sending me off to warm up again.

Finally, with 93 minutes on the clock, he told me I was going on. I stripped off my tracksuit top before running onto the pitch. The ball had already gone out for a throw, and just after the throw in was taken, the referee blew his whistle. I was on the pitch for less than 20 seconds and didn't really understand why he had sent me on. I guess he made the substitution to run the clock down. The only thing that softened the blow was that, at the time, I was on a £3,000 appearance fee, so it was the easiest three grand I've ever made!

But it wasn't about the money, I wanted to play, so I went to see Gareth after the game and asked how I could be expected to prove my worth to the squad if I'm only given 20 seconds. He was learning on the job – he admitted as much to me – so he wouldn't get everything right.

He started me ten days later against Bristol City in the FA Cup where I scored our second goal in a 2-2 draw. It was my second goal in four starts which proved my belief that if I played, I would score.

After a few more substitute appearances, I started my final game of the season on 14th April 2007 at home to Aston Villa. I played the full 90 minutes for the first time in three and a half years. Ironically, it was my final match for Middlesbrough.

It was a strange game. We lost 3-1 at home and for the first time I heard different noises from the fans. When I joined the club, they were always 100% behind me, but now I could sense their frustration and heard some negative comments towards me. It was heart breaking as I was a confidence player who liked to please people, and this was the first time I was ever the focal point of the supporter's discontent. It had gone full circle and it was affirmation that I wasn't the same player anymore. No matter what happens in your career, you always want the supporters behind you. They'd read about my injuries in the newspapers, but they hadn't seen what I'd endured in order to get back into the team. If I misplaced a pass, there were some groans and a few people started telling me I was shit. In reality it was only one or two, but it may as well have been 10,000. It's no coincidence that I didn't play again for the club after that. It felt like the final nail in the coffin.

The fans wanted me to be my old self straight away, but I needed game time to get back to my best. Had I been given more starts that season, I know I would have scored goals and maybe I'd have earned a new contract, but it's all if, buts, and maybes.

I think the supporters were also dissatisfied with the team in general as we'd gone from a team who were getting to cup finals, to a struggling side. The big-name players had stopped coming in and the club was at the start of a downward spiral that eventually resulted in relegation a few seasons later.

After the Villa game, I was told to go and see Gareth and I knew exactly what was coming. I couldn't get out of his office quick enough.

"Malcolm, I'd like to thank you for your service to this football

Team Umbro - Magaluf 2002 left to right:
me, Gavin, Simon & James Trigg.

Me and Simon with those legendary
Police sunglasses (Magaluf 2002).

The Derby fans were incredible. I loved
nothing more than celebrating with them.

In happier times with John Gregory.
I really believed he would save us.

Training, playing and celebrating with Fabrizio Ravanelli, one of my idols growing up. It was always a pleasure to share the same pitch as him.

Going out with a bang. One of my favourite Derby County goals was ironically my last (vs Stoke City 18/02/03). Just 13 days later I signed for Middlesbrough F.C.

A happy day after finally securing my move to Middlesbrough F.C. on deadline day 2003, along with my Derby County pal Chris Riggott and Michael Ricketts.

Scoring my first goal at the Riverside for Boro (vs Charlton 22/03/03).

Celebrating that special feeling with Colin Cooper and skipper Gareth Southgate.

One of the funniest people I met on the journey.
Steve 'Harry' Harrison with 'the Doc'.

Snowy training
days at Rockliffe.

Feeling on top of the world, celebrating at the Riverside with the
Boro supporters after scoring the first goal (vs West Brom 05/04/03).

aying against Premier League Hall of Famer, Thierry Henry (vs Arsenal 24/08/03).

When my injuries hit, the Boro gym became my second home.

Me with the Carling Cup 2004. Smiling on the outside but really hurting on the inside. Not every picture tells the true story.

Playing European football with Middlesbrough (vs Banik Ostrava 30/09/04).

On the comeback trail again (vs West Ham 17/04/06).

Back in the team with a goal (vs Aston Villa 25/11/06). Sadly this was to be the last Premier League goal I scored. My teammates knew exactly what it meant to me.

My first (and only) Leeds United goal (vs Stockport 28/12/08) with Luciano Becchio.

With Niall Horan at the 1D show, with step-daughters Eva (middle) and Nya (left).

Meeting and marrying Emma in 2017 was the missing piece of the jigsaw puzzle. (Our wedding day August 2017).

Leo Anthony Christie.

Zac Christie.

Flynn Christie.

My four a side team. My boys from left to right: Zac, Leo and Flynn (Christmas 2021).

club. You are aware that your contract expires in June and unfortunately, we won't be offering you a new one. I want to wish you all the best for the future."

I understood why my contract wasn't being renewed – I hadn't played – but I remained hopeful that I'd find another club and be able to resurrect my career elsewhere. After all, I'd only just turned 28 and was available on a free transfer.

I ran down the rest of my contract and finally left Middlesbrough in June 2007, four and a half years after arriving. I was upset, really cut up about it. I had hopes and expectations of taking my career to the next level when I had joined Boro; winning trophies, playing for England, scoring lots of goals, and I left as a bit part player, having missed out on the club's glory years.

On my last day at Middlesbrough, I went around saying goodbye to everyone and I was choked up. Despite my injury nightmare, the training ground had become my home, the players and staff had become my friends. I felt I was leaving with unfinished business.

I'm sure Chris Moseley and Grant Downie, our physios, were glad to see the back of me, though! I say that in jest, of course. I'm sure they learnt a lot from working with me and I imagine, like all of us, that there are things they would do differently if they could rewind the clock.

Leaving was the right thing for me and for the club, I needed to get away from football for a bit and reset. It's hard for me to say, but I wasn't raring to get back into the game at that stage. Part of me had given up and I'd begun to fall out of love with the beautiful game.

CHAPTER 22
Into the depths of Hull

For the first time in my career, I found myself without a club and without a plan.

In my head, I was convinced that someone was going to take a chance on me, why wouldn't they? I was a proven Premier League player who could score goals. I didn't mind if it was one of the newly promoted clubs, Sunderland, Birmingham, or especially Derby who came in for me. A return to Pride Park would have been a dream come true.

After everything I'd been through, I was finally fit. I think the problem was that people didn't know I was fit because I hadn't played at Middlesbrough. I'd scored two goals in six starts, which wasn't bad, but when you take into account all my substitute appearances, it skewered my goals to game ratio.

I sat by the phone, day after day, waiting for it to ring. I was expecting a long list of potential suitors forming an orderly queue, but there was no interest at all. I didn't know what to do and my over thinking held me back:

Do I ring my agent every day or will I be bothering him?

If I don't call him, will he think I don't want a new club?

My agent, Paul Martin, was one of the best around, also dealing with a lot of the big players. I hadn't really brought much to the table in recent years in terms of marketing, endorsements, sponsorship, or signing on fees and, by that stage, clearly clubs weren't breaking down the door to sign me, so I guess I wasn't too high up on his list of priorities. I don't know, and will never know, how hard he was working behind the scenes for me, but I'd like to think that he'd begun to put feelers out in January 2007 when it was becoming obvious that my Middlesbrough days were numbered.

As we inched closer to the start of pre-season, I was wondering how much I should be doing fitness wise. The last thing I wanted was to train on my own and pull my calf while running because if I got injured, I'd never find a new club. I was in a horrible quandary of not knowing what to do, so I just sat by the phone and did nothing.

Finally, at the end of July 2007, Paul rang and said that Stoke City were interested in talking to me. I should have been jumping for joy that someone was showing some interest in me, but my mind wasn't right, and I felt thoroughly underwhelmed. They had been languishing in middle of the Championship and I thought I was better than Stoke. I thought I was better than the Championship. I told Paul I'd think about it.

Within days, I received another call informing me that Barnsley were interested. *Fucking hell,* I thought. I wasn't thrilled with the prospect of Stoke, now Barnsley!

"What kind of figures are we talking?" I asked Paul, who was being quite coy.

"We're looking about £3,000 a week," he replied.

That's a lot of money in any walk of life, but in the final year of my Middlesbrough contract I'd been on £12,000 a week, so it was a 75% pay cut for me. I lived to my means like most people do and there aren't many who wouldn't find a 75% pay cut tough. But I got my head around it and agreed to go and talk to both clubs.

Arriving at the Britannia Stadium in Stoke, I was impressed with the facilities. I'd played there before, so knew all about the passionate fans. The manager, Tony Pulis, introduced himself to me and explained his plans for the club.

I'd only ever seen Tony on television where he is very well spoken, articulate, and interesting to listen to, but in person, I've never heard anyone swear so much in my life! He must find it a real struggle not to swear in interviews. I told him that I was fit and raring to go. Tony explained that although Stoke were renowned for playing with a big target man up front, he saw me as a different option, someone with pace who could get round the back of the defence.

He showed me around the ground and when we stood in one of the executive lounges, looking down at the lush, green turf, I recalled the fond memory of scoring my final goal for Derby

County on that very pitch. I began to feel excited as I visualised myself scoring goals, wearing the famous red and white shirt.

It was an encouraging meeting; we shook hands, and the agreement was that Paul would negotiate my contract with the chairman, Peter Coates, and all being well, I'd be a Stoke City player before the start of the season.

The following day, Paul asked if I'd speak to Barnsley out of courtesy. I felt really positive about the Stoke deal, excited even, but I agreed to phone Simon Davey, Barnsley's manager. Simon went through his plans for the club and said that he would love to have me on board. They were due to go on a tour of America and he told me they'd like me to join them out there so I could get to know the lads. Simon told me he'd let his chairman and Paul sort out the contract. I didn't know whether or not I should have told him about my meeting with Stoke, but decided not to mention it.

For the first time in a very long time, I felt wanted. I'd realised by then that I wasn't going to be a Premier League player, so I phoned Paul, explained that I was happy with either club, and I left it with him to broker the deal.

A week later, nothing had happened.

Two weeks later, still nothing had happened.

I couldn't understand it. I'd met with Tony Pulis, and he said he wanted to sign me. I'd spoken to Simon Davey, and he said he wanted to sign me.

Why the silence? Have they seen my medical records? I wondered.

I eventually got hold of Paul and it emerged that both deals were off. There was no explanation at the time, although I did find what had actually happened 18 months later.

It transpired that my agent was trying to high ball both clubs and play them off against each other. Little did he know that Stoke's chairman, Peter Coates, was good friends with Barnsley's chairman, Gordon Shepherd, and they caught him trying to inflate my wages which pissed them both off, so they pulled out. You can argue that my agent was just doing his job, trying to get me as much money as possible, but it backfired massively, costing me a contract and the chance to re-establish myself as a footballer.

The knock-on impact was huge. The football community is very tight knit, so when other clubs heard that Barnsley and Stoke had pulled out, there was another stigma attached to me. He's been released from Middlesbrough, two Championship clubs have spoken to him and not offered him anything, so something must be wrong.

A few more weeks passed, we were almost at the start of season when Paul rang and told me that Nottingham Forest, who were in League One, were interested.

"Forest?" I replied. "I was a Derby player, there is no way I can sign for them. Can you not get me back to Derby? I love the club and the fans love me."

"I've tried, Malcolm. I've spoken to Billy Davies, but he doesn't want you because he's heard you're a big time Charlie."

I was shocked as that couldn't have been further from the truth, I don't know who he'd spoken to because I'd never met him. I'd be surprised if anyone I've ever worked with described me as a big time Charlie, that just wasn't who I was.

With no other offers on the table, I decided to go to the City Ground and meet Forest's manager, Colin Calderwood. As soon as I pulled into the car park, I knew I couldn't sign for them. I didn't want to do it. I knew if I signed it would hurt the Derby fans who had always been so good to me, it would tarnish my legacy with the Rams.

Colin told me all about his ambitious plans to win promotion back to the Championship. Neil Lennon was there too, and he came in to welcome me and say that he was looking forward to playing with me. We had a nice positive chat, and I got the vibe that he wanted to sign me, but the move never materialised. There was no way I could have gone there; I'd have been hated by the Derby fans forever.

We didn't discuss numbers with Forest, but I got the impression that we were talking somewhere in the region of £1,500 a week – a 90% pay cut. I still remained hopeful that Paul could pull a rabbit out of the hat and find me a Championship club.

But when the season kicked off, I still didn't have a club. I considered asking Gareth Southgate if I could train at Middlesbrough to keep myself fit, but I couldn't risk picking up another injury, so I spent my days at home, watching football on the television. I found it hard to leave the house because when I did, people asked me which team I was going to sign for? I didn't have the answer, and the questions were a constant reminder that I couldn't find a club, so once again I cut myself off from the outside world.

There was a glimmer of hope at the start of September when my phone finally rang. It was Paul calling to tell me that Phil Brown had offered me a trial at Hull City who were in the Championship.

A trial? Oh my God, what the hell has happened here? I thought.

In the space of three months, I had gone from being a Premier League player, to a 75% pay cut in the Championship, then a 90% pay cut in League One, and now my agent's ringing around, begging people to give me a trial. How the hell did I find myself in that position?

I was still only 28 and I was in the same position I'd been in when I was aged 18, talk about full circle. You can imagine how this was affecting me mentally.

I knew I had to get myself back on the conveyor belt, and while half of me was appreciative that someone wanted to take a look, the other half couldn't believe that I was on trial. But I swallowed my pride and saw it as an opportunity to go there and show that I could still perform. I didn't get paid a penny during the two months I was at Hull, I had to pay all my own travelling expenses, so it was actually costing me to play. That's how desperate I was to get my career back on track.

My trial turned out to be the most mentally demoralising time I ever experienced in football. It drained the life out of me, and it was a miracle that I actually came back from that experience to play again.

I hated every second of my two months at Hull, from the minute I arrived to the minute I left. I got the impression that Phil Brown was just doing my agent a favour. I didn't get that sense that he wanted me, not like I had felt from Pulis, Davey, and Calderwood. He didn't seem bothered, and rarely took the time to speak to me. His assistant was Brian Horton, a manager who'd been round the block, he was really friendly, and we got on well.

The Middlesbrough dressing room was full of laughter and jokes. In contrast, Hull's was cold; very serious, quiet, and everyone had their head down. It would have been different if I'd gone there on a contract, but because I was only on trial, I think the strikers saw me as a threat, like I was coming in to take their positions, so they never really took the time out to welcome me.

Hull's main centre forward was Dean Windass. Dean had been one of the strikers who left Middlesbrough in January 2003, just before I joined, so I don't imagine he was particularly thrilled to see me turn up at Hull. He was the heart and soul of the dressing room with his funny banter and snide put downs.

The banter at Boro was light hearted, but at Hull it could be quite deep, sometimes nasty. I'm all for banter, but not when you're just insulting people.

There were some good lads there though. Ian Ashbee was the captain and he showed me around the club. He'd been a youngster at Derby before I was in the first team, and I liked him.

Boaz Myhill, the goalkeeper, was another lovely guy who took time out to welcome me, as did Sam Ricketts, a Welsh international defender, who had spent a short spell on loan at Nuneaton, so we spent a bit of time reminiscing.

The training facilities were shocking and, to make matters worse, the kit man didn't have any training gear for me when I arrived on my first day. "No one told me you were coming," he said, before cobbling some kit together. Great start!

Nevertheless, aware that I had nowhere else to go, I tried my hardest for the duration of my trial, even though I was training with the reserves or youth team most of the time. A strange situation that only normally happens when established players have been frozen out in a bid to try and force them out of the club, not something a manager would do to a trialist. I'd never felt so unwanted at any level in football.

The kids were a decent bunch, and I soon got my fitness back and played in a reserve match against North Ferriby. I did pretty well until I came off with a dead leg. *Here we go again,* I thought, but I only missed a couple of days training and was back in time for our next reserve game which was against Scunthorpe United. I played really well, scoring twice in a 3-2 win and felt the sharpest I had for a long time.

I arrived at the training ground the next day feeling positive. I never lost the thrill of scoring a goal, it didn't matter what level, I just loved scoring.

So, I was in the dressing room, getting ready for a warm down, when the first team arrived ahead of their training session and Dean Windass approached me, "How did you get on last night?"

"Yeah, good thanks," I replied. "We won 3-2."

"Did you score?"

"Yes, I got two," I declared proudly.

"Well, if you can't score against them you want to be hanging your boots up," he said before walking off. I immediately felt totally deflated. I'd previously scored goals against big teams like Manchester United, Spurs, and Newcastle in the Premier League, but getting a brace against Scunthorpe reserves was a big thing for me at that stage in my road to recovery.

That one little comment affected me massively. I don't think there was any malice in it, but it sent me right back to the bottom of the hill. He went on to score the winning goal at Wembley and he probably doesn't even remember it, but I've never forgotten what he said. Maybe it shouldn't have affected me as much as it did, but after everything I'd been through, it did.

It didn't help that communication with the manager was non-existent. I read in a newspaper one day that Phil had told the press that I was having a good couple of weeks, and he might look at offering me a contract. *Fucking hell, any chance you could come and speak to me,* I thought. I probably should have gone to see him, but I was terrified of doing something to upset him as I was that desperate for a contract, even though I absolutely hated it there.

I didn't think it was possible, but things got even worse.

I picked up a little knock one day in training and although it was nothing serious, by the time I got home, I was in a bit of pain. The club phoned me that night to say that the first team were away the following day and that there wouldn't be anyone at the training ground, so I was to report to a school in Hull to do my training there.

"Bearing in mind I've hurt my ankle, will there be a physio there?" I asked.

"No, the physios will be with the first team, but you need to go so we can see if your ankle is alright," they replied.

"I know my ankle isn't right and I think it would be better to rest it. I know my body," I argued.

"No, Malcolm. You need to come in so we can take a look at it," I was told firmly.

So, the next day, I drove from Middlesbrough to Hull. I was

commuting because my first son was due to be born any day, so I wasn't going to stay in a hotel. I arrived at the school field where the reserves were training because the pitches at the training ground were flooded, and got changed in the back of the car like a Sunday league player.

I ran onto the pitch and the coach asked how my ankle was. I explained that it still hurt, and he told me to go home and rest it! My commute was an hour and a half each way, which isn't a fun drive with an injured ankle. It was only a knock and I was fully recovered after two days.

In October, Fraizer Campbell joined us on loan from Manchester United, and Phil Brown was all over him. Fraizer was a good player who knew where the back of the net was, and I honestly thought he'd go on to be a world beater. Sadly, he didn't reach his full potential, although he did enjoy a very good career. With Brown signing another striker, that meant that I moved further down the pecking order.

The final straw for me came a few weeks later when I received a phone call from the fitness coach who informed me that as the first team had a day off, the reserves would be training at the KC stadium, adding an additional 30 minutes to my journey. When I walked in the dressing room the kit man asked me what I was doing there. I couldn't believe it. I explained that I'd been told to report to the ground.

"We didn't know you were coming and haven't got any kit for you," he told me. I was livid. The rest of the players had their heads down as usual, no one offered me any of their spare kit, so I just walked out. My head had pretty much gone by this point.

I called Paul from the car park and explained what had happened. "I need to get out of here, Paul. I don't know how on earth I've ended up here, but I'm not coming back." I've never been treated so badly in my life. I've never been made to feel so small. It was ruining me mentally.

I didn't speak to Phil Brown to tell him that I had left, he'd avoided me the whole time I was there anyway. I just thought I'd leave and find a new club, but the chances of that happening reduced drastically when I read the following quote on the internet:

Hull boss Phil Brown has confirmed he will not be offering the 28-year-old a contract at the KC Stadium. Brown told BBC Radio Humberside: "We've had a good look at Malcolm but decided not to give him a deal."

I couldn't believe it. He hadn't had a good look at me at all, he'd stuck me with the reserves and the kids, and didn't even have the courtesy of speaking to me during my whole time there. He treated me like a piece of shit on his shoe. I didn't expect superstar treatment, but a little bit of respect wasn't too much to ask for.

That statement was a downright lie. It was my decision to leave Hull, not Brown's. At that stage I wouldn't have signed for him for all the money in the world.

The problem was that prospective clubs were put off because they assumed there must have been a reason why Hull didn't sign me. There must have been a problem with me. I still to this day cannot understand why he said what he did.

A horrible experience.

It was another nail into the coffin that contained my football career.

CHAPTER 23
One last chance

I'd been around the professional scene long enough to understand that my time at Hull wasn't normal, and I made a vow that even if I went on another trial, it wouldn't be as bad as that. I wouldn't allow myself to be treated that poorly again. Sometimes in life you have to go through the negative times to appreciate the good. I learnt a lot of lessons from my experience at Hull that stood me in good stead for the future – how not to treat people for a start.

The phone didn't ring for a while after my departure from Hull, or Hell to be more accurate. They weren't a big club or a fashionable one, so not winning a contract there didn't really send out a great message to other teams. I was back to square one, but I was OK because something really positive had happened to me – I had become a father.

My son, Flynn, was born in October 2007 and that was such an amazing thing. After everything I'd been through since leaving Middlesbrough, his birth was a good distraction and, with Christmas approaching, I decided to take a breather and spend some time away from football to enjoy the festivities with my family.

In January 2008, my agent rang and asked me if I was interested in talking to Dennis Wise, the manager of Leeds United.

"Absolutely!" was my instant response.

Yes, they were playing in League One, but Leeds were a massive club and ticked all the boxes. I'd played against them and knew first hand how good their support was. I'd experienced their top class training facilities when I'd trained there with England. Leeds were a sleeping giant. We didn't speak about a contract as money was secondary, I just wanted to play football. Seven months earlier

I had baulked at a 75% pay cut, now the finances didn't even cross my mind. It just goes to show how quickly things can change in football.

I drove to Thorp Arch, the Leeds training ground, and just as I was pulling into the car park, my phone rang. The caller ID displayed a number I didn't recognise.

"Hi Malcolm, it's Nigel Clough from Burton Albion. What are you up to?"

"Believe it or not, I've just arrived at the Leeds training ground," I replied.

"You're joking. Well, if it doesn't work out for you there, please give me a call," Nigel said. I really appreciated his call. It gave me a confidence boost to know that I was still wanted in football.

I got on well with Dennis Wise from the start which was so important. I needed to connect with someone who understood my journey, appreciated what I'd been through, and Dennis got me straight away. He explained his plans for the club, which were to win promotion back to the Championship that season, and he told me that he was expecting me to come in and compete for a spot up front. It was a positive conversation, exactly what I needed at the time.

When I met the players, I was pleased to find that the dressing room was great and the banter was good natured. It was just a brilliant club.

We had some really good young players in the squad who went on to play at a higher level; Jermaine Beckford, Jonny Howson, Frazer Richardson, Luciano Becchio, Robert Snodgrass, and Fabian Delph, a player who I knew would go right to the top.

There was a wealth of experience in the ranks as well, including David Prutton, the former Nottingham Forest and Southampton midfielder, ex-Chelsea striker Tore Andre Flo, and former England international Alan Thompson. It was a good mix of lads who got on well with each other on and off the pitch, and they made me feel welcome from day one.

Training was good fun, lively and sharp, and it was an easy commute for me – everything was perfect. By this stage I'd accepted that I wasn't a Premier League player anymore, maybe I wasn't even a Championship player, but at least I was finally a footballer again.

After a good week of training, I felt that I was getting back to myself. There were flashes and glimpses that showed people what I was capable of. I remember scoring a bicycle kick during one training session and some of the lads were full of praise, telling me it was Premier League class, while others were taking the mick, telling them to leave me alone. I felt that I fitted in and had earned the respect of the other players which was exactly what I needed.

On 14th January 2008, Dennis called me into his office to tell me that he had been impressed with my performances in training and said he was going to offer me a pay-as-you-play deal. I was over the moon. OK, it wasn't a full contract, but it was a big step up from a trial. I knew that once I'd made it into the first team and started scoring goals, he'd have no choice but to offer me a permanent contract.

My agent negotiated a deal where I'd be paid £1,000 a game, but I'd have probably done it for free because I loved it so much at Leeds. I honestly believed that this was the moment I'd resurrect my career.

So, the next day, a Tuesday, I arrived at Thorp Arch full of excitement. I'd been selected for a reserve game that evening, so the plan was for me to do a bit of light training, grab some lunch, take a medical, and sign my contract.

As I stepped onto the training pitch, I was thinking, *This is brilliant. Do the training, sign my contract, play the match. Back on the wagon, back on my football journey.*

We were doing a crossing and finishing drill when Tom Elliott, a 17-year-old striker, swung a ball in. It was slightly behind me, so I had to twist my body to get a shot at goal and as soon as I connected with the ball . . . BANG – I felt something go in my back. I ended up on the floor because of the way I'd twisted, and when I tried to stand up the whole of my lower back went into spasm, like I was suffering from cramp. I suddenly felt a fizzing feeling across my back and I knew that something was very wrong.

My teammates came over to see how I was. I said that I was fine, trying to brush it off, but I knew I wasn't. They helped me up and I leaned back to stretch it out and . . . boom, it spasmed again. *I've done something horrendous here,* I thought.

I trudged off the training pitch, towards the changing rooms, and my back spasmed another four times. The dressing room door was stiff, and I couldn't even open it, so I had to knock on it and wait for someone to let me in. I went straight in to see the physios and told them something was wrong with my back. It was lunchtime so they told me to grab a bite to eat first and then they'd have a look.

I walked to the canteen in agony, pain shot through my body with every step I took. I tried to get by and pretend it wasn't too bad, but I couldn't even carry my tray back to the table. Dennis Wise sat with me and asked if I was alright. "Don't worry, Gaffer, it's just a pulled muscle," I replied, desperately hoping that was all it was.

Dennis and the physios were great, they sent me for a scan that same afternoon, even though they didn't need to because I hadn't signed the contract at that stage, and I was still technically a free agent.

As soon as the specialist walked into the room, I could tell from the sombre look on his face that the news was not going to be good. "Malcolm, you have fractured your spine," he told me. I was absolutely shell shocked.

I had put so much force through my lower spine when I twisted to kick the ball that I had cracked one of the pars, a bone that joins the vertebras together. You just couldn't make it up. The contract was waiting in the office, on the table, for me to sign. Literally twenty minutes after my I hurt my back, I would have signed.

I was inconsolable. Dennis spoke to me and said that they'd get me fit and playing again, but I wasn't sure. I needed to get away from football for a bit and get my head right because I knew that if I was to come back from this, I would need a considerable amount of mental strength.

The specialist advised me that I needed an operation to fuse my back, but as I wasn't officially a player, I'd have to pay for it myself. I considered it, but it was expensive, and I hadn't earned any money in almost a year – I paid my own travel and expenses whilst at Leeds and Hull and wasn't paid a penny – so I decided to go down the conservative route.

I need to make this clear, Leeds were fantastic to me. They did everything they could to help me, especially Harvey Sharman, the Head physio. I cannot sing his praises enough. Harvey advised me to rest for three months, before sending me for another scan – that Leeds would pay for – and then he'd devise an exercise programme to improve my core stability in a bid to get me back to a position where I could play again.

While I was coming to grips with my new injury nightmare, Dennis Wise, the one manager who had trusted me, who'd given me an opportunity, left Leeds to become Director of Football at Newcastle United. We were top of the league at the time, and I have to say, it felt like a strange decision for him to leave.

I was concerned about my future, but Gary McAllister took over and he was great with me. I'd played against him, had an enormous amount of respect for him, and he told me he was quite happy for the physios to continue to treat me.

At the end of the 2007/08 season, the first in my career that I didn't make a single appearance, I sat and watched the fortunes of the clubs I almost joined:

Stoke City finished second in the Championship, winning promotion to the Premier League.

Barnsley survived a relegation battle and reached the semi-final of the FA Cup which was played at Wembley.

Nottingham Forest were promoted to the Championship after finishing second in League One.

Leeds United were beaten by Doncaster at Wembley in the Play-Off Final.

And Hull City. Well, they were promoted to the Premier League after beating Bristol City 1-0 in the Play-Off Final, with Dean Windass scoring the winning goal at Wembley. It didn't really surprise me as they had solid, experienced pros, but it did stick in the throat a bit after the terrible experience I'd had there.

You couldn't make it up; these clubs that I coulda woulda shoulda, all went on to achieve success. Playing at Wembley was another lifelong ambition of mine, so to see Barnsley, Hull, and Leeds achieving it in the season I was close to signing for them was really hard. There was a dark cloud that hung over my head, constantly following me around. It almost like everything was conspiring to torment me mentally.

*****

While I was out injured, I dipped my toe into the media side, doing a bit of commentary work for the BBC in London. I was paid £300 a game, but I had to make my own way to and from London, so when you factor in the train journey, travel to and from the studio, and food, it was actually costing me to do it, but I really enjoyed my commentary duties and was hoping it might lead to other work. When I got myself into a position where I could start running again, I decided to focus on my football career instead of the media side.

In September 2008, I was ready to resume training and McAllister allowed me to train with Leeds again, he joined in too and was still a quality player. It was an incredible gesture from him. I think it inspired the younger players to see me around the place, trying to recapture my former glories after bouncing back from yet another injury nightmare. I spent hours in the gym and did far more running than ever before, and soon started to feel fit and positive again.

The players were great, even though they still saw me as an injured player, and I knew that my career was on a knife edge. Mentally I felt exhausted, but I knew I was wanted by the club and that really helped. Gary McAllister had told me that if I could get fit again, he'd offer me the same pay-as-you-play deal that was previously on the table, so I had that carrot dangled in front of me. I worked tirelessly every day and I'm proud that I managed to come back from what could, and probably should, have been a career-ending injury.

In November 2008, 10 months after breaking my back, I finally signed a contract with Leeds, and soon after, I made my debut in the first round of the FA Cup away at Northampton Town. I started up front alongside Jermaine Beckford and it felt so good to be back. Although there were only 4,000 fans inside Sixfields Stadium, they were so loud, and I felt the hairs stand up on end as we kicked off. This was credit to all my hard work.

I'd learnt to adapt my style of play, so I was letting Beckford do what I used to. He was the young, hungry striker making the runs, and I was coming short, holding the ball up, and looking to play him in. I enjoyed the new role and played my part in a deserved 5-2 victory, with Jermaine grabbing a hat-trick.

I made my home debut a few days later, coming on for the last half an hour of our league game against Colchester at Elland Road. The Leeds fans were absolutely amazing. They didn't know what had happened behind the scenes, but they gave me such a warm reception which meant a great deal to me. Home and away our support was incredible, even though we were in League One.

After the match, McAllister told me that if I could play four or five times that he'd sign me, which was fantastic to hear and gave me something to work towards.

But then he was sacked!

Another manager who had shown faith in me was out the door, and as I still didn't have a full contract, I was effectively back on trial again.

Former Leeds player Simon Grayson came in to be the new manager. He knew that I wasn't on a full contract, so he was either going to have a good look at me or get rid of me. He realised I could do a job for him, but I think he also wanted to bring his own players in, rather than make do with Dennis and Gary's signings.

In Grayson's second match in charge, against Stockport, the scores were tied at 1-1 when he brought me and Jonny Howson on for the last 25 minutes. Ten minutes later, Fabian Delph had given us the lead and towards the end of the game I scored my first goal for Leeds. Our goalkeeper, Casper Ankergren, launched a long ball that I chased and hit on the half volley. As I watched the ball fly into the net, I was overcome with emotion. It was two years since my last goal, and I made the most of my celebration in front of the jubilant Leeds fans.

It was the final goal I ever scored.

Grayson started to bring his own players in, beginning with the arrival of Lee Trundle, a very good player full of tricks and skills and, even though I played a couple more times for Grayson, I knew by then that the writing was on the wall.

During one training session, I felt a little twinge in my back, nothing major, so I carried on playing and tried to ignore it. Reality kicked in a couple of days later when I bent over to pick up Flynn, who had just turned one, and my back went into spasm. I knew it wasn't right and even though I realised that it was only going to get worse, and maybe even lead to a bigger injury, I kept quiet because I knew if I said anything to the physio, my career would likely be over.

I was waiting for a moment, some kind of sign, that said, "Malcolm, you're done."

That moment came on 24th January 2009.

We were playing Peterborough United at home, ironically my local team. I'd worked hard and performed well in training all week as I was fired up to play against the team who had rejected me when I was a kid. I saw it as my chance to show the Posh what they had missed out on. Although, you never really know whether you'll be in the squad or not until the manager announces the team. I'd played in our previous three games, so expected to be on the bench at least as I still had a lot to offer the team.

I sat in the dressing room with the lads while Grayson announced the squad, and my name was missing. One of the lads turned around and said, "Bloody hell, that's bit harsh. You don't get paid unless you play, so why didn't he tell you earlier to save you the journey?" I was thinking the same thing, as was Paul Telfer who was in a similar position to me.

I turned to Telf and said, "That's a bit shit, isn't it? We've trained all week, travelled all the way here, and we're not getting picked or being paid."

We went to the bar area and people were telling me that I might as well go home, but I wanted to stay and cheer on the team. I decided to go back down to the dressing room to wish the lads well for the match.

As I was about to turn the corner towards the changing rooms, my ears pricked up as I heard Simon Grayson yelling. "I'm not being fucking dictated to about who I have to put in my squad. I don't care if he's being paid or not, I'm not fucking picking him."

His comments saddened me, and I immediately felt myself begin to shake with the shock of what I'd just heard. That was the moment I decided that I was done. I turned around, walked out of Elland Road, and drove home.

That was it, I retired from football.

I didn't speak to Grayson again; I just didn't turn up for training on the Monday. I didn't make an announcement to say that I was retiring, and my phone never rang.

I was done, and no one cared.

My overriding emotion was one of pure relief. My injury problems had started way back in November 2003 and had dragged on through to January 2009; we're talking over five years of injury hell. That's a long time.

Deep down, I knew that if I carried on playing something bad would have happened to my back. I'm 100% certain of that. I'd been on the edge of a cliff for so long. All the cards were stacked against me. I'd worked so hard to get back into the game, I'd done absolutely everything I could to get fit, and I knew that I was never going to be the same player. The mental torture that I'd endured for so long was finally over. I made the decision on my terms which was so important as I needed to be the one who closed the book.

When I look back, I sometimes question whether I should have been more honest with the physios and maybe they could have rehabbed me through it. But in my heart, I know I made the right decision to retire. I'd fought for so long; I had no more fight left in me.

People around me had lived through the nightmare with me and they were relieved when I ended it. It's tough to admit, but I'd fallen out of love with football, and football had fallen out of love with me. I'd had the dream as a boy, lived it as a man and by the age of 29, it had soured and was all over.

I wore the number 28 shirt for Leeds although most fans have forgotten that. To be honest, most fans have forgotten I even played for Leeds! I'm a bit of a comedy figure for United fans now; whenever you see things on the internet like 'Here's a list of random players who played for Leeds,' my name is mentioned. I don't care about that, though. Although I didn't represent them as often as I would have liked, I am incredibly proud to have played for Leeds United.

CHAPTER 24

Piecing together the jigsaw

My purpose in life was to play football and score goals, it's all I'd ever really done since I was a kid. When I awoke on 25th January 2009, the thought struck me like a free kick in the face – *I'm no longer a professional footballer. What am I supposed to do now?*

One thing I knew for certain was that I wanted nothing to do with football; I didn't want to watch it, I didn't want to talk about it, I didn't even want to think about it.

When you have spent your whole life chasing and living your dream, putting your heart and soul into something you love doing, something that was everything, how on earth are you supposed to flick a switch and do something else? I'd fallen out of love with football, my passion, what else was going to be out there for me?

And who was I? For my entire adult life, I'd been Malcolm Christie, the footballer. Now what was I? I had lost my identify.

Things had fallen off a cliff financially. Since I left Middlesbrough in June 2007, I'd earned the total sum of £5,000, a grand for each of my five appearances for Leeds. I realise that I was well paid during my career, but I wasn't as well paid as people thought. I started on £800 a week at Derby in 1998, and that had increased to £3,000 by the time I left in 2003. A lot of money, yes, but not in the realms of other Premier League players, like my Derby strike partner, Fabrizio Ravanelli, who was on £40,000.

Half my wages went to the tax man, the agent took a big chunk too, and as I know only too well, a footballer's career is short. When you consider that I was only paid a wage as a footballer for nine years and that money had to last me for the rest of my life, it's not as much as it seems.

My Middlesbrough contract contained performance related

bonuses, so I received an extra £3,000 for every game I played and £1,000 a goal. There were bonuses for cup performances and league positions. I've done the calculations and you're talking around £750,000 that I lost out on through injuries.

I was very fortunate in that I had a nice house, decent cars, exotic holidays, and designer clothes. I lived like a stereotypical footballer, but I was also conservative with my money. I look back and wish I had been a bit more extravagant. As a kid, I always wanted a Ferrari, and I could have afforded one at one time, but I chose not to. My mum had dad had taught me the value of money, so I made sure I invested it well. Dad sorted my finances out until I broke into the first team at Derby which is when the vultures began circling and I signed up with a financial advisor. My dad was very frugal with my cash, risk averse, and invested it safely into property. In contrast the financial advisors drew up complex plans and investments and, with hindsight, I should have allowed my dad to continue looking after me. He always had my best interests at heart.

I had medical insurance, so I worked with the Leeds physio, the PFA, doctors, and other medical professionals to try and make a claim, but the insurance company refused to pay out, claiming that I had a degenerative problem that caused my back injury which was not true at all. I'd paid hundreds of thousands of pounds into my policy over the years and when I needed them, they did nothing.

I'd had an agent and a financial advisor during my career, but as soon as it was over, they stopped calling. You find out who your real friends are when you become an ex-footballer, all these people who wanted to know me when I was on the up disappeared the moment I retired.

I had to tighten the purse strings and that had massive repercussions on my home life. When someone has only ever known you as a footballer earning a good income, it becomes hard when the money dries up. As well as the financial adjustments I needed to make, I was trying to mentally adjust to the end of my career, and each day became a recurring nightmare.

A footballer's life is glamorous when we're playing regularly, scoring goals, and everything is going well, but dealing with retirement can be a very bleak time.

I've read a report that states that a staggering 80% of footballers develop problems with their body that effect their later life; osteoarthritis, knee and hip replacements, and general mobility issues the most common. Just under half declare bankruptcy within five years of retiring, and 75% of ex-players are divorced by the time they turn 50. I hope and pray that there is more support for players when they hang up their boots than there was when I finished.

I was fortunate that I was in a position where I didn't need to work, although in some ways that can be dangerous. Flynn was almost 18 months old, so it was easy for me to become a stay-at-home dad. He became my purpose, the reason for getting out of bed in the morning because there was always something that needed to be done, whether that was changing a nappy or going out to do the weekly food shop. It was a massive thing for me to have the opportunity to be around Flynn, watching him grow up.

I still lost weeks and months, shutting myself off from the outside world, but Flynn's presence stopped me from going down the ultimate dark holes. I became Malcolm, Flynn's dad, instead of Malcolm, the worthless human being, which is probably where I would have ended up.

I did nothing for years, absolutely nothing. I thought I was quite happy, feeling safe in my own world. But I wasn't happy. I was on a painful, downward slope with many dark days. It's a hard story for me to tell. The cloud that had followed me during the latter days of my career evaporated the moment I walked away from the game, but it was quickly replaced by a fog that surrounded me. A fog so thick that I couldn't see where I was going.

I felt myself becoming bitter about things. When I heard that Middlesbrough had been relegated in 2009, I felt a bit of a buzz. It's a horrible thing for me to admit, I didn't wish ill on them, and I felt for the fans, but part of me began to take pleasure in other's misery.

I should have spoken up and told people how I felt, but that's not what we do in England is it? When you see a friend and ask them how they are, how do they respond? "I'm fine." "Alright." But are they? Most of the time you're not alright, something is worrying you, something has annoyed you.

There was no reason for me to put my hand up and ask for help because in my head, I thought I was OK. We need to do more to probe our friends and family to check that they really are OK. It's only by taking the time to show a genuine interest in how they are feeling that we will get them to open up. Allowing people to live in their own heads is not healthy. As I learnt, your own mind is not a safe place.

I want this story, my journey, to help someone, even if it's just one person. I want you to know that it's OK to admit when you're struggling. That it's OK to ask for help. I wish I had spoken up as things would have been massively different for me.

I enjoyed my time with Flynn, but I also knew I needed something else to do, I just couldn't figure out what. People suggested I join a gym, but that was the last place I wanted to be because the gym was the scene of many a nightmare. The gym scared me because it put me back into the mindset of an injured footballer. At least then, I'd had Gareth Southgate or Andrew Davies to bounce off, and a physio setting me targets and showing encouragement. I saw the gym as a stepping stone back into football, but now I was retired, I couldn't see the point. It took me 10 years before I was finally over the ordeal and was able to step foot into a gym.

I began to realise that the corridor I was walking led to a cliff and if I didn't change things soon, I'd end up falling straight off the edge, so I decided to do something about it. Although by that stage I hated football, I didn't know anything else, so I contacted Pat Lally at the PFA to enquire about a coaching course. Darlington Football Club were running a level one training course for their Under 16 team and I was invited to join them. I didn't feel any passion for coaching, I was just doing it for the sake of it, a bit like when I had done my A levels all those years earlier.

Neil Bailey, the regional PFA coach, and Craig Liddle, the Darlington Academy manager, were running the course and they thought it was admirable that I was prepared to learn alongside the kids.

It was the first time I'd sat in a classroom for years, and I felt totally out of place surrounded by 14 and 15 year-olds. Neil handed out a book, which was basically a manual of how to play football. I flicked through the pages and felt like I was back at the bottom of the hill. We then went out onto the training field to be taught how to do a warm up and how to set cones up. I hadn't kicked a ball since retiring and these kids were running rings around me. I couldn't finish the course, I just wasn't in the right place mentally to try and get back into football. I still felt traumatised from my experiences, so I went home at the end of day one and didn't go back. I think that deep down I was still grieving for my career, maybe I should have buried a football or something symbolic like that to help me get over it.

The only good news for me at that point was that I was the proud father of another child, Zac, so when Flynn was ready to go to school, I resumed my role as stay-at-home dad for Zac.

Eventually, I decided to make something of myself again; I'd done it before, I wanted to do it again. I enjoyed speaking to people and I liked cars, so I chose to become a car salesman. I composed a letter that I sent to every dealership in the North East. It was a revealing letter that explained who I was, what I'd done and my aims for the future.

I later learned through sales that if you throw enough shit at the wall, some of it will stick, and lo and behold, the phone rang.

The first call I received was from Nissan in Middlesbrough. As I pulled into the car park, I felt a nagging feeling and thought, *Is this what I really want?* I felt worried that they knew all about me because I'd written everything down and exposed myself emotionally.

The place was a little run down, but the interview went well and I was offered a job straight away. The money wasn't anywhere in the league of what I had earned, but that wasn't important. I just needed something to do to get me out of the house. To reclaim my life back.

I felt a little pressured into making a decision there and then which I couldn't do. I needed time to think, although part of me got a warm feeling, pleased that someone wanted me again. It was definitely a boost to the ego.

My second interview was with Ian Pinnegar, the Dealer Principal at Aston Martin in Houghton-le-spring. There is a bit of prestige with Aston Martin, and I remember thinking, *That's a bit more me.* I'm not being a snob, but if you're offered the choice of working for Aston Martin or Nissan, unless you're a Nissan enthusiast, why wouldn't you choose Aston Martin?

The interview went well, and I was offered the job on the spot, not before I was asked if I still had contacts in the game. I didn't really because I had cut off all ties by then, but that wasn't the right thing to say, so I told him that I'd played with or against most of the players in the England squad. It was true, but it wasn't like I had John Terry's number on speed dial. His eyes lit up though, thinking he had a direct link into the Premier League.

After a few days deliberating, I accepted Ian's offer and I became part of the motor trade. It only took a couple of days for me to realise how cut throat the industry is and how naïve I was.

I'd made an appointment with someone who was interested in a car. I was feeling pleased with myself, straightening my tie in anticipation of what could be my first ever sale when one of my fellow salesmen came over and told me he'd just sold the car over the phone. I was absolutely fuming that he'd sold it when he knew I had made an appointment for someone, but that was the way the sales world worked. Dog eat dog, every man for himself.

Aston Martin used to run some ride and drive events for the wealthy individuals we called the big hitters. We'd invite them for a day out at the Aston Martin facility where they'd blast cars around the track. My boss had booked four guys in for a session, and he asked me to take them. It was a nine-hour round trip, so I'd have no chance to sell any cars that day which wasn't great as the bulk of my wage was earned through commission. I asked if I'd get the chance to drive some cars and my boss told me I might.

I was the new boy and had to learn the ropes, so I reluctantly agreed to go. When we arrived at the track I asked if I'd be able to drive some cars and was told no, so I spent four hours sitting in a waiting room, watching the big hitters come in after driving yet another car, asking them if they were having fun.

It wasn't all bad though as I was given some cheese sandwiches and a packet of crisps!

The next day, one of my colleagues asked how the day had gone, giving me a bit of banter because they knew it was a waste of time. "That was a long old job," I replied, before adding, "I felt like a glorified taxi driver."

Little did I know that the Sales Manager was standing around the corner, listening to what I was saying, and he stormed out and said, "Welcome to the real world."

I didn't know what to do, although I felt angry with the way he'd spoken to me. While most people I worked with were great, there was a lot of bitterness towards me from others because I'd achieved something in football, and they loved nothing more than putting me down.

I stayed in the industry for a number of years, working at different dealerships where I met some wonderful people, like Vince Ravenhall and Ray Reed. I wasn't doing what I loved, and selling cars wasn't my passion, but Vince and Ray provided some camaraderie and banter, and the sales meetings were fun because we had a laugh. I was promoted to sales manager and was gradually getting my mojo back.

But I still wasn't the old me. I still couldn't accept that my career was over. There were many times when I played out the fairy tales in my head, the alternative reality, the life I could have led had I not been injured. I was a professional footballer for 11 years and spent almost six years out injured.

Six years of hell.

The fact that I kept coming back and getting injured again traumatised my body and damaged my mental health. I wonder if things would have been better if my first leg break had been an instant career ender. It would have been hard to deal with, I know that, but maybe I would have been able to satisfy my mind and start afresh.

Eventually, my marriage broke down which was hard as it naturally meant I didn't see my children as often as I had when I lived with them. I never dealt with setbacks well, and I had no one around me because I had fallen out with my parents when I was at Middlesbrough.

As Steve McClaren used to say, "It's all about defining moments." You have them in your life, and you just have to hope that they go your way. My defining moments, in some respects went well, but when they did go wrong, they went really wrong. I had the wrong people around me at Middlesbrough, and I pushed my parents away. I regretted that every single day. I should have been stronger, and I shouldn't have allowed myself to be manipulated by others. I missed them so much, but my pride prevented me from contacting them and apologising, even though I knew that was exactly what I should have done.

Things started to change for me when Zac turned five. Flynn

was already playing for Wynyard Football Club and Zac also signed on for them. When I took them to their training sessions I felt a little buzz, I wanted to be out there with them. I was living in a flat with a good-sized lounge at the time, so I bought a mini goal and a beach ball, and we played football for hours. I taught Zac how to kick a ball, we did keepy uppies, headers, volleys, and then I'd go in goal while he took shots. I found myself getting back into the game.

Flynn is a good player, but doesn't have the same passion for football that I had, whereas his brother absolutely loves the game. Zac has a lot of talent and he's in the Bournemouth academy now. I can see a little bit of me in him, although he is a midfielder who prefers creating goals to scoring them.

Thanks to my sons, I began to fall in love with football again.

As the boys got older, they started to ask me questions about my career which gave me the opportunity to look back on some positive moments, instead of focussing on the scars from the latter years. At first it felt like I was telling the story of someone else, but as time went on, I started to relive the good memories. I went into the loft and brought down some clippings that my mum and dad had saved for me. Zac, Flynn, and I spent hours going through the clippings and watching old videos of me in action on YouTube. I wanted them to be proud of me.

In late 2014, I met Emma who later became my wife. I think after all the bad moments and experiences I had been through in the previous years, in some respects, I must have been due some luck. Meeting, and falling in love with Emma, is the best thing that has ever happened to me and I'm eternally grateful she came into my life when she did.

I knew straight away that Emma shared my values. I wasn't earning thousands of pounds a week when we met, but that didn't matter to Emma, she saw me as a normal person, not a footballer.

We spoke in depth about my career, my past life and where I was at. She realised straight away what I was missing in my life which was my family. Emma is amazing; she told me I needed to stop over thinking things and just pick up the phone and ring my parents. I had no idea how difficult it must have been for them all those years. They spoke about me in the past tense, almost as if I was dead, even though they knew I wasn't. That was how they coped with my absence. There wasn't a day that went by that I didn't think about them and wish that things were different.

With Emma's support and encouragement, in 2015, I finally picked up the courage to phone my dad. My heart was pounding as I dialled the familiar number. When he answered, I couldn't speak, it was too emotional. Dad knew it was me and he said, "It's alright, Son, take your time." It was the hardest phone call that I'd ever had to make. Forget all the calls from agents, reporters, and football clubs, this was the most important phone call of my life.

When I eventually managed to control my emotions, I told my dad that I was in a different place in my life now, and he understood. It was late at night when I called, so my mum was in bed. It would have been even harder to talk to Mum, but I called her the next day. It was lovely to reminisce with my parents about the past and it brought back some fond memories.

Reconnecting with my parents and trying to rebuild that relationship was a massive piece of the jigsaw. I'd realised that the pieces weren't going to suddenly land in my lap, I'd have to go out and find them. I needed Emma to show me that.

I've since come to realise that some things in life are just not meant to be, and when that happens, you need to be able to put them to one side and move on with the things that do matter. It's only through experience that you understand the things that are important to you. When I was 19 or 20, I simply didn't know what that was, but in my 40s I realise that family is everything.

In 2018, my third son Leo Anthony Christie was born, a first son for Emma and another for my five-a-side team. Zac has continued to excel at his football and Flynn is more academic. I'm incredibly proud of my three boys, as I am of my step daughters, Eva and Nya.

I've spoken to them to make sure that they know the value of a good family unit. Whatever their future holds, whatever they achieve in their lives, and whatever struggles they face, they know I will always be there for them. I just hope that I can pass on some of the lessons I learned so they don't make the same mistakes that I did.

I left the motor industry in 2019. It wasn't my dream; it wasn't where I wanted to spend the next 10-15 years of my life. I wanted to look back and forward at the same time and rediscover my love for football.

I've also come to accept what I achieved as a footballer. There was a time when I hated when people recognised me as I didn't want to talk about football. Although the moments are few and far between, I now enjoy the times when I am recognised as it gives me the chance to babble on about my career!

One evening, Emma and I took Eva and Nya to the Metro Radio Arena, Newcastle, to watch the boy band One Direction. We had great seats on the third row and when the concert started, the girls, who were big fans, went crazy, dancing and singing along to the songs. In fact, so was I!

The arena, as you can you imagine, was full of young girls and I, a six foot tall man with dark hair and a beard, must have stuck out like a sore thumb.

During the gig, Niall Horan, the band's singer and guitarist, put his thumb up to me. I waved and he waved back. It was almost like he knew me which was strange.

A few minutes later he wandered over to the side of the stage where someone handed him a flag. He held it in my direction and that was when I spotted that it had a Derby County badge on it, so I started cheering.

Emma turned to me and asked, "Is he doing that to you?"

"I think so," I replied before turning to the girls, telling them, "I think one of the band members has recognised me."

"Shut up," they said together. They didn't expect me to be recognised by one of the biggest boy bands in the world.

After the interlude, a security guard came over and asked me if I was Malcolm Christie. When I told him I was he said, "Great. Niall is over the moon that you're here as he's a big Derby fan. He's asked if you could meet him after the show."

Bloody hell!

"Emma, you'll never guess what," I said to my wife. "Niall has invited us back stage."

"No way," she said in disbelief. When I told the girls they were screaming their heads off.

When the concert finished, we hung around in our seats before the security guard escorted us back stage. It felt like I was famous again. It was brilliant to be able to take the girls to meet their idols. It was a dream come true for them.

Niall and I had a long chat and it transpired that he and his brother Greg, are huge Derby fans who used to travel over from

Ireland in the late 1990s with their dad, Bobby, to watch our home games. Niall explained that he used to wait for me in the car park and ask for my autograph, wearing his Derby shirt with 'Christie 10' on the back. I was his hero, and he said he even cut his hair like me when he was a boy! It was such a surreal moment.

We took some photographs together, and he kindly gave the girls some Derby County embossed guitar plectrums that he'd used in the show. It was a great night.

I've also began to enjoy the rare occasions when I am back in the spotlight. I've appeared on *Soccer AM* a couple of times, and I've done a bit more commentary and although I don't like watching myself on the television, I really enjoy the media side. I'm not pining to be on television or the radio, but if the door was open, I would quite happily step through it.

For now, I'm focussing on my coaching academy, Christie Coaching, teaching children all about the attacking side of the game. I take the things that I learnt from playing under some of the best coaches in the world, combine that with the aspects that worked for me in the Premier League, and share that experience with the next generation.

Looking forward, I'd love to get back into professional football, whether that's as a manager, assistant or coach, I don't know. I have rekindled my passion for the game. My hunger and determination to make something of myself is as strong as ever before. I've taken my UEFA B badge and I'm hoping that opens some doors.

My journey is unique; I've achieved success and made mistakes; I've experienced the highs of the game and the very lows. I've also lived a life outside football. As Head of Sales, I won awards, learnt how to manage people, how to have difficult conversations, and I was responsible for hiring and firing. They are all skills that are transferable into football management and coaching.

Wherever my journey takes me, it's important that my family are by my side.

I'll let you in on a little secret. Sometimes, after training when all the kids have gone home and I'm alone on the field, I'll pretend to be Bryan Robson running with the ball before smashing it into the empty goal. Even though there is no one there, I still get that unbelievable buzz when the ball ripples against the back of the net.

After all, scoring goals, it's the best feeling in the world.

The best of the best

Writing this book has reminded me of the many wonderful players I am fortunate enough to have played with and against, so I've decided to don the manager's hat and select two sides; the first consists of my former teammates, the second those I've lined up against.

It's certainly not been an easy decision; the competition for both teams is fierce. Here are my line ups.

My all-time teammate eleven

Formation: 4-3-3

Goalkeeper: Mark Schwarzer

This was a very tough decision as there isn't a lot between Mark and Mart Poom. Both were fantastic goalkeepers, who enjoyed long international careers, but the reason I've gone for Schwarzer is his temperament.

When we did a shooting drill in training, the ultimate insult to a goalkeeper is chipping them, so if you attempted to chip Poom, he'd come charging out and try to volley the ball at you because he was so angry! It's fair to say that Mart Poom, like most goalkeepers, was eccentric.

In contrast, Schwarzer was quite normal, a very laid back and chilled out Australian. They both had a mistake in them, but Mark was able to recover mentally from a mistake quicker than Poom.

Mark was a big presence, a good guy, very funny and a great shot stopper, especially from the penalty spot. Like most Boro fans, I'll never forget him saving Robbie Fowler's last-minute penalty in the final game of the 2004/05 season that sent us into Europe.

Defender: Gareth Southgate

I've already said a lot about Gareth, but for me, he was Middlesbrough's rock and a big factor behind Boro achieving what we did as a club. As a leader, as a player, and as a person, he was someone I wanted to be like. He gave his all in everything he ever did, whether that was in training, matches, or in the gym.

Gareth very rarely made a mistake and had very few faults. I'd lined up against him before I played with him, and I remember thinking that he'd be quite easy to come up against because I was quicker than him. But Gareth read the game so well he always managed to get to the ball slightly earlier than me and he didn't give me an inch of space.

Even though he had won trophies and captained his country, he remained one of the most respectful and humble people I have ever met. After a game, my parents would often join us in the Players' Lounge for a drink, and Gareth would speak to all the families to make everyone feel welcome. My mum used to adore him; he'd always give her a little kiss on the cheek. He had an ability to made everyone feel special and that's one of the reasons he is so well respected.

When I talk to the young players I work with now, I tell them that Gareth is the role model they should aspire to.

Defender: Igor Stimac

What Gareth was to Middlesbrough, Igor was to Derby.

He was my first captain and such a well respected guy, with a big presence and an aura around him. No one had a bad word to say about him. He played and trained like it was the World Cup Final which made us all raise our levels.

Even though he only spent four years at Derby, Igor is a club legend and even has a lounge at Pride Park named after him. The fans still love him, and I have nothing but fond memories of Igor. He was such an important player to us that when we lost him to West Ham in 1999, it marked the start of Derby's decline.

Defender: John Terry

I had the pleasure of playing with and against John. I first met him in 2000 when I joined up with the England Under 21s. He was training with some unbelievable players at Chelsea, and he taught me how the top players are expected to train. The idea was that you should work so hard on the training pitch that the match almost becomes easy.

He was a leader from an early age and was someone I knew was destined for bigger and better things. What he achieved at Chelsea was magnificent, captaining the club to every major honour in the game.

Defender: Ashley Cole

Ashley wasn't a regular for the Under 21s when I played with him, he was just breaking into the Arsenal team, so no one really knew a lot about him. As soon as I saw him in training, I could see he was quality.

Blessed with bags of pace, he was very hard to get past, exceptional going forward and he developed into one of the most complete full backs of his generation. He was one of the most important members of the great Arsenal and Chelsea sides of the 2000s and 2010s and became a mainstay in the England squad.

To be around him when he was just a fledgling talent, it was great to see him go on to achieve what he did. At one stage, Ashley was the best left back in the world.

Midfielder: Stefano Eranio

As a footballer you cross paths with lots of people. Most don't leave a lasting impression, but occasionally you work with someone whose impact stays with you forever. Stefano is in that category.

Before he joined Derby, Eranio was a member of the all-conquering AC Milan team of the 90s, winning multiple Serie As, Italian Cups, and the Champions League, but he was so humble. He was such a lovely man, and I don't remember him ever arguing with anyone.

He was unbelievable with the ball. I will always remember one time at Derby, we'd been training in a park and as part of the cool down we walked around the perimeter for 45 minutes. Stefano did keepy uppies the whole way round, and the ball didn't hit the ground once. I couldn't believe it. I know it's a bit fanboyish, but I was in awe and told all the lads what he'd just done.

Around the training ground, he always looked immaculate,

arriving in a suit - he even smelt nice! The man oozed class. I am full of admiration for Stefano, and it was an honour to play with him.

I'll never forget a volley he scored against West Brom in the FA Cup. Danny Higginbotham swung a ball in that Stefano then hit with a side swipe. That goal was all about technique and timing.

I remember feeling emotional when he said his goodbyes to the fans on the pitch after the final home game of the 2000/01 season. It was Stefano who chipped the ball to me for my goal at Old Trafford, and I'll always be grateful to him for that.

Midfielder: Michael Carrick

When I saw Michael's talents first hand, I was shocked because he was so good. He showed me the standard that was expected of England players. His touch was incredible, he could control anything and did it with such ease.

Michael had so much ability, but his biggest talent was that he never gave the ball away. I knew straight away that he was going to achieve something big in his career which he did, winning the Premier League and Champions League with Manchester United.

Midfielder: Georgi Kinkladze

This was the hardest position to fill as it was a toss-up between Kinkladze and Juninho.

I would have loved to have played with Juninho during his first spell at Middlesbrough because he was assisting everyone, but during his second spell his game had evolved and he was playing a little further up the pitch, scoring and taking shots himself, rather than providing the chances for others.

In contrast, when I look back at the highlights of my Derby County career, Kinkladze assisted most of my goals which is why I've picked him ahead of Juninho.

When we signed Georgi, Steve Round sat us all down and played a video showcasing Kinkladze's highlight reel which included moments of magic from his time at Manchester City and Ajax.

My jaw hit the floor and I couldn't wait to play with him.

At times, no one could get near him, and he was unplayable in some games. His only weakness was that if he didn't fancy it, or if the weather wasn't quite right, he just didn't perform. I couldn't understand it because if he'd been switched on all the time, I'm convinced he would have been a top, top player.

Georgi liked to keep himself to himself off the pitch. His English wasn't great, although sometimes I think he spoke better English than he let on. On the rare occasions we spoke, he'd say, "Malcolm, you make the runs and I'll find you." That was music to my ears.

Kinkladze was a genius at spotting my movement and playing the ball at the right time. I knew all I needed to do was to create enough space and nine times of 10 he would find me. I loved playing with him, and I doubt I'd have scored the number of goals I did if I didn't have the supply from him.

Striker: Fabrizio Ravanelli

A huge hero of mine as a kid. As I was on the early part of my journey, playing for Deeping Rangers, Rav was at the top of his game, scoring in the 1996 Champions League Final for Juventus. If someone had told me at the time, that one day I'd be playing up front with him I'd have never believed them.

I often look back at pictures of myself and Rav and remember the wonderful memories. There was a misconception about Rav, I remember reading articles saying that he was disruptive, but I never saw anything other than a hard-working player, a great guy and a huge asset to us.

I think we did well when we played together. Even though we were part of the Derby side who were relegated, we scored regularly throughout the season.

In many ways he was the perfect strike partner for me at that time. I learnt so much from him in training and in matches he'd advise me on where to stand and where to run.

I think he was frustrated that his legs had gone by the time he joined Derby and I used to look at him and think, *If I can take your hold up play and you can have my pace, we'd be unstoppable.*

Rav was an iconic figure who made an instant impact on the Premier League during his solitary season at Middlesbrough. Like most kids at the time, I would pull my shirt over my head, copying his trademark celebration. I obviously couldn't tell him that when I played with him, so I kept all the fan boy stuff to myself!

To play with Rav was a dream come true.

Striker: Jermain Defoe

Quite simply the best natural finisher I have ever seen.

When I was first called up to the England Under 21 squad, I was full of confidence thinking, *I'm going away with England so I must be really good.* But as soon as I saw Jermain, I realised that he was on a totally different level to me, and I knew I had a lot of work to do.

During shooting drills, Defoe would finish everything: left foot, right foot, headers, close range, long range – he'd score them all.

If I was a defender, Jermain would have been the type of player I'd hate to play against. Quick, sharp, good movement, could hold the ball up well, and was capable of spinning behind, you'd have to be on your toes for the whole game. He's scored goals wherever he's been and that's the sign of a proper striker.

Striker: Mark Viduka

Middlesbrough fans will remember him fondly, as do I. It is one of the biggest regrets of my career that I didn't get the opportunity to enjoy a run of games playing alongside Mark because he would have been the ideal strike partner for me.

We trained a lot together and clicked naturally. He held the ball up so well, could spot my runs, and his selfless style of play meant he was always looking to find me. If we'd partnered each other for a season or two, I know I would have scored a lot of goals.

Big, strong, powerful, Mark didn't take any messing. I saw him and Ugo Ehiogu go at it a few times, he went at it with Chris Riggott too. Mark didn't mind sticking his elbow in during training if it meant getting the ball.

He was a pure winner, with good feet and someone who knew where the goal was. I'll never forget the four goals he scored for Leeds against Liverpool.

He had a really laid-back attitude and was often the last to arrive for training. If we had to report for 10 a.m. and I was pulling into the car park at 9.59 a.m., I'd be jogging, desperately trying to be on time. But Mark would stroll in late holding his wash bag, without a care in the world. He didn't arrive late to annoy people, it was just his style, so he got away with it.

Manager: Jim Smith
Assistant: Steve McClaren
Coach: Steve Round

I couldn't leave out any of these three because they were all a huge part of my journey. They made me the player I became and the man I am today.

Jim gave me the opportunity to achieve my dream of becoming a professional footballer. I know I didn't cost him a lot of money but for him to spend money on me when he didn't have a clue if I was going to make it was still a gamble. There weren't any other teams who were willing to do that at that time.

Steve McClaren was a great foil for Jim. Where Jim was old school, Steve was much more tactically astute, putting on bright, lively training sessions. Each session felt different to the last which isn't easy to do. He kept it fresh and made the lads want to train.

Steve Round was very much a sponge, taking on-board all the information he was picking up from Jim and from McClaren. He wasn't massively experienced as a coach when I joined Derby, but he learnt so much so quickly, and when you look at his CV which includes Manchester United, Arsenal, Newcastle, and Everton, it shows how highly regarded he is in the game.

If I can be half as good a coach as the two Steves, I'll be very proud.

Honourable mentions

There are two players who didn't make my first eleven who deserve an honourable mention.

Midfielder: Juninho

Some people reading this may question why I haven't included him in my best eleven. It was so close, but as I've mentioned, I enjoyed my better years with Kinkladze.

However, Juninho means so much to the Middlesbrough supporters that I simply have to mention him here.

He was a wonderful player, a magician with the ball, and a joy to watch. With all that he'd achieved in the game he could have been quite cocky, arrogant even, but he was anything but. Juninho was such a nice, down-to-earth guy, who got on with everyone. Managers, coaches, staff, players, everyone loved him, which is testament to his personality.

He was an emotional guy who loves the club, and my everlasting memory of Juninho is seeing him in tears, sitting on the pitch when Middlesbrough had been relegated in 1997.

Striker: Jimmy Floyd Hasselbaink
Another player who I looked up to. I'm not so sure that we could've formed a partnership, but what I saw from Jimmy was hunger, drive, and a winning mentality. He demanded so much from people and that's something I look back on and wish I'd had in my own locker.

*****

My all-time opponents eleven
Formation: 3-5-2

Goalkeeper: Peter Schmeichel
Schmeichel was one of my heroes growing up. I used to enjoy going in goal when I was a kid, messing about at the park with my brother and our friends.

I remember having the goalkeeper kit that Schmeichel wore for United in the 1993/94 season. It was a white shirt, with quite a lairy yellow and blue spray pattern, and came with elbow pads. So when Gavin and I went across to the college field to play, I'd wear Reusch gloves, the United shirt, and pretend to be Peter Schmeichel.

I actually played one match as a goalkeeper for my brother's fruit and veg team, Pauley's. I was playing for Nuneaton at the time, but I used to go along to watch the lads and on one occasion, the goalkeeper didn't turn up, so I put some gloves on and went in goal. We lost the game 6-1, though. At one stage, I decided to go on a mazy run, so I rolled the ball to myself, took on about four players and shot, but their goalkeeper pulled off a great save.

For me to have the opportunity to play against someone I'd pretended to be was brilliant, and even better when I managed to score past him for Derby when he was playing for Aston Villa. There is a photograph of me putting the ball past him, with Schmeichel diving in vain to save it. That's one of my favourite images.

He was part of that great United team that helped me fall in love with football, but it's not just that he was one of my heroes, I've picked him because he is one of the greatest goalkeepers to ever play the game.

Defender: Gary Neville

When I think of defenders that I've had a tough time against, Neville is right up there. He was the ultimate right back. OK, so he was never going to beat three or four players going forward, but he was almost impossible to get past.

I remember an occasion at Old Trafford when he used his experience to win a penalty. We were both in the Derby penalty area, running for the ball, when he grabbed my arm and fell to the floor. He was still holding my arm when he fell which caused me to lean towards him, and when he let go of me, it looked like I'd barged him to the ground. Jeff Winter, the referee, bought it and gave United a penalty. I looked down at Neville, lying on the floor, and he gave me a little wink. I just thought, *You've absolutely done me there!* Fortunately for us, Mart Poom saved Paul Scholes' spot kick.

I think if you ask most players of my era who was the best right back in the Premier League at that time, Neville would be mentioned nine times out of 10.

Defender: Jaap Stam

Another Manchester United hero of mine. I've seen some photos of him from earlier in his career when he had a full head of hair, and he looks very different. When he lost his hair, he looked quite scary! There aren't many players I've played against where I've actually felt a bit of fear and felt intimidated by them, but Jaap was one.

He had an aura and a presence, and was a really solid defender. I played against him when he was at United and again in a friendly game when Derby played Lazio, and they were both very tough matches.

I could have picked Rio Ferdinand, John Terry, or Nemanja Vidic but, for me, the experience of playing against Stam was completely different because I was completely in awe of him. Not many players have had that effect on me.

Defender: Ashley Cole
He is the only player who appears in both teams which tells you how highly I rate him.

Midfielder: David Beckham
When I was younger, I used to write to the young Manchester United players requesting autographs, in case they became really famous one day. Beckham was one of those who sent me a personal autograph which I still treasure.

He developed into a superstar, married a pop star, became a fashion icon, but that all glossed over the fact that he was a very good footballer. In many ways he was underrated. You don't play for United, Real Madrid, AC Milan, Paris Saint Germain, and captain England if you're not a great player.

He was unbelievable; his range of passes, his touch, the goals he scored, and the sheer number of goals he created. He was brave, good in the air, amazing at set pieces, he had a bit of everything. He was the complete midfielder.

I would have loved to have played alongside him. With the runs I made, I know he would be able to find me, and what a dream it would have been to be the one getting on the end of some of those trademark whipped crosses.

Another iconic photograph I have hanging on my wall, is celebrating my goal for Derby at Old Trafford in 2001, with Beckham standing in the background.

Midfielder: Xavi
I've already mentioned the game I played for England against Spain when they gave us a real footballing lesson. We got absolutely trounced. I even tried to get back into midfield to help out because we were being completely overran, and that was because of Xavi.

He was so good as a youngster and it's frightening to think how good he must have been in his prime. He grew into one of the greatest midfield players of all time and I'm proud to be able to say I've shared a pitch with him, even though I couldn't get anywhere near him!

Midfielder: Steven Gerrard
A bit of a controversial choice for me because he was a Liverpool player and for me growing up, Liverpool were the enemy.

Frank Lampard was in contention because he was a great goalscoring midfielder and a strong leader, but you need a Steven Gerrard type midfielder in your team which is why Gerrard has got the nod. He had everything, and in my opinion, was a more complete player than Lampard.

Gerrard encapsulated everything that Liverpool were about. He was so determined, passionate and aggressive. He forced others to raise their level and was the man behind Liverpool's success in the 2000s. Not many players can take a game by the scruff of the neck like Gerrard did in both the 2005 Champions League Final and 2006 FA Cup Final.

Midfielder: Paul Scholes

When you hear people like Xavi, Zinedine Zidane, and Pele, all these top players praising Scholes, you have to take note.

I played against him a few times and I don't ever recall seeing Scholes give the ball away which is unheard of. A positive player too, his line of vision was always forward, he rarely played the ball backward, and like Beckham, his range of passing was superb.

I remember him breaking onto the scene at United as a striker, so I took note as that was the position I played. But he adapted his game to become a top midfielder, one of the best this country has ever produced.

Scholes was a one club man which is a great achievement, but to do it at Manchester United where he won everything is unbelievable.

Midfielder: Cristiano Ronaldo

I'm often asked to chip in with my opinion on the ongoing debate: who is best – Ronaldo or Messi?

I've seen Cristiano Ronaldo's talents up close and, in my opinion, he is the better player. I played against him a couple of times when he was transitioning from a skilful player, full of tricks, to one of the most prolific goal scorers in the history of the game.

I've included him as a midfielder because I played against him when he was a winger. Before he became a striker, he was a brilliant wide man, capable of taking defenders on before playing inch perfect balls to the strikers. It would have been an absolute dream to play alongside him.

For him to score goals at the highest level at the grand old age of 37 is amazing. Whatever age I am, even when I'm not on this planet anymore, he will still be regarded as one of the best ever. To have shared a pitch with such an amazing talent is incredible for me to look back on.

One of the greatest players of all time.

Striker: Thierry Henry

I had the privilege of standing in a wall at Pride Park in a match against Arsenal. I remember feeling awestruck, thinking, *Thierry Henry is taking a free kick here.* He curled the ball up and over the wall, I turned and watched the ball fly into the top corner. It was an amazing free kick, one of that you dream of taking yourself. It was so good that I felt like applauding him even though he'd just scored against us!

Henry was so quick, he was so powerful, and he had a few seasons at Arsenal when he was unplayable, he really was. He had tough time at the start of his Arsenal career, joining the club as a winger and I remember there were some doubts over him, but he developed into an awesome attacker who defenders genuinely feared.

I've already spoken about how much I hated missing games through injury, but there was one match I'm glad I didn't take part in. In January 2006, Arsenal beat Middlesbrough 7-0, with Henry scoring a hat trick. He absolutely annihilated us in that match, one of the best individual performances I have ever seen.

He broke Ian Wright's goalscoring record at Arsenal which is no mean feat. He wasn't just a good goal scorer, he scored good goals. Free kicks, headers, volleys, close range, long range, it didn't matter.

Henry's trademark goal was cutting in from the left before curling the ball in with his right foot. He must have practised that move over and over again, and he got it down to a fine art.

One of the best goals I've ever seen was scored by Henry, against United, unfortunately. Henry flicked the ball up on the edge of the box and volleyed it into the net. It was the kind of goal you look at as a fellow player and just think, *Wow!*

Striker: Alan Shearer

Shearer holds the record for scoring the most Premier League goals which says it all really.

As a striker myself, I looked up to Alan both before and during my career because in terms of pure goal scoring ability, he was the best. To have the privilege of playing against Shearer and seeing what he meant to the Newcastle fans was unreal. He was a God to the Geordie fans.

I used to curse him when I was younger because he rejected Manchester United twice and was one of the main reasons Blackburn pipped United to the Premier League title in 1995.

Alan Shearer scored some unbelievable goals – I'll always remember that volley against Everton from outside the box – and has set the benchmark for all other strikers.

When he retired, I heard him say that when he was through on goal, he didn't try and be too precise, he just put his foot through it. That is unheard of, most forwards are taught how to finish. As you're running through on goal, you decide whether to place it or go for power, you decide whether to go left, right or down the middle. Shearer didn't even think about it which shows you how naturally goal scoring came to him.

I scored 30 Premier League goals. Shearer scored 260 – it's incredible. What is even more amazing is that he scored all those goals playing for Blackburn and Newcastle. Can you imagine how many he'd have scored if he had joined Manchester United and had Beckham, Giggs and Scholes providing chances for him?

Manager: Sir Alex Ferguson

The greatest manager of all time. I have so much respect for Sir Alex, even though I didn't play for him, because he was the manager of my heroes.

The first time I met him was in 1999, just after he'd led United to the treble, and I asked for his autograph in the tunnel after our game against them. It was a surreal moment as almost ten years earlier, I'd been jumping for joy on the sofa when Mark Robins scored the goal that saved his job.

The rest is history.

Sir Alex completely revolutionised English football; developed so many talented youngsters, brought the right players in at the right time, and wasn't afraid to make the tough decisions when needed.

In many ways, he was an old school manager, a strict disciplinarian like Jim Smith, and I think I'd have enjoyed playing for him because I always performed better when I was a little afraid of the gaffer. I definitely would have been scared of receiving the famous hair-dryer treatment!

He achieved everything in the game, and I don't think anyone will ever be able to emulate his success.

Honourable mentions

I've spent hours agonising over this team, and there are a few players who didn't made the starting line-up, but deserve a mention.

Midfielder: Frank Lampard

A fantastic attacking midfielder, in many ways he was almost like a centre forward. I trained with him when I was first called up for the England Under 21s, but I'm not sure I'd have liked to play with him because he'd be making the same runs as me.

Frank was a technically gifted player, who just didn't lose the ball. The first time I saw him in training, we were doing a keep ball exercise with one of us in the middle trying to get the ball off the others. It didn't matter if you smashed it to him at 100 miles an hour or mishit it, Lampard would control it or lay it off first time. He made it look so easy.

Midfielder: Patrick Vieira

A leader of men, Vieira was a strong solid midfield player who was a big part of Arsenal's Invincible team and France's World Cup winning squad. He didn't have any weaknesses that I can think of. His temperament was questioned a few times because of the number of red cards he received, but that was all part of the package.

Midfielder: Roy Keane

Roy was similar in stature to Vieira. I looked up to Roy and with his fearsome reputation, I expected him to be this big monster, so it was strange when I played against him for the first time, and I realised that he wasn't quite as big as I had imagined. He was very vocal, commanded respect, and very much ran the game. Not just from his own players, but also the opposition and the referee too, such was his presence.

Midfielder: Paul Gascoigne

Gazza is a national icon. One of my most vivid childhood memories is of Gavin and myself crying with Gazza during Italia 90. During that tournament, he was an absolute joy to watch and when, 12 years later, I found myself on the same pitch as him, I had to pinch myself.

Gascoigne is one of the most technically gifted English players of all time and it meant a lot for me to have the opportunity to play against Gazza, someone who was a big reason for me falling in love with the game.

Striker: Michael Owen

Even though we were a similar age, I used to look up to Michael. He burst onto the scene while I was working at Somerfield, and his style of play reminded me a little bit of the way I played for Northborough and Deeping. Owen was a far superior player to me, but we both liked to keep the game simple. Like me, he didn't score many goals outside the box, he was a pure finisher. It was all about getting on the end of things, getting played through and finding the back of the net.

I had the honour of playing against him, just a couple of weeks before he won the Ballon d'Or, and I saw first-hand his incredible talent when he scored the only goal of that game.

During his prime, he was a terrifying prospect for defenders, at both club and international level.

Striker: Ruud van Nistelrooy

My dream was always to be the centre forward for Manchester United, even while I was playing, and I watched on in envy as Ruud was actually doing it. I reluctantly accepted that he probably was a bit better than me.

I had great admiration for what he achieved in his five years at Old Trafford, not just his incredible goal scoring record of 95 league goals in just 150 appearances, but the way he bounced back from a devastating cruciate knee injury. I can't help but respect the man.

He was a natural finisher, whether that was scoring with his head, his foot, or even his shin, and was always in the right place at the right time, getting on the end of the endless supply of chances created by Beckham, Giggs, and Ronaldo.

Ruud had a sixth sense of positional play which is so important for a centre forward. There were so many times in my career when I positioned myself in a certain place in the hope that the ball would land kindly and a lot of time it did. Ruud was one of the best at that. People would say that he got a bit lucky when the ball fell to him, but it wasn't luck at all. When the ball was bouncing about, Ruud would instinctively know where the ball was likely to fall. That's something you either have or you don't, and Ruud most certainly had it.

Striker: Wayne Rooney

I first played against Rooney when he was breaking into the first team at Everton. Although he was only 17, he already carried a big reputation and was clearly going to become a quality player. But what really surprised me was his aggression. At one point in the game, the referee gave us a free kick and Rooney went ballistic, going after the ref, effing and blinding which was unheard of, especially for such a young player. I'd always been brought up to respect referees, so it was an eye opener for me as the ref did nothing about it!

I knew he was going to be a good player, but what he achieved at Manchester United was incredible. He was ahead of his years, and nothing fazed him. A big money move to a club like United at 18 would be a daunting prospect for most players, but it didn't bother Rooney one bit as evidenced by a hat trick on his debut.

I'm reminded of Steve McClaren's defining moments speech. Wayne's defining moment was *that* goal against Arsenal as a 16-year-old.

Special mention: Ryan Giggs

I idolised Ryan Giggs. When I was 13, he was the pin up boy that all the girls at school fancied, so I decided that I wanted to look like him. I rang the hairdressers myself and asked how much it would cost to have my hair permed. It was £30, which was a lot of money for me, so I asked my mum. Her shocked response was, "What? You want to have your hair permed? I've got a perm!"

"Yes, mum, I want to look like Ryan Giggs," I replied.

"Erm, well, if you're sure," she said.

With Mum's blessing – and £30 in cash – I walked to the

barber's shop in Stamford and had my hair permed. I'll never forget the smell of the perm.

What the hell was I thinking?

When I got home, I immediately put on the full Manchester United kit, including my Reebok boots, and posed for a photo, holding a Mitre football (the kind they used in the Premier League at the time).

That was how much I loved football, I couldn't just watch it on the television, I couldn't just play the game, I wanted to look like a footballer. Sadly, I didn't get the same level of female attention that Giggs enjoyed!

I was devastated when he didn't give me his shirt when I asked after I'd played against him for the first time. Maybe I should have told him that I had once had my hair permed because I wanted to look like him. On second thoughts, maybe not!

A few years ago, I was on holiday with Emma in Dubai, and while we were sitting in a restaurant, I noticed Ryan Giggs walk in and stroll straight past me. Now at the time, I was almost 40, I'd been a professional footballer for 10 years, I'd played against him many times, but I was still completely star struck. I didn't want to disturb his meal, so I didn't say anything to him, but looking back, I wish I'd gone over and said hello. I would have had to remind him who I was, but I'm sure once he heard my name, he'd remember me.

My love of football has gone the full circle and I am once again, a football fan.

Afterword by Niall Horan

For as long as I can remember I've been a Derby County fan. My dad started supporting the club in the early 70s and when he had money, he would take himself over to Derby, by ferry and train, to see the mighty Rams. I was taken to my first game when I was six or seven. At that time we were a decent Premier League side.

As a seven year-old, I had my heroes, and a lot of them were in the shape of Derby County footballers. The one that stood out to me as a young lad was Malcolm. As youngsters we are very impressionable. I would do my hair like Malcolm, have 'Christie' on the back of my shirt until I was forced back to Horan because, "If you have Horan on the back and Christie leaves next season, you'll still have this shirt." I also wore it baggy because, "You'll grow into it!"

I loved how Malcolm played. He stood out like a sore thumb as he had the ability to take a game by the scruff of the neck, no matter how big or small. His movement off the ball was brilliant and he was always there to score the perfect striker's goal from within the 18 yard box or take on multiple players to score, as we saw at Old Trafford on that famous afternoon.

Malcolm was clearly missed when he went to Boro, and maybe apart from Stevie Howard or Chris Martin, I don't think we've had a stand out goal scorer like him since.

I'm not one to get star struck but one night I was stood on stage with the lads in Newcastle and I looked out into the crowd, as you do. I looked down and saw a man with black hair and thought, *That's Malcolm fucking Christie!* My mind was blown. The last time I'd seen Malcolm Christie I was standing outside the players' entrance at Pride Park, waiting for his autograph like all the other young kids at the time. Now I'm standing on stage years later and he's there watching me. Life does some weird, weird, stuff sometimes. Inevitably we met up backstage with his kids and lovely lady, took a picture or two, and had a reminisce of the good times.

A great Premier League striker he was and I'm glad that both Derby and Boro fans can remember him fondly for all the great goals scored, and fantastic times together.

Niall Horan
June 2022

Acknowledgements

To my wife Emma, my rock and soul-mate. Your unconditional love is what keeps me going every day.

My boys Flynn, Zac, and Leo, the best gift anyone could ever give me is being your father. Dream big my sons.

It was a number of years ago when my mum said your story would make a good book, well here it is mum. I ultimately achieved my boyhood dream but could never have done it without the help, love, and support of my parents. The best mum and dad you could ever wish for.

To my brother Gavin, thank you for being the best 'supporter' on the journey, and looking out for me, always.

To the teams I played for, Northborough, Deeping Rangers, Pauley's, Nuneaton Borough, Derby County, Middlesbrough, Leeds United, and England, with each team came a different story and I'm eternally grateful for everyone connected with each club that helped me. From the Managers to all the wonderful coaches and support staff right through to the dinner ladies and cleaners.

I had the pleasure of playing with some wonderful players over the years and I thank each and every one of my teammates, I'm proud to say I never had an argument with any of you, maybe it was the way I was brought up. My mum always told me it's nice to be important but it's more important to be nice!

Thank you to all the supporters of the great teams I played for, your support over the years is without question what kept me going through both the good times and the obvious bleak times.

Thank you to Dave Essam of Frontline Recruitment for his support with the production of this book. Dave is a big Derby fan and coaches Long Eaton under 11s.

Thanks also to John Fearnehough of Chevin Homes, and Kyle Hassall of The Boathouse, for their support with the production of this book.

And finally to my author, Mathew, for listening to my life story over the past year, almost like a therapist! I'm sure we'd both agree it's been worthwhile. . .

Thank you

Malcolm
June 2022

Malcolm has collaborated with Mathew Mann to write his autobiography. Mathew has ghost written several books including Minding My Own Football Business by Barrie Pierpoint, You Must Be Joachim by Julian Joachim, and I Get Knocked Down by Danny Wilson.

Mathew would like to thank:

Malcolm for taking me into your confidence and for giving me the opportunity to help tell your unique story.

The team at Morgan Lawrence: Barrie Pierpoint (Director), Harry Worgan, Peter Taylor, Amy Memory, and Lee Clark.

My wife Holly for your continued support and encouragement.

And my children, Dylan and Eve, who are my inspiration.

Youth and amateur career statistics

	Appearances	Goals
Northborough 1992 - 1993	18	38
Deeping Rangers 1993 - 1998	118	137
Pauley's 1998	12	31
Total	**148**	**206**

Semi-professional and professional career statistics

	Appearances	Goals
Nuneaton Borough 1998	21 + 1 sub	14
Derby County 1998 - 2003	101 + 28 sub	36
Middlesbrough 2003 - 2007	29 + 20 sub	9
Leeds United 2008 - 2009	2 + 3 sub	1
England (Under-21) 2000 - 2002	8 + 3 sub	3
Total	**161 + 55 sub**	**63**

Message from Kyle Hassall

I remember the first time I watched Derby live like it was yesterday. It was the final home game of the 1995/96 season, and we beat Crystal Palace 2-1 to clinch promotion to the Premier League. And so began my romance with Derby County.

Jim Smith had an eye for a player, bringing in stars such as Igor Stimac, Stefano Eranio, and Paolo Wanchope, off of whom helped us finish 12th, 9th and 8th in our first three Premier League seasons.

When one goalscoring hero (Wanchope) left, another arrived – Malcolm Christie. I was at Old Trafford in 2001 when Malcolm scored the only goal of the game to keep us in the Premier League. What a goal it was too!

I was also in the crowd when Malcolm scored a brace against Manchester United in the season we were finally relegated to the Championship.

It was such a magical period for the club, and I have some wonderful memories of that era.

Although I moved from Derby to Worcester in 2014, my love of the club continued. I now own two restaurants and a sports bar in Worcestershire, as well as an outside bar and catering business. I am also a member of the West Midlands Derby County Supporters' Club, based at my restaurant the Boathouse. We host Q&As with former players, including Jacob Laursen, and we've held several charity events where we've auctioned off Derby County memorabilia.

We've got some more Q&As planned for the future – including one with Malcolm Christie – so if you're ever in the Worcestershire area, why not pop in and say hello. And if you wear your Derby shirt, you'll receive a 10% discount on your meal!

www.theboathouseupton.co.uk
www.thymecatering.co.uk
www.mojitosupton.co.uk
Bar7 upton sports bar

Message from Chevin Homes

Chevin is proud to support and help promote Malcolm Christie's story, portrayed so openly in this book.

When Malcolm approached us for our support, we were not only proud to be asked, but touched by the honesty of the reality of the dream that we all had as amateur footballers, that has been lived out by Malcolm – rising meteorically to play in the Premier League.

At Chevin Homes, we have the privilege of meeting many of the Derby County players in our capacity as Preferred Partner in Property. We provide rental accommodation and bespoke new build houses that are popular with players and staff.

This isn't just business for us, though – we are lifelong Derby County fans. Meeting and helping the players not only makes you feel proud and satisfied but takes you back to the days as an innocent youngster at the Baseball Ground where you idolised players – and often strikers like Malcolm.

Fans love goal scorers and for me, my Derby County journey as a fan began around 1985 – ironically at our lowest ebb in the old Division Three when Bobby Davison was the shining light providing excitement with his pace and goals. The club's rise from that low point to Division One in two seasons was intoxicating. I was hooked from then on and have had a season ticket almost every year since.

The club's fast rise in those days, mirrors Malcolm's rapid rise to success. I was there when Malcolm made his debut in January 2000 scoring twice - a new hero was born! He'll always be remembered most fondly by Derby fans for the goal at Old Trafford in 2001 that kept the club in the Premier League.

That period in the late 90s and early 2000s was the last time Derby's fans enjoyed watching a successful Premier League team with Malcolm joined by the likes of Stimac, Eranio, Baiano, and Wanchope.

Now relegated to League One, fans have their own dreams to be back in the big time but of course, for a footballer like Malcolm it's a moment in time that can never be repeated – that's the reality of the dream.

Index

INDEX

INDEX

INDEX

INDEX